Whillans's Tax Tables

Budget Edition 2013

Edited by

Claire Hayes CTA

Kevin Walton MA

Julie Ward CTA

Consultant Editor

Rebecca Benneyworth BSC, FCA, MBE

Members of the LexisNexis Group worldwide

United Kingdom	LexisNexis, a Division of Reed Elsevier (UK) Ltd, Halsbury House, 35 Chancery Lane, London, WC2A 1EL, and London House, 20-22 East London Street, Edinburgh EH7 4BQ
Australia	LexisNexis Butterworths, Chatswood, New South Wales
Austria	LexisNexis Verlag ARD Orac GmbH & Co KG, Vienna
Benelux	LexisNexis Benelux, Amsterdam
Canada	LexisNexis Canada, Markham, Ontario
China	LexisNexis China, Beijing and Shanghai
France	LexisNexis SA, Paris
Germany	LexisNexis Deutschland GmbH, Munster
Hong Kong	LexisNexis Hong Kong, Hong Kong
India	LexisNexis India, New Delhi
Italy	Giuffrè Editore, Milan
Japan	LexisNexis Japan, Tokyo
Malaysia	Malayan Law Journal Sdn Bhd, Kuala Lumpur
New Zealand	LexisNexis NZ Ltd, Wellington
Poland	Wydawnictwo Prawnicze LexisNexis Sp, Warsaw
Singapore	LexisNexis Singapore, Singapore
South Africa	LexisNexis Butterworths, Durban
USA	LexisNexis, Dayton, Ohio

First published in 1948

© Reed Elsevier (UK) Ltd 2013

Published by LexisNexis
This is a Tolley title

ISBN for this volume: 9781405778992

Printed and bound by CPI Group (UK) Ltd, Croydon, CR0 4YY

Visit LexisNexis at www.lexisnexis.co.uk

Preface

Welcome to the new Edition of Whillans's Tax Tables. All of the usual material that you need to refer to is here again; to make the book as user friendly as possible, we have organised it so that each topic is covered on a separate page. In particular, I would like to draw your attention to the section on penalties. With the new penalty regime for late filing and late payment being rolled out gradually, it is important to keep on top of the latest position. In our penalties section you can see at a glance which penalty regime is in force for which periods, across all of the taxes.

Rebecca Benneyworth

Administration

Bank base rates

Period	Rate
from 5 March 2009	0.50%
5 February 2009–4 March 2009	1.00%
8 January 2009–4 February 2009	1.50%
4 December 2008–7 January 2009	2.00%
6 November 2008–3 December 2008	3.00%
8 October 2008–5 November 2008	4.50%
10 April 2008–7 October 2008	5.00%
7 February 2008–9 April 2008	5.25%
6 December 2007–6 February 2008	5.50%
5 July 2007–5 December 2007	5.75%
10 May 2007–4 July 2007	5.50%
11 January 2007–9 May 2007	5.25%
9 November 2006–10 January 2007	5.00%
3 August 2006–8 November 2006	4.75%
4 August 2005–2 August 2006	4.50%
5 August 2004–3 August 2005	4.75%
10 June 2004–4 August 2004	4.50%
6 May 2004–9 June 2004	4.25%
5 February 2004–5 May 2004	4.00%
6 November 2003–4 February 2004	3.75%
10 July 2003–5 November 2003	3.50%
6 February 2003–9 July 2003	3.75%
8 November 2001–5 February 2003	4.00%
4 October 2001–7 November 2001	4.50%
18 September 2001–3 October 2001	4.75%
2 August 2001–17 September 2001	5.00%
10 May 2001–1 August 2001	5.25%
5 April 2001–9 May 2001	5.50%
8 February 2001–4 April 2001	5.75%
10 February 2000–7 February 2001	6.00%
13 January 2000–9 February 2000	5.75%
4 November 1999–12 January 2000	5.50%
8 September 1999–3 November 1999	5.25%
10 June 1999–7 September 1999	5.00%
8 April 1999–9 June 1999	5.25%
4 February 1999–7 April 1999	5.50%
7 January 1999–3 February 1999	6.00%
10 December 1998–6 January 1999	6.25%
5 November 1998–9 December 1998	6.75%
8 October 1998–4 November 1998	7.25%
4 June 1998–7 October 1998	7.50%
6 November 1997–3 June 1998	7.25%
7 August 1997–5 November 1997	7.00%
10 July 1997–6 August 1997	6.75%

Due dates for tax

Capital gains tax

Normally 31 January following end of year of assessment. (TMA 1970 s 59B)

(See also *Extended due dates* under **Income tax**, below.)

Corporation tax

Must be paid electronically for tax due on or after 1 April 2011.

Generally (TMA 1970 s 59D)

9 months and 1 day after end of accounting period.

Instalments for larger companies (TMA 1970 s 59E, SI 1998/3175)

A 'large company' is any company responsible for paying the bank levy, and one whose augmented profits (see p 63) exceed £1.5m a year, divided by 1 plus the number of any active associated companies. A company is not a large company in respect of an accounting period if its total liability for that period is not more than £10,000, or if its profits for an accounting period are £10m or less and it was not a large company in the 12 months preceding that accounting period. For most large companies (those with no ring fence profits) the amount of each instalment for a 12 month accounting period will be one quarter of its total liability. The amount of each instalment for any accounting period longer than 3 months but shorter than 12 months is calculated using the formula $3 \times CTI/n$ where CTI is the amount of a company's total liability for that accounting period, and n is the number of months in the accounting period. The due dates of instalments are as follows:

    1st instalment: 6 months and 13 days from start of accounting period (or date of final instalment if earlier);

    2nd instalment: 3 months after 1st instalment, if length of accounting period allows;

    3rd instalment: 3 months after 2nd instalment, if length of accounting period allows;

    Final instalment: 3 months and 14 days from end of accounting period.

Close companies: tax on loans to participators

9 months and 1 day after the end of the accounting period. To be included in instalment payments for large companies (see above) (TMA 1970 s 59E(11)).

Income tax

Payments on account (TMA 1970 s 59A, SI 1996/1654)

A payment on account is required where a taxpayer was assessed to income tax in the immediately preceding year to an amount exceeding the amount of tax deducted at source in respect of that year (subject to a de minimis limit, see below).

The payment on account (which includes Class 4 NIC) is made in 2 equal instalments due on:

    (a)   31 January during the year of assessment, and

    (b)   31 July in the following year of assessment.

No payments on account are required where either:

    (a)   the aggregate of the liability (including Class 4 NIC) for the preceding year (net of tax deducted at source) is less than £1,000 (£500 for 2008/09 and previous years (SI 2008/838)); or

    (b)   more than 80% of the taxpayer's income tax and Class 4 NIC liability for the preceding year was met by tax deducted at source (including PAYE).

Final payment (TMA 1970 s 59B, Sch 3ZA)

Balance of income tax due for a year of assessment (after deducting payments on account, tax deducted at source and credits in respect of dividends, etc) is due on:

31 January following end of year of assessment (TMA 1970 s 59B(4)).

Extended due dates:

    (a)   If a taxpayer has given notice of liability within 6 months of the end of the year of assessment , but a notice to make a return is not given until after 31 October following the end of the year of assessment, the due date is 3 months after the notice is given (TMA 1970 s 59B(3)).

    (b)   If tax is payable as a result of a taxpayer's notice of amendment, an HMRC notice of correction or an HMRC notice of closure following enquiry, in each case given less than 30 days before the due date (or the extended due date at (a) above), the due date is on or before the day following the end of a 30-day period beginning on the day on which the notice is given (TMA 1970 s 59B(5), Sch 3ZA).

    (c)   If an assessment other than a self-assessment is made, tax payable under the assessment is due on the day following the end of a 30-day period beginning on the day on which notice of the assessment is given (TMA 1970 s 59B(6)).

The extensions under (b) and (c) do *not* alter the due date for *interest purposes* (see p 3).

Interest on overdue tax see p 3.

Remission of tax see p 6.

Repayment supplement see p 6.

Inheritance tax

(IHTA 1984 s 226)

Chargeable transfers other than on death, made between:

6 April and 30 September	–	30 April in next year.
1 October and 5 April	–	6 months after end of month in which chargeable transfer is made.

Chargeable events following conditional exemption for heritage etc property and charge on disposal of trees or underwood before the second death:

    – 6 months after end of month in which chargeable event occurs.

Transfers on death:

Earlier of   (*a*)   6 months after end of month in which death occurs, and

           (*b*)   delivery of account by personal representatives.

Tax or extra tax becoming payable on death.

Chargeable transfers and potentially exempt transfers within 7 years of death.

    – 6 months after end of month in which death occurs.

PAYE and national insurance

(SSCBA 1992 s 15, SI 2001/1004, SI 2003/2682)

Employer's tax and Class 1 national insurance payable under PAYE.	In-year payments – 14 days after end of tax month or quarter to which it relates (extended to 17 days where payments are made by electronic means). Final payment for tax year – 19 April following deduction year (extended to 22 April where payments are made by electronic means).
Class 1A national insurance.	19 July following year in which contributions due (extended to 22 July where payments are made by electronic means).
PAYE settlement agreement and Class 1B national insurance.	19 October following year to which agreement relates (extended to 22 October where payments are made by electronic means).
Class 2 national insurance.	From April 2011 due in 2 instalments on 31 January and 31 July.
Class 4 national insurance.	See under income tax on p 2.

Paying HMRC

HMRC have a number of bank accounts. They provide an A–Z list of taxes for details of the respective account to which payments should be made. See www.hmrc.gov.uk/tools/bankaccounts/index.htm.

Interest on overdue tax

FA 2009 ss 101–104, Schs 53–54A introduced provisions to harmonise interest regimes across all taxes and duties. Implementation will be staged over a number of years. The provisions apply to income and capital gains tax self-assessment from 31 October 2011 (SI 2011/701). For details of dates from which interest is payable see **harmonised interest regime** p 8. For amounts outstanding immediately prior to 31 October 2011 the old rules under TMA 1970 s 86 have effect up to and including 30 October 2011, and the new rules under FA 2009 ss 101 and 103 have effect thereafter.

Where the harmonised interest regime does not yet apply interest runs from the due date (see p 2) to the date of payment, on the amount outstanding.

Interest is payable gross and is not tax deductible.

Income tax, capital gains tax, NICs Class 1, 1A, 4 and (from 6.4.99) 1B, and (from 1.10.99) stamp duty, SDRT and (from 26.9.05) stamp duty land tax

Period	Rate
from 29 September 2009	3.0%
24 March 2009–28 September 2009	2.5%
27 January 2009–23 March 2009	3.5%
6 January 2009–26 January 2009	4.5%
6 December 2008–5 January 2009	5.5%
6 November 2008–5 December 2008	6.5%
6 January 2008–5 November 2008	7.5%
6 August 2007–5 January 2008	8.5%
6 September 2006–5 August 2007	7.5%
6 September 2005–5 September 2006	6.5%
6 September 2004–5 September 2005	7.5%
6 December 2003–5 September 2004	6.5%
6 August 2003–5 December 2003	5.5%

Surcharge on unpaid income tax and capital gains tax before 1 April 2011 (TMA 1970 s 59C)

For tax years before 2010–11, where income tax or capital gains tax became payable and all or part of it remained unpaid the day following 28 days after the due date, the taxpayer was liable to a surcharge of 5% of the unpaid tax. A further surcharge of 5% was levied on any of the tax remaining unpaid six months and one day from the due date. Interest was payable on the surcharge from the expiry of 30 days beginning on the day on which the surcharge was imposed until the date of payment chargeable at the above rate. Penalties for late filing of returns and late payment of tax have been reformed. A new system has been introduced (see **penalties** p 12) and the previous rules have been repealed for tax years 2010–11 onwards. The new rules are to be phased in over several years. The penalties for late payment apply for PAYE including CIS and student loan deductions and pension schemes from 6 April 2010, and for bank payroll tax from 31 August 2010. They apply to IT and CGT from 6 April 2011 and to other taxes from a date to be determined (FA 2009 Sch 56 and F(No 3)A 2010 Sch 10).

Corporation tax

Interest runs from the due date (see p 2) to the date of payment. For instalment payments by large companies for accounting periods ending after 30 June 1999, a special rate of interest runs from the due date to the earlier of the date of payment and nine months after the end of the accounting period (after which the normal rate applies).

Corporation tax self-assessment (accounting periods ending after 30 June 1999)

Period	Normal rate
from 29 September 2009	3.0%
24 March 2009 to 28 September 2009	2.5%
27 January 2009–23 March 2009	3.5%
6 January 2009–26 January 2009	4.5%
6 December 2008–5 January 2009	5.5%
6 November 2008–5 December 2008	6.5%
6 January 2008–5 November 2008	7.5%
6 August 2007–5 January 2008	8.5%
6 September 2006–5 August 2007	7.5%
6 September 2005–5 September 2006	6.5%
6 September 2004–5 September 2005	7.5%
6 December 2003–5 September 2004	6.5%
6 August 2003–5 December 2003	5.5%
6 November 2001–5 August 2003	6.5%

Period	Special rate for instalment payments (except where still unpaid nine months after end of accounting period)
from 16 March 2009	1.50%
16 February 2009–15 March 2009	2.00%
19 January 2009–15 February 2009	2.50%
15 December 2008–18 January 2009	3.00%
17 November 2008–14 December 2008	4.00%

Period	Special rate for instalment payments (except where still unpaid nine months after end of accounting period)
20 October 2008–16 November 2008	5.50%
21 April 2008–19 October 2008	6.00%
18 February 2008–20 April 2008	6.25%
17 December 2007–17 February 2008	6.50%
16 July 2007–16 December 2007	6.75%
21 May 2007–15 July 2007	6.50%
22 January 2007–20 May 2007	6.25%
20 November 2006–21 January 2007	6.00%
14 August 2006–19 November 2006	5.75%
15 August 2005–13 August 2006	5.50%
16 August 2004–14 August 2005	5.75%
21 June 2004–15 August 2004	5.50%
17 May 2004–20 June 2004	5.25%
16 February 2004–16 May 2004	5.00%
17 November 2003–15 February 2004	4.75%
21 July 2003–16 November 2003	4.50%
17 February 2003–20 July 2003	4.75%
19 November 2001–16 February 2003	5.00%

Corporation tax pay and file (accounting periods ending after 30 September 1993)

Period	Rate
from 29 September 2009	3.0%
24 March 2009– 28 September 2009	1.75%
27 January 2009–23 March 2009	2.75%
6 January 2009–26 January 2009	3.50%
6 December 2008–5 January 2009	4.25%
6 November 2008–5 December 2008	5.00%
6 January 2008–5 November 2008	6.00%
6 August 2007–5 January 2008	6.75%
6 September 2006–5 August 2007	6.00%
6 September 2005–5 September 2006	5.25%
6 September 2004–5 September 2005	6.00%
6 December 2003–5 September 2004	5.25%[1]
6 August 2003–5 December 2003	4.25%
6 November 2001–5 August 2003	5.00%

[1]   This rate was corrected by HMRC (see news release HMRC 27/05 of 6 September 2005) and is higher than that previously used (5%). No attempt will be made to recover any further interest which may be due unless, exceptionally, a liability is reviewed.

Income tax on company payments (due on or after 14 October 1999)

Period	Rate
from 29 September 2009	3.0%
24 March 2009– 28 September 2009	2.5%
27 January 2009–23 March 2009	3.5%
6 January 2009–26 January 2009	4.5%
6 December 2008–5 January 2009	5.5%
6 November 2008–5 December 2008	6.5%
6 January 2008–5 November 2008	7.5%
6 August 2007–5 January 2008	8.5%
6 September 2006–5 August 2007	7.5%
6 September 2005–5 September 2006	6.5%
6 September 2004–5 September 2005	7.5%
6 December 2003–5 September 2004	6.5%
6 August 2003–5 December 2003	5.5%
6 November 2001–5 August 2003	6.5%

Inheritance tax

Interest runs from the due date (see p 3) to the date of payment.

Period	Rate
from 29 September 2009	**3%**
24 March 2009–28 September 2009	0%
27 January 2009–23 March 2009	1%
6 January 2009–26 January 2009	2%
6 November 2008–5 January 2009	3%
6 January 2008–5 November 2008	4%
6 August 2007–5 January 2008	5%
6 September 2006–5 August 2007	4%
6 September 2005–5 September 2006	3%
6 September 2004–5 September 2005	4%
6 December 2003–5 September 2004	3%
6 August 2003–5 December 2003	2%
6 November 2001–5 August 2003	3%

Remission of tax

By concession, arrears of tax may be waived if they result from HMRC's failure to make proper and timely use of information supplied by the taxpayer or, where it affects the taxpayer's coding, by his or her employer. The concession also applies to information supplied by the Department for Work and Pensions affecting the taxpayer's entitlement to a retirement, disability or widow's pension (see Concession A19). The concession only applies where the taxpayer could reasonably have believed that his or her affairs were in order and (unless the circumstances are exceptional) where the taxpayer is notified of the arrears more than 12 months after the end of the tax year in which HMRC received the information indicating that more tax was due.

Interest on overpaid tax

Income tax, capital gains tax, Class 1, 1A, 4 and (from 6.4.99) 1B national insurance contributions and (from 1.10.99) stamp duty and stamp duty reserve tax and (from 26.9.05) stamp duty land tax

FA 2009 ss 101–104, Schs 53–54A introduce provisions to harmonise interest regimes across all taxes and duties. Implementation will be staged over a number of years. The provisions will apply to income and capital gains tax self-assessment from 31 October 2011. For details of the periods for which interest is repayable see **harmonised interest regime** p 8. For amounts outstanding immediately prior to 31 October 2011 the old rules under TA 1988 s 824 and TCGA 1992 s 283 have effect up to and including 30 October 2011, and the new rules under FA 2009 ss 102 and 103 have effect thereafter.

Calculated as simple interest on the amount of tax repaid. The supplement is tax free.

Period	Rate
from 29 September 2009	**0.50%**
27 January 2009–28 September 2009	0.00%
6 January 2009–26 January 2009	0.75%
6 December 2008–5 January 2009	1.50%
6 November 2008–5 December 2008	2.25%
6 January 2008–5 November 2008	3.00%
6 August 2007–5 January 2008	4.00%
6 September 2006–5 August 2007	3.00%
6 September 2005–5 September 2006	2.25%
6 September 2004–5 September 2005	3.00%[1]
6 December 2003–5 September 2004	2.25%[1]
6 August 2003–5 December 2003	1.50%[1]
6 November 2001–5 August 2003	2.25%[1]

[1] These rates were corrected by HMRC (see HMRC 27/05, 6 September 2005) and are lower than those previously used. No attempt will be made to recover amounts overpaid by HMRC unless, exceptionally, a repayment is reviewed.

Income tax

(TA 1988 s 824; FA 1997 s 92; ITTOIA 2005 s 749, SI 2011/701)

From 1996–97 for amounts which become repayable up to and including 30 October 2011 (from 1997–98 for partnerships whose trade, profession or business commenced before 6 April 1994) repayment supplement applies to:

(a)   amounts paid on account of income tax
(b)   income tax paid by or on behalf of an individual
(c)   late payment penalties for income and capital gains tax self-assessment under FA 2009 Sch 56
(d)   penalties incurred by an individual under any provision of TMA 1970

but excluding amounts paid in excess of the maximum the taxpayer is required to pay.

Except for tax deducted at source, the repayment supplement runs *from* the date on which the tax or penalty was paid *to* the date on which the order for repayment is issued. For tax deducted at source, repayment supplement runs from 31 January after the end of the tax year for which the tax was deducted.

Capital gains tax

(TCGA 1992 s 283, SI 2011/701)

From 1996–97 for amounts which become repayable up to and including 30 October 2011 repayment supplement runs *from* the date on which the tax was paid *to* the date on which the order for repayment is issued.

Inheritance tax

(IHTA 1984 s 235)

Repayments of inheritance tax or interest paid carries interest *from* the date of payment *to* the date on which the order for repayment is issued. Before 29 September 2009, the prescribed rates for unpaid tax applied equally to repayment supplements. From 29 September 2009, the rate is 0.5%.

Companies

Corporation tax self-assessment (accounting periods ending after 30 June 1999)

Normal rates

Rates on overpaid corporation tax in respect of periods after normal due date (SI 1989/1297 reg 3BB).

Period	Rate
from 29 September 2009	**0.5%**
27 January 2009–28 September 2009	0%
6 January 2009–26 January 2009	1%
6 December 2008–5 January 2009	2%
6 November 2008–5 December 2008	3%
6 January 2008–5 November 2008	4%
6 August 2007–5 January 2008	5%
6 September 2006–5 August 2007	4%
6 September 2005–5 September 2006	3%
6 September 2004–5 September 2005	4%
6 December 2003–5 September 2004	3%
6 August 2003–5 December 2003	2%
6 November 2001–5 August 2003	3%

Special rates

For instalment payments by large companies and early payments by other companies, a special rate of interest runs from the date the excess arises (but not earlier than the due date of the first instalment) to the earlier of the date the repayment order is issued and nine months and one day after the end of the accounting period, after which the normal rate of interest (as above) applies.

Rates on overpaid instalment payments and on corporation tax paid early (but not due by instalments).

Period	Rate
from 21 September 2009	**0.5%**
16 March 2009–20 September 2009	0.25%
16 February 2009–15 March 2009	0.75%
19 January 2009–15 February 2009	1.25%
15 December 2008–18 January 2009	1.75%
17 November 2008–14 December 2008	2.75%
20 October 2008–16 November 2008	4.25%
21 April 2008–19 October 2008	4.75%

Period	Rate
18 February 2008–20 April 2008	5.00%
17 December 2007–17 February 2008	5.25%
16 July 2007–16 December 2007	5.50%
21 May 2007–15 July 2007	5.25%
22 January 2007–20 May 2007	5.00%
20 November 2006–21 January 2007	4.75%
14 August 2006–19 November 2006	4.50%
15 August 2005–13 August 2006	4.25%
16 August 2004–14 August 2005	4.50%
21 June 2004–15 August 2004	4.25%
17 May 2004–20 June 2004	4.00%
16 February 2004–16 May 2004	3.75%
17 November 2003–15 February 2004	3.50%
21 July 2003–16 November 2003	3.25%
17 February 2003–20 July 2003	3.50%
19 November 2001–16 February 2003	3.75%
15 October 2001–18 November 2001	4.25%
1 October 2001–14 October 2001	4.50%
13 August 2001–30 September 2001	4.75%
21 May 2001–12 August 2001	5.00%
16 April 2001–20 May 2001	5.25%
19 February 2001–15 April 2001	5.50%
21 February 2000–18 February 2001	5.75%
24 January 2000–20 February 2000	5.50%

Corporation tax pay and file (accounting periods ending before 1 July 1999)

Period	Rate
from 29 September 2009	0.50%
27 January 2009–28 September 2009	0.00%
6 January 2009–26 January 2009	0.50%
6 December 2008–5 January 2009	1.25%
6 November 2008–5 December 2008	2.00%
6 January 2008–5 November 2008	2.75%
6 August 2007–5 January 2008	3.50%
6 September 2006–5 August 2007	2.75%
6 September 2005–5 September 2006	2.00%
6 September 2004–5 September 2005	2.75%
6 December 2003–5 September 2004	2.00%
6 August 2003–5 December 2003	1.25%
6 November 2001–5 August 2003	2.00%

Harmonised interest regime

(FA 2009 ss 101–104, Schs 53–54A; SI 2011/701; SI 2013/280)

A harmonised interest regime is being phased in for all taxes and duties and applies to income and capital gains tax self-assessment from 31 October 2011. It applies to tax agent dishonest conduct penalties from 1 April 2013 (see p 20). Planned implementation dates for other taxes and duties covered in this publication are not yet clear. For amounts outstanding immediately prior to 31 October 2011, the previous legislation for income and capital gains tax self-assessment (TMA 1970 s 86, TA 1988 s 824 and TCGA 1992 s 283) had effect up to and including 30 October 2011, and the new legislation applies thereafter. The measure provides for differential interest charged and paid by HMRC to be based around the Bank of England base rate. The current rates are as set out on p 3 and p 6 – 3.0% for late payment interest and 0.5% for repayment interest.

Late payment interest runs from the start date to the date of payment. The start date is generally the date on which the amount becomes due and payable, but special rules apply as follows:

Where an amount is due as a result of—
- (a) an amendment or correction to an assessment or self-assessment; or
- (b) an HMRC assessment in place of, or in addition to, an assessment made by the taxpayer; or
- (c) an HMRC assessment in place of an assessment which ought to have been made by the taxpayer,

the start date is the date it would have been if the original assessment or self-assessment had been complete and accurate and made on the date (if any) by which it was required to be made, and the tax had been due and payable as a result of the original assessment or self-assessment.

Repayment interest runs from the start date until the date the payment or repayment is made. The start date in the case of an amount paid to HMRC is the later of—
- (i) the date the amount was paid to HMRC; and
- (ii) the date on which the amount became due and payable to HMRC (in a case where the amount has been paid in connection with a liability to make a payment to HMRC, and it is to be repaid by them).

The start date, in the case of an amount which has not been paid to HMRC and which is payable by virtue of a return or a claim having been submitted, is the later of—
- (1) the date (if any) on which the return or claim was required to be submitted; and
- (2) the date on which the return or claim was submitted.

The start date in the case of the carry back of losses or averaging claims is 31 January following the *later* tax year in relation to the claim.

Special relief

(TMA 1970 Sch 1AB para 3A; FA 1998 Sch 18 para 51BA)

From 1 April 2011 a new statutory 'special relief' is available which allows HMRC to give effect to a claim for repayment or discharge of an amount of tax that a person is liable to pay, but which the person believes is not due or, if it has been paid, was not due, where the usual time limits for such relief have expired. Relief is only available to taxpayers in receipt of an income tax or corporation tax self-assessment determination made by HMRC in the absence of a self-assessment return being submitted, and where the following specific conditions are met: (a) it would be unconscionable for HMRC to seek to recover the amount or to refuse to repay it if it has already been paid; (b) that the person's tax affairs are otherwise up to date, or arrangements have been put in place to HMRC's satisfaction, to bring them up to date as far as possible; and (c) the person has not previously claimed special relief, or its concessionary predecessor equitable liability, whether or not such a claim was successful. This latter condition may be waived in exceptional circumstances. There is no time limit for claiming the relief.

Certificates of tax deposit

Certificates are not available for purchase for use against corporation tax or PAYE liabilities. Certificates are available to individuals, partnerships, individual partners, trustees, personal representatives and companies for the payment of income tax, Class 4 national insurance contributions, capital gains tax, inheritance tax, petroleum revenue tax or petroleum royalty. Minimum first deposit £500; subsequent deposits not less than £250 or amount required to bring total deposits up to £500 (ie where total deposits have fallen below that amount). Interest is paid gross and is chargeable to tax. It will only be paid for the first six years of a deposit. A deposit bears interest for the first year at the rate in force at the time of the deposit and for each subsequent year at the rate in force on the anniversary of the deposit.

Date	Amount	Held for (mths in yr)	Pay't of tax %	Cashed %
11.6.04–5.8.04	Under £100,000	no limit	1.00	0.50
	£100,000 or over	under 1	1.00	0.50
		1–under 3	3.75	1.75
		3–under 6	3.50	1.75
		6–12	3.75	1.75
6.8.04–4.8.05	Under £100,000	no limit	1.25	0.50
	£100,000 or over	under 1	1.25	0.50
		1–12	3.75	1.75
5.8.05–3.8.06	Under £100,000	no limit	1.00	0.50
	£100,000 or over	under 1	1.00	0.50
		1–under 3	3.50	1.75
		3–under 6	3.25	1.50
		6–12	3.00	1.50
4.8.06–9.11.06	Under £100,000	no limit	1.75	0.75
	£100,000 or over	under 1	1.75	0.75
		1–under 3	4.25	2.00
		3–under 6	4.25	2.00
		6–12	4.00	2.00
10.11.06–11.1.07	Under £100,000	no limit	1.50	0.75
	£100,000 or over	under 1	1.50	0.75
		1–under 3	4.00	2.00

Date	Amount	Held for (mths in yr)	Pay't of tax %	Cashed %
		3–under 6	4.00	2.00
		6–12	3.75	1.75
12.1.07–10.5.07	Under £100,000	no limit	1.50	0.75
	£100,000 or over	under 1	1.50	0.75
		1–under 3	4.25	2.00
		3–under 6	4.00	2.00
		6–12	4.00	2.00
11.5.07–5.7.07	Under £100,000	no limit	2.00	1.00
	£100,000 or over	under 1	2.00	1.00
		1–under 3	4.75	2.25
		3–under 6	4.50	2.25
		6–12	4.50	2.25
6.7.07–6.12.07	Under £100,000	no limit	2.25	1.10
	£100,000 or over	under 1	2.25	1.10
		1–under 3	5.00	2.50
		3–under 6	4.75	2.25
		6–12	4.75	2.25
7.12.07–7.02.08	Under £100,000	no limit	3.00	1.50
	£100,000 or over	under 1	3.00	1.50
		1–under 3	5.50	2.75
		3–under 6	5.00	2.50
		6–under 9	4.75	2.25
		9–12	4.50	2.25
8.02.08–10.04.08	Under £100,000	no limit	2.00	1.00
	£100,000 or over	under 1	2.00	1.00
		1–under 3	4.50	2.25
		3–under 6	4.25	2.00
		6–under 9	4.00	2.00
		9–12	3.75	1.50
11.04.08–8.10.08	Under £100,000	no limit	2.00	1.00
	£100,000 or over	Under 1	2.00	1.00
		1–under 3	4.75	2.25
		3–under 6	4.50	2.25
		6–under 9	4.25	2.00
		9–12	4.25	2.00
9.10.08–6.11.08	Under £100,000	No limit	2.50	1.25
	£100,000 or over	under 1	2.50	1.25
		1–under 3	5.25	2.50
		3–under 6	5.00	2.50
		6–under 9	5.00	2.50
		9–12	4.75	2.25
7.11.08–4.12.08	Under £100,000	No limit	1.75	0.75
	£100,000 or over	under 1	1.75	0.75
		1–under 3	4.50	2.25
		3–under 6	4.25	2.00
		6–under 9	4.25	2.00
		9–12	4.00	2.00
5.12.08–8.1.09	Under £100,000	No limit	0.00	0.00
	£100,000 or over	under 1	0.00	0.00
		1–under 3	2.50	1.25
		3–under 6	2.50	1.25
		6–under 9	2.50	1.25
		9–12	2.25	1.00
9.1.09–5.2.09	Under £100,000	No limit	0.00	0.00
	£100,000 or over	under 1	0.00	0.00
		1–under 3	1.50	0.75
		3–under 6	1.25	0.50
		6–under 9	1.25	0.50
		9–12	1.25	0.50
6.2.09–5.3.09	Under £100,000	No limit	0.00	0.00
	£100,000 or over	under 1	0.00	0.00

Date	Amount	Held for (mths in yr)	Pay't of tax %	Cashed %
		1–under 3	1.00	0.50
		3–under 6	1.00	0.50
		6–under 9	1.00	0.50
		9–12	0.75	0.25
6.3.09–	Under £100,000	No limit	0.00	0.00
	£100,000 or over	under 1	0.00	0.00
		1–under 3	0.75	0.25
		3–under 6	0.75	0.25
		6–under 9	0.75	0.25
		9–12	0.75	0.25

Student loan deductions

	Percentage	Threshold
2013–14	9%	£16,365 per year £1,363.75 per month £314.71 per week
2012–13	9%	£15,795 per year £1,010.25 per month £303.75 per week
2005–06 to 2011–12	9%	£15,000 per year £1,250 per month £288.46 per week

Filing dates

Corporation tax

(FA 1998 Sch 18 paras 14, 15; SI 2003/282 reg 3(2A))

The return must be filed on the latest of the following dates—

(a) 12 months from the end of the period for which the return is made;
(b) where the company makes up its accounts for a period not exceeding 18 months, 12 months from the end of that period;
(c) where the company makes up its accounts for a period exceeding 18 months, 30 months from the start of that period;
(d) 3 months from the date of issue of the notice requiring the return.

From 1 April 2011 all company returns for accounting periods ending after 31 March 2010 must be filed online. Computations and, in most cases, accounts must be submitted in iXBRL format.

Income tax and capital gains tax

(TMA 1970 ss 8, 8A, 12AA; SI 2003/2682 reg 186)

Basic position for paper returns.	On or before 31 October following end of tax year.
Basic position for electronic returns.	On or before 31 January following end of tax year.
Paper return and notice to file return issued after 31 July but on or before 31 October following end of tax year.	Within 3 months of date of notice.
Electronic return and notice to file return issued after 31 July but on or before 31 October following end of tax year.	On or before 31 January following end of tax year.
Paper or electronic return and notice to file return issued after 31 October following end of tax year.	Within 3 months of date of notice.
Paper return and taxpayer wishes tax underpayment of less than £3,000[1] to be coded out.	On or before 31 October following end of tax year.
Electronic return and taxpayer wishes tax underpayment of less than £3,000[1] to be coded out.	Before 31 December following end of tax year.

[1] Applies to self-assessment underpayments of less than £2,000 before 2011–12.

Withdrawal of self-assessment notice

HMRC may withdraw a notice to file a self-assessment tax return in certain circumstances. The statutory power has effect for returns for 2012–13 onwards but has already been used by HMRC on a concessionary basis. Penalties for failure to make a return may be cancelled.

Penalties

Penalties — modernised penalty regime

A new modernised penalty regime is being rolled out to all taxes and duties with the exception of tax credits. The penalty regime in force in respect of various defaults is set out below. Planned implementation dates for other taxes and duties are not yet clear.

Inaccuracy in return or other document

Applies to	Commencement date	Penalty details
IT, CGT, CT, VAT, CIS, NIC Classes 1 and 4[1] (FA 2007 Sch 24)	Return periods starting 1 April 2008 where the return is due to be filed on or after 1 April 2009	Penalty based on potential lost revenue Careless inaccuracy — 30% Deliberate but not concealed — 70% Deliberate and concealed — 100%
IHT, all other taxes and duties (except tax credits)	Return periods starting 1 April 2009 where the return is due to be filed on or after 1 April 2010, or where the liability arises on or after 1 April 2010; for IHT in respect of deaths from 1 April 2009	*Reductions for disclosure* Unprompted disclosure minimum penalties nil, 20% and 30% Prompted disclosure minimum penalties 15%, 35% and 50%
Class 1A NIC	2010–11 returns	
Corporation tax credit, return by registered pension scheme	Return periods starting 1 April 2009 where the return is due to be filed on or after 1 April 2010	
IT, CGT but offshore matter (FA 2010 Sch 10)	6 April 2011	Penalties above are increased by either 0%, 50% or 100% depending on the territory concerned (see table on pp 17–18 for a list of territories in each category)

[1] The penalties under FA 2007 Sch 24 will apply to RTI returns from the date of Royal Assent to the Finance Bill 2013.

Inaccuracy in return or other document as a result of third party providing incorrect (or withholding) information

Applies to	Commencement date	Penalty details
IT, CGT, CT, VAT, IHT, CIS, NIC Classes 1 and 4, all other taxes and duties (except tax credits) (FA 2007 Sch 24)	1 April 2009 where the return is due to be filed on or after 1 April 2010	100% of potential lost revenue Subject to reduction for disclosure as for inaccuracies above.
Class 1A NIC	2010–11 returns	

Failure to notify HMRC of an error in an assessment (within 30 days)

Applies to	Commencement date	Penalty details
IT, CGT, CT, VAT, CIS, NIC Classes 1 and 4 (FA 2007 Sch 24)	1 April 2008 where the return is due to be filed on or after 1 April 2009	30% of potential lost revenue *Reductions for disclosure* Unprompted disclosure minimum penalty nil Prompted disclosure minimum penalty 15%
IHT, SDLT, all other taxes and duties except tax credits	1 April 2009 where the return is due to be filed on or after 1 April 2010	
Class 1A NIC	2010–11 returns	

Failure to notify chargeability (includes failure to register for VAT)

Applies to	Commencement date	Penalty details
IT, CGT, NIC Class 4 (Class 2 similar provisions but in separate legislation) (FA 2008 Sch 41)	2009–10	Penalty based on potential lost revenue Failure to notify — 30% Deliberate but not concealed — 70% Deliberate and concealed — 100%
CT	Accounting periods ending on or after 31 March 2010	*Reductions for disclosure* Unprompted disclosure minimum penalties nil (within 12 months late), 10% (more than 12 months late), 20% and 30% Prompted disclosure minimum penalties 15%, 35%, 50%
All other taxes and duties	Obligations arising on or after 1 April 2010	
IT, CGT but offshore matter (FA 2010 Sch 10)	6 April 2011	Penalties above are increased by either 0%, 20% or 100% depending on the territory concerned (see table on pp 17–18 for a list of territories in each category)

Failure to make returns on time

Applies to	Commencement date	Penalty details
Bank Payroll Tax	31 August 2010	Initial penalty £100 Failure continues for more than three months — with notice — £10 per day for up to 90 days Six months late — greater of 5% of the tax due and £300 12 months late — same penalty as for 6 months late unless deliberately withholding the return
IT, CGT, NIC Class 4 (FA 2009 Sch 55)	6 April 2011	Deliberate withholding of the return more than 12 months — 70% of tax due (minimum £300) Deliberate and concealed withholding of the return more than 12 months — 100% of tax due (minimum £300)
Return by Registered Pension scheme (FA 2009 Sch 55)	1 April 2011	*Reductions for disclosure* Unprompted disclosure minimum penalty 20% and 30% Prompted disclosure minimum penalties 35% and 50%
CIS returns (FA 2009 Sch 55)	6 October 2011	Initial penalty £100 After two months — £200 Six months late — greater of 5% of the tax due and £300 12 months late — same penalty as for 6 months late unless deliberately withholding the return Deliberate withholding of the return more than 12 months — 70% of tax due (minimum £1,500) Deliberate and concealed withholding of the return more than 12 months — 100% of tax due (minimum £3,000) *Reductions for disclosure* Unprompted disclosure minimum penalty 20% and 30% Prompted disclosure minimum penalties 35% and 50% Special rules apply to the first returns made on registration for CIS so that the maximum total penalty that can apply for the initial and second fixed penalties for all such returns is £3,000. Subsequent tax-geared penalties may still be incurred. Where a CIS return only relates to persons registered for 'gross payment' a tax-geared penalty after 6 months or 12 months cannot apply. In these cases the person is liable to the fixed amount penalty.
IT, CGT but offshore matter (FA 2010 Sch 10)	6 April 2011	Penalties above for a return later than 12 months which has been withheld are increased by either 0%, 50% or 100% depending on the territory concerned (see table on pp 17–18 for a list of territories in each category)
PAYE Real Time Information. Failure during a tax month to make a return on or before the filing date	6 April 2014 in relation to 2014–15 onwards[1]	First failure — nil Second and subsequent failure — an amount calculated in accordance with regulations yet to be announced Failure continues for more than three months — with notice — 5% of tax due

[1]   For 2013–14 the rules in the PAYE table on p 17 under "failure to submit returns" still apply.

Failure to pay tax on time

Applies to	Commencement date	Penalty details
PAYE, NIC Class 1, CIS, student loan deductions. (FA 2009 Sch 56)	2010–11 liabilities (on a risk assessed basis at present)	Penalty based on number of late payments in a year applied to the amounts paid late 1 late payment — nil 2, 3, 4 late payments — 1% 5, 6, 7 late payments — 2% 8, 9, 10 late payments — 3% 11, 12 late payments — 4% Any amount paid 6 months late — 5% Any amount paid 12 months late — 5%
NIC Class 1A and 1B (SI 2001/1004 reg 67B)	2010–11	31 days late — 5% 6 months late — 5% 12 months late — 5%
Bank Payroll Tax	31 August 2010	5% 5 months late — 5% 11 months late — 5%
Tax due by Registered Pension schemes (FA 2009 Sch 56)	Payments due 30 September 2010	31 days late — 5% 6 months late — 5% 12 months late — 5%
IT, CGT payable under self-assessment	6 April 2011 for self-assessment for 2010–11 onwards	31 days late — 5% 6 months late — 5% 12 months late — 5%

Offshore penalties — territory categories

Category 1

Anguilla	Estonia	Japan	Portugal[4]
Aruba	Finland	Korea, South	Romania
Australia	France[2]	Latvia	Slovakia
Belgium	Germany	Lithuania	Slovenia
Bulgaria	Greece	Malta	Spain[5]
Canada	Guernsey[3]	Montserrat	Sweden
Cayman Islands	Hungary	Netherlands (not including Bonaire, Sint Eustatius and Saba)	USA (not including overseas territories and possessions)[6]
Cyprus	Ireland	New Zealand (not including Tokelau)	
Czech Republic	Isle of Man	Norway	
Denmark (not including Faroe Islands or Greenland)[1]	Italy	Poland	

[1] Faroe Islands and Greenland are in Category 2.
[2] Includes overseas Departments of France; the overseas collectivities of France are in Category 2.
[3] Includes Alderney and Sark.
[4] Includes Madeira and the Azores.
[5] Includes the Canary Islands and other overseas territories of Spain.
[6] The overseas territories and possessions of the USA are in Category 2.

Category 2

Territories not listed in Categories 1 or 3 (other than the UK) will be in Category 2. Crown Dependencies and Overseas Territories of the UK are, unless listed, in Category 2.

Albania	Costa Rica	Kyrgyzstan	Saint Lucia
Algeria	Curaçao	Lebanon	Saint Vincent and the Grenadines
Andorra	Cuba	Macau[1]	San Marino
Antigua and Barbuda	Democratic People's Republic of Korea	Marshall Islands	Seychelles
Armenia	Dominica	Mauritius	Sint Maarten
Bahrain	Dominican Republic	Micronesia, Federated States of	Suriname
Barbados	Ecuador	Monaco	Syria
Belize	El Salvador	Nauru	Tokelau
Bonaire, Sint Eustatius and Saba	Gabon	Nicaragua	Tonga
Brazil	Grenada	Niue	Trinidad and Tobago
Cameroon	Guatemala	Palau	United Arab Emirates
Cape Verde	Honduras	Panama	Uruguay
Colombia	Iran	Paraguay	
Congo, Republic of the	Iraq	Peru	
Cook Islands	Jamaica	Saint Kitts and Nevis	

[1] China and Hong Kong are in Category 2.

Personal tax and corporation tax

Offence	Penalty
Failure to notify chargeability to income or capital gains tax within six months of tax year or to corporation tax within one year of accounting period (TMA 1970 s 7; FA 1998 Sch 18).	*Up to tax liability still unpaid after 31 January following tax year (IT or CGT) or one year after end of accounting period (CT).* **Repealed for failures on or after 1 April 2010.**
Failure to render return for income tax or capital gains tax (TMA 1970 ss 93, 93A).	*(a) Initial penalty of £100 (or tax due if less);* *(b) upon direction by Commissioners, further penalty up to £60 for each day failure continues;* *(c) if failure continues after six months from filing date, and no penalty imposed under (b), a further penalty of £100 (or tax due if less);* *(d) if failure continues after one year from filing date, a further penalty up to amount of tax due.* **Repealed and replaced by penalty under FA 2009 Sch 55 above for 2010–11 onwards.**
Failure to render return for corporation tax (FA 1998 Sch 18 paras 17, 18).	*(a) £100 if up to three months late (£500 if previous two returns also late);* *(b) £200 if over three months late (£1,000 if previous two returns also late);* *(c) if failure continues, on final day for delivery of return or, if later, 18 months after return period, 10% of tax unpaid 18 months after return period (20% of tax unpaid at that date if return not made within two years of return period).*
Failure to maintain records supporting personal and trustees' returns of partnership returns (TMA 1970 s 12B).	Up to £3,000.
Fraudulently or negligently making an incorrect statement in connection with a claim to reduce payments on account (TMA 1970 s 59A(6)).	Up to the amount (or additional amount) payable on account if a correct statement had been made.
Fraudulently or negligently delivering incorrect return or accounts or making an incorrect claim for an allowance, deduction or relief (TMA 1970 ss 95, 95A; FA 1998 Sch 18 para 89).	*Up to amount of tax underpaid by reason of incorrectness for (IT and CGT) the tax year (or following tax year and any preceding tax year) in which the return or claim is delivered, (CT) the accounting period(s) to which the return or claim relates.* **Repealed for returns or claims for periods to which penalty under FA 2007 Sch 24 applies (see p 12).**

Offence	Penalty
Failure to notify within charge to corporation tax within three months after the beginning of the first accounting period and any subsequent accounting period not following on immediately from the end of a previous accounting period. With effect for accounting periods beginning on or after 22 July 2004 (FA 2004 s 55).	(a) Initial penalty up to £300; and (b) a continuing penalty up to £60 for each day on which the failure continues. **Repealed for accounting periods ending after 31 March 2010.**
Deliberately or recklessly failing to pay corporation tax due in respect of total liability of company or fraudulently or negligently making claim for repayment (TMA 1970 s 59E(4); SI 1998/3175 reg 13).	Penalty not exceeding twice amount of interest charged under SI 1998/3175 reg 7.
Failure to register as self-employed (and liable to Class 2 NIC) within three months after month in which self-employment begins (SI 2001/1004 reg 87).	Up to £100. **Repealed for obligations arising after 5 April 2009.**

PAYE

Offence	Penalty
Failure to submit return P9D or P11D (benefits in kind) by due date (6 July following subsequent tax years) (TMA 1970 s 98(1)).	(a) Initial penalty up to £300; and (b) continuing penalty up to £60 for each day on which the failure continues.
Fraudulently or negligently submitting incorrect return P9D or P11D (TMA 1970 s 98(2)).	Penalty up to £3,000. **Does not apply from 1 April 2009 when penalty for careless or deliberate error under FA 2007 Sch 24 applies.**
Failure to submit returns P14 (individual end of year summary), P35 (annual return), P38 or P38A (supplementary returns for employees not on P35) by due date (19 May following tax year) (TMA 1970 s 98A)[1].	(a) First 12 months: penalty of £100 for each 50 employees (or part thereof) for each month the failure continues; (b) failures exceeding 12 months: penalty up to amount of PAYE or NIC due and unpaid after 19 April following tax year.
Fraudulently or negligently submitting incorrect forms P14, P35, P38 or P38A (TMA 1970 s 98A).	Penalty up to the amount of tax due. **Repealed from 1 April 2008 in relation to documents for tax periods commencing on or after that date.**
Failure to submit returns P11D(b) (Class 1A NIC returns) by due date (6 July following tax year, but by concession until 31 March 2013, 19 July applies) (SI 2001/1004 reg 81(2)).	(a) First 12 months: penalty of £100 for each 50 employees (or part thereof) for each month the failure continues (but total penalty not to exceed total Class 1A NIC due); (b) failures exceeding 12 months: a penalty not exceeding the amount of Class 1A NIC due and unpaid after 19 July following tax year.
Fraudulently or negligently submitting incorrect form P11D(b) (2001/1004 reg 81(1) before substitution by SI 2010/721).	Up to the difference between the amount paid and the amount which should have been paid if the return had been correct. **Does not apply from 2010–11 when FA 2007 Sch 24 applies.**
Failure to submit information in connection with mandatory e-filing from 2004–05 onwards (SI 2003/2682 as amended by 2009/2029 reg 14).	Penalty based on number of employees not exceeding £3,000 for 1,000 or more employees.

[1]   See p 14 for penalties for failure to make returns on time under PAYE Real Time Information from 6 April 2014 for 2014–15 onwards.

Inheritance tax returns and information

Offence	Penalty
Failure to deliver an account within 12 months of death (unless tax is less than £100 or there is a reasonable excuse) (IHTA 1984 s 245).	(a) Initial penalty of £100 (or the amount of tax payable if less); (b) further penalty up to £60 (where penalty determined by court or tribunal) for each day on which the failure continues; (c) if failure continues after six months after the date on which account is due, and proceedings not commenced, a further penalty of £100 (or amount of tax payable if less); and (d) if failure continues one year after end of the period in which account is due, and IHT is payable, a penalty not exceeding £3,000.

Offence	Penalty
Failure to submit account or notify HMRC under IHTA 1984 s 218A if a disposition on a death is varied within six months of the variation and additional tax is payable (IHTA 1984 s 245A(1A), (1B)).	(a) Initial penalty up to £100; (b) further penalty up to £60 (if determined by court or tribunal) for each day on which the failure continues; (c) up to £3,000 if failure continues after 12 months from date notification is due.
Failure to provide information etc under IHTA 1984 s 218 concerning a settlement by a UK-domiciled settlor with non-resident trustees (IHTA 1984 s 245A(1)).	(a) Initial penalty up to £300; and (b) further penalty up to £60 (where penalty determined by court or tribunal) for each day on which the failure continues.
Failure to provide documents etc under IHTA 1984 s 219A(1) or (4) (IHTA 1984 s 245A(3)).	(a) *Initial penalty up to £50; and* (b) *further penalty up to £30 (where penalty determined by court or tribunal) for each day on which the failure continues.* **Repealed with effect from 1 April 2010 and replaced by penalties under FA 2008 Sch 36 (see p 20).**
Taxpayer fraudulently or negligently delivering, furnishing or producing incorrect accounts, information or documents (IHTA 1984 s 247; FA 2004 s 295(4), (9)).	*(Accounts etc delivered after 22 July 2004)* *Penalty up to the amount of tax payable.* **Repealed for accounts etc to which penalty under FA 2007 Sch 24 applies (see p 12).**
Person other than the taxpayer fraudulently or negligently delivering, furnishing or producing incorrect accounts, information or documents (IHTA 1984 s 247(3); FA 2004 s 295(4), (9)).	Up to £3,000.
Incorrect return etc: Assisting in or inducing the delivery, furnishing or production of any account, information or document knowing it to be incorrect (IHTA 1984 s 247(4)).	*Up to £3,000.* **Repealed with effect from 1 April 2013. See now tax agent dishonest conduct penalties under FA 2012 Sch 38 (see p 20).**

Special returns of information

Offence	Penalty
Failure to comply with a notice to deliver a return or other document, furnish particulars or make anything available for inspection under any of the provisions listed in column 1 of the table in TMA 1970 s 98.	(a) Initial penalty up to £300; (b) further penalty up to £60 for each day on which the failure continues.
Failure to furnish information, give certificates or produce documents or records under any of the provisions listed in column 2 of the table in TMA 1970 s 98.	(a) Initial penalty up to £300; and (b) further penalty up to £60 for each day on which the failure continues.
Fraudulently or negligently delivering any incorrect document, information etc required under the above provisions (TMA 1970 s 99; SI 2013/279).	Penalty up to £3,000. **Repealed with effect from 1 April 2013. See now tax agent dishonest conduct penalties under FA 2012 Sch 38 (see p 20).**
Failure to deduct income tax at source from payments of interest or royalties under ITA 2007 Part 15 where the exemption does not apply and the company did not believe or could not reasonably have believed that it would apply (TMA 1970 s 98(4A)–(4E)).	(a) Initial penalty up to £3,000; and (b) further penalty up to £600 for each day on which the failure continues.
Advance pricing agreements: Fraudulently or negligently making a false or misleading statement in the preparation of, or application to enter into, any advance pricing agreement (TIOPA 2010 s 227).	Penalty up to £10,000.
Declaration of non-UK residence: Fraudulently or negligently making a false or misleading declaration of non-UK residence to a deposit-taker or building society under ITA 2007 ss 858-861 (TMA 1970 s 99B).	Penalty up to £3,000.

Other offences by taxpayers, agents etc

Offence	Penalty
Falsification of documents. Intentionally falsifying, concealing or destroying documents required under TMA 1970 ss 20A (repealed with effect from 1 April 2013) or 20BA (TMA 1970 s 20BB).	On summary conviction, a fine up to the statutory maximum (£5,000); on conviction on indictment, imprisonment for a term not exceeding two years or a fine or both.
Failure to produce documents etc for the purposes of an enquiry under TMA 1970 s 19A or under FA 1998 Sch 18 para 27 (TMA 1970 s 97AA; FA 1998 Sch 18 para 29).	(a) Initial penalty of £50; and (b) further penalty up to £30 (if determined by HMRC) or £150 (if determined by tribunal) for each day on which failure continues. **Repealed on or after 1 April 2009**.
European Economic Interest Groupings– Offences in connection with the supply of information:	
(i) failure to supply information	Initial penalty up to £300 per member of the Grouping at the time of failure and after direction by the tribunal: continuing penalty up to £60 per member of the Grouping at the end of the day for each day on which the failure continues.
(ii) fraudulent or negligent delivery of an incorrect return, accounts or statement	Up to £3,000 for each member of the Grouping at the time of delivery.
(TMA 1970 s 98B).	
Assisting in the delivery of incorrect returns, accounts or information (TMA 1970 s 99: SI 2013/279).	Penalty up to £3,000. **Repealed with effect from 1 April 2013. See new tax agent dishonest conduct penalties under FA 2012 Sch 38 on p 20.**
Certificates of non-liability to income tax: Fraudulently or negligently giving such a certificate for the purposes of receiving interest gross on a bank or building society account, or failing to comply with an undertaking given in such a certificate (TMA 1970 s 99A).	Penalty up to £3,000.
Refusal to allow a deduction of income tax at source (TMA 1970 s 106).	£50.
Obstruction of officer in inspection of property to ascertain its market value (TMA 1970 s 111).	Up to £50. **Repealed with effect from 1 April 2010 and replaced by penalties under FA 2008 Sch 36 (see below).**
Construction Industry Scheme: (pre 1 April 2007 scheme) Failure by contractor to check validity of registration card (TA 1988 s 566(2B)–(2E)).	Up to £3,000. **Repealed for payments after 5 April 2007.**
(pre 1 April 2007 scheme) Fraudulent attempt by sub-contractor to obtain or misuse a sub-contractor's certificate (TA 1988 s 561(10), (11)).	Up to £3,000. **Repealed for payments after 5 April 2007.**
Construction Industry Scheme: (post 31 March 2007 scheme) Making false statements etc for the purpose of obtaining a gross payment certificate (FA 2004 s 72).	Up to £3,000.
Fraudulent evasion of income tax (TMA 1970 s 106A).	On summary conviction, imprisonment for up to six months or a fine up to the statutory maximum (£5,000); on conviction on indictment, imprisonment for up to seven years or a fine or both.
Enterprise investment scheme relief: Issue by a company of a certificate of approval for such relief fraudulently or negligently or without the authority of HMRC (ITA 2007 s 207).	Not exceeding £3,000.
Treasury consent: Creation or transfer of shares or debentures in a non-resident subsidiary company without the consent of HM Treasury (TA 1988 s 766).	On conviction on indictment— (a) imprisonment for not more than two years or a fine, or both; or (b) in the case of a UK company, a fine not exceeding the greater of £10,000, or three times the tax payable by the company attributable to income and gains arising in the previous 36 months. **Repealed with effect from 1 July 2009**.
Failure of a company to maintain records (other than those only required for claims, etc, or dividend vouchers and certificates of income tax deducted where other evidence is available) (FA 1998 Sch 18 para 23).	Penalty not exceeding £3,000.

Offence	Penalty
Failure to notify notifiable proposals or notifiable arrangements, or failure to notify the client of the relevant scheme reference number under the provisions of FA 2004 ss 306–319 (TMA 1970 s 98C).	(*a*) Up to 31 December 2010 an initial penalty not exceeding £5,000; (i) From 1 January 2011 in the case of provisions under FA 2004 ss 308(1) and (3), 309(1) and 310 up to £600 per day in 'initial period' (but a tribunal can determine a higher penalty up to £1 million); (ii) From 1 January 2011 in the case of provisions in FA 2004 ss 312(2), 312A(2), 313ZA, 313A, 313B, 313C an initial penalty up to £5,000. Where a disclosure order is made the amount in (i) above is increased up to £5,000 per day that failure continues from ten days after the order is made. (*b*) a continuing penalty not exceeding £600 for each day on which the failure continues after imposition of initial penalty. Where a disclosure order is made the amount is increased up to £5,000 per day that failure continues from ten days after the order is made.
Failure to notify scheme reference number etc under FA 2004 s 313(1);	Penalty of £100 in respect of each scheme to which the failure relates;
for second failure, occurring within three years from the date on which the first failure began;	penalty of £500 in respect of each scheme to which the failure relates;
for subsequent failures, occurring within three years from the date on which the previous failure began. (TMA 1970 s 98C; FA 2004 s 315(1)).	penalty of £1,000 in respect of each scheme to which the failure relates.
Failure to comply with HMRC investigatory powers under FA 2008 Sch 36.	(*a*) an initial penalty of £300;
Failure to comply with an information notice within FA 2008 Sch 36 Pt 1 or deliberately obstructing an HMRC officer in the course of an inspection of business premises under FA 2008 Sch 36 Pt 2 which has been approved by the First-tier Tribunal. Applies to IT (including PAYE and CIS), CT, CGT, VAT and certain foreign taxes with effect from 1 April 2009. Extended to IHT, SDLT and other taxes from 1 April 2010 and to Bank Payroll Tax (BPT) from 31 August 2010.	(*b*) if failure/obstruction continues, a further penalty up to £60 per day; (*c*) if failure/obstruction continues after penalty under (*a*) imposed, a tax-related amount determined by the Upper Tribunal.
Carelessly or deliberately providing inaccurate information or an inaccurate document in response to an information notice.	Up to £3,000 per inaccuracy.
Failure of a senior accounting officer to ensure a company maintains appropriate tax accounting arrangements (FA 2009 Sch 46).	£5,000.
Failure of a senior accounting officer to provide a certificate stating whether the company had appropriate tax accounting arrangements (FA 2009 Sch 46).	£5,000.
Failure to notify Commissioners of name of senior accounting officer (FA 2009 Sch 46).	£5,000.
Failure of a third party to notify the contact details of a debtor (FA 2009 Sch 49).	£300.
Tax agent failure to comply with file access notice (FA 2012 Sch 38).	(*a*) an initial penalty of £300. (*b*) if failure continues, a further penalty up to £60 per day.
Tax agent engaging in dishonest conduct (FA 2012 Sch 38).	£5,000 minimum to £50,0000 maximum subject to the quality of disclosure and compliance with any access notice, with possible special reduction of £5,000 penalty to nil at HMRC's discretion.

Mitigation of penalties

HMRC have discretion to mitigate or entirely remit any penalty or to stay or compound any penalty proceedings (TMA 1970 s 102).

Interest on penalties

Penalties under TMA 1970 Parts II (ss 7–12B), IV (ss 28A–43B), VA (ss 59A–59D) and X (ss 93–107), and FA 1998 Sch 18 carry interest at the prescribed rate (see p 3): TMA 1970 s 103A. For tax years before 2010–11, surcharges on unpaid income tax and capital gains tax carried interest under TMA 1970 s 59C. Surcharges have been replaced by a modernised penalty regime (see p 12).

Publishing details of deliberate tax defaulters

From 1 April 2010 HMRC have the power to publish the names and details of taxpayers who are penalised for deliberate defaults leading to a loss of tax of more than £25,000 (FA 2009 s 94).

Tax agent dishonest conduct

From 1 April 2013, in addition to the penalties listed above, HMRC have the power to publish names and details of tax agents who incur penalties for dishonest conduct over £5,000 (FA 2012 Sch 38; SI 2013/279).

Failure to provide security

A person who fails to comply with a requirement imposed under the PAYE regulations to give security or further security is liable on summary conviction to a fine not exceeding level 5 on the standard scale (ITEPA 2003 s 684(4A)).

Time limits for claims and elections

Whenever possible, a claim or election must be made on the tax return or by an amendment to the return (TMA 1970 s 42 and FA 1998 Sch 18 paras 9, 10, 67 and 79). Exceptions to this general rule are dealt with in TMA 1970 Sch 1A. Except where another period is expressly prescribed, a claim for relief in respect of income tax and capital gains tax must be made within four years after the end of the tax year (for claims made before 1 April 2010 such claims had to be made within five years from the 31 January following the year of assessment to which they related). (TMA 1970 s 43(1); FA 2008 Sch 39 para 12.) The time limit for claims by companies is four years from the end of the accounting period to which it relates (six years for claims made before 1 April 2010) (FA 1998 Sch 18 para 55; FA 2008 Sch 39 para 45).

The tables below set out some of the main exceptions to the general limits.

Income tax

Claim	Time limit
Trading losses: Loss sustained in a trade, profession or vocation to be set against other income of the year or the last preceding year. Extended to certain pre-trading expenditure by ITTOIA 2005 s 57 (ITA 2007 s 64).	One year after 31 January next following tax year in which loss arose.
Unrelieved trading losses to be set against capital gains (TCGA 1992 ss 261B, 261C).	One year after 31 January next following tax year in which loss arose.
Losses of new trade etc: Loss sustained in the first four years of a new trade, profession or vocation to be offset against other income arising in the three years immediately preceding the year of loss. Extended to certain pre-trading expenditure by ITTOIA 2005 s 57 (ITA 2007 s 72).	One year after 31 January next following tax year in which loss arose.
Property business losses: Claim for relief against total income (ITA 2007 s 124).	One year after 31 January next following tax year specified in claim.
Loss on disposal of unlisted shares: Loss on disposal of shares in an EIS company or a qualifying trading company to be offset against other income of the year of loss or the last preceding year (ITA 2007 s 132).	One year after 31 January next following tax year in which loss arose.
Gift aid: Election to treat donations to charity under gift aid made after 5 April 2003 as made in the previous tax year (ITA 2007 s 426).	On or before date on which donor delivers tax return for the previous tax year and not later than 31 January after that year.

Capital gains

Claim	Time limit
Assets of negligible value: Loss to be allowed where the value of an asset has become negligible (TCGA 1992 s 24(2)).	Two years after end of chargeable period of deemed sale (and reacquisition).
Assets held on 31 March 1982: Events occurring prior to 31 March 1982 to be ignored in computing gains arising after 5 April 1988 (TCGA 1992 s 35(5), (6) as amended).	Two years after end of accounting period in which first relevant disposal made after 31.3.88; or such further time as HMRC may allow (corporation tax). *One year after 31 January next following tax year in which first relevant disposal made after 5.4.88 (**capital gains tax for tax years before 2008–09 only**).*
Main residence: Determination of main residence for principal private residence exemption (TCGA 1992 s 222(5)(a)).	Two years after acquisition of second residence.
Relief for loans to traders: Losses on certain loans to traders to be allowed as capital losses at the time of claim or 'earlier time' (TCGA 1992 s 253(3A)).	Two years after the end of the tax year or accounting period of loss.
Relief for loans to traders (payments by guarantor): Losses arising from payments by guarantor of certain irrecoverable loans to traders to be allowed as capital losses at time of claim or 'earlier time' (TCGA 1992 s 253(4), (4A)).	Four years after the end of the tax year or accounting period in which payment made (for claims before 1 April 2010, five years after 31 January following tax year in which payment made (capital gains tax); six years after end of accounting period in which payment made (corporation tax)).
Election for valuation at 6 April 1965: Gain on a disposal of an asset held at 6 April 1965 to be computed as if the asset had been acquired on that date. An election once made is irrevocable (TCGA 1992 Sch 2 para 17).	Two years after end of accounting period in which disposal made; or such further time as HMRC may allow (corporation tax). *One year after 31 January following tax year in which disposal made (**capital gains tax for tax years before 2008–09 only**).*

Corporation tax

Claim	Time limit
Trading losses: Loss sustained by a company in a trade in an accounting period to be offset against profits of that accounting period and profits of the preceding year. Extended to certain pre-trading expenditure by CTA 2009 s 61 (CTA 2010 s 37(7)).	Two years after end of loss-making period; or such further period as HMRC may allow.
Group relief: Group relief to be given for accounting periods ending after 30 June 1999. The surrendering company must consent to the claim (FA 1998 Sch 18 paras 66–77).	The last of: (a) one year from filing date of claimant company's return for accounting period for which claim is made; (b) 30 days after end of an enquiry into return; (c) if HMRC amend return after an enquiry, 30 days after issue of notice of amendment; (d) if an appeal is made against amendment, 30 days after determination of appeal; (or such later time as HMRC may allow).
Non-trading deficit on loan relationship: Claim for non-trading deficits on loan relationships (including non-trading debits on derivative contracts) in an accounting period to be: (a) offset against profits of same period or carried back (CTA 2009 s 460);	Two years after end of accounting period in which deficit arose (or such later time as HMRC may allow).
(b) treated as non-trading deficit of subsequent accounting period to be carried forward to succeeding accounting periods (CTA 2009 s 458).	Two years after end of that subsequent accounting period.
Intangible assets: Election to replace accounts depreciation with fixed writing-down allowance of 4% (CTA 2009 s 730).	Two years after end of the accounting period in which asset was created or acquired.
Research and development: Claim for tax relief to be made, amended or withdrawn in company tax return (or amended return) (FA 1998 Sch 18 paras 83E).	One year from the filing date for return or such later time as HMRC may allow.
UITF 40 spreading adjustment: Election to treat it as arising and charged in an accounting period rather than spreading it over three to six years (FA 2006 Sch 15 para 13).	One year from filing date for return.

Capital allowances

Claim	Time limit
Corporation tax claims: Claims, amended claims and withdrawals of claims in respect of corporation tax capital allowances (CAA 2001 s 3(2), (3)(b); FA 1998 Sch 18 para 82).	The last of: (a) one year after filing date of claimant company's return for accounting period for which claim is made; (b) 30 days after end of enquiry into return; (c) If HMRC amend the return after an enquiry, 30 days after issue of notice of amendment; (d) if appeal is made against amendment, 30 days after determination of appeal; (or such later time as HMRC may allow).
Short life assets: Plant or machinery to be treated as a short life asset (CAA 2001 s 85(2)).	One year after 31 January after tax year in which chargeable period ends (income tax); two years after end of chargeable period (corporation tax).
Connected persons: Succession to a trade between connected persons to be ignored in computing capital allowances (CAA 2001 s 266).	Two years after date of the succession.
Sales between persons under common control treated as made at the lower of open market value and tax written down value (CAA 2001 s 570(5)).	Two years after date of the disposal.

Exchanges

Recognised stock exchanges

The following is a list of countries with exchanges which have been designated as recognised stock exchanges under ITA 2007 s 1005; CTA 2010 s 1137. Unless otherwise specified, any stock exchange (or options exchange) in a country listed below is a recognised stock exchange provided it is recognised under the law of the country concerned relating to stock exchanges.

HMRC may make an order designating a market in the UK as a recognised stock exchange.

Country	Date of recognition
Australian Stock Exchange and its stock exchange subsidiaries	22 September 1988
Austria[3]	22 October 1970
Bahamas	
Bahamas International Securities Exchange	19 April 2010
Belgium[3]	22 October 1970
Bermuda	4 December 2007
Brazil	
Rio De Janeiro Stock Exchange	17 August 1995
São Paulo Stock Exchange	11 December 1995
Canada	
Any stock exchange prescribed for the purposes of the Canadian Income Tax Act	22 October 1970
Cayman Islands Stock Exchange	4 March 2004
China	
Hong Kong – Any stock exchange recognised under Section 2A(1) of the Hong Kong Companies Ordinance	26 February 1971
Cyprus	
Cyprus Stock Exchange	22 June 2009
Denmark	
Copenhagen Stock Exchange	22 October 1970
Estonia	
NASDAQ OMX Tallinn	5 May 2010
European Wholesale Securities Market	18 January 2013
Finland	
Helsinki Stock Exchange	22 October 1970
France[3]	22 October 1970
Germany[3]	5 August 1971
Greece	
Athens Stock Exchange	14 June 1993
Guernsey[3]	10 December 2002
Iceland	31 March 2006
Irish Republic[3]	22 October 1970
Italy[3]	3 May 1972
Japan[3]	22 October 1970
Korea	10 October 1994
Lithuania	
NASDAQ OMX Vilnius	12 March 2012
Luxembourg[3]	21 February 1972
Malaysia	
Kuala Lumpur Stock Exchange	10 October 1994
Malta Stock Exchange	29 December 2005
Mauritius Stock Exchange	31 January 2011
Mexico	10 October 1994
Netherlands[3]	22 October 1970
New Zealand	22 September 1988
Norway[3]	22 October 1970
Poland	
Warsaw Stock Exchange	25 February 2010
Portugal[3]	21 February 1972
Russia	
MICEX Stock Exchange	5 January 2011
Singapore	30 June 1977

Country	Date of recognition
South Africa	
Bond Exchange of South Africa	16 April 2008
Johannesburg Stock Exchange	22 October 1970
Spain[3]	5 August 1971
Sri Lanka	
Colombo Stock Exchange	21 February 1972
Sweden	
Stockholm Stock Exchange	16 July 1985
Swiss Stock Exchange	12 May 1997
Thailand	10 October 1994
United Kingdom	
London Stock Exchange	19 July 2007
PLUS-listed Market	19 July 2007
LIFFE Administration and Management	26 September 2011
United States	
Any stock exchange registered with the SEC as a national securities exchange[1]	22 October 1970
Nasdaq Stock Market[2]	10 March 1992

[1]   'National securities exchange' does not include any local exchanges registered with Securities and Exchange Commission.

[2]   As maintained through the facilities of the National Association of Securities Dealers Inc and its subsidiaries.

[3]   i.e., a stock exchange according to the law of the country concerned relating to stock exchanges.

Recognised futures exchanges

The following is a list of exchanges which have been designated as recognised futures exchanges under TCGA 1992 s 288(6). By concession, those exchanges were recognised futures exchanges for the tax year of recognition onwards.

Recognised futures exchanges	Date of recognition
International Petroleum Exchange of London	6 August 1985
London Metal Exchange	6 August 1985
London Gold Market	12 December 1985
London Silver Market	12 December 1985
CME Group (formerly Chicago Mercantile Exchange and Chicago Board of Trade)	19 December 1986
New York Mercantile Exchange	19 December 1986
Philadelphia Board of Trade	19 December 1986
Mid America Commodity Exchange	29 July 1987
Montreal Exchange	29 July 1987
Hong Kong Futures Exchange	15 December 1987
Commodity Exchange (Comex)	25 August 1988
Sydney Futures Exchange	13 October 1988
Euronext (London International Financial Futures and Options Exchange)	22 March 1992
OM Stockholm	18 March 1992
OMLX (formerly OM London)	18 March 1992
New York Board of Trade	10 June 2004

Recognised investment exchanges and clearing houses

The following is a list of investment exchanges and clearing houses recognised as investment exchanges under the Financial Services and Markets Act 2000 and able to carry out investment business in the UK.

Recognised investment exchanges	Date of recognition
London Stock Exchange plc	22 November 2001
LIFFE Administration and Management	22 November 2001
The London Metal Exchange Ltd	22 November 2001
ICE Futures Europe	22 November 2001
EDX London Ltd[1]	1 July 2003
ICAP Securities & Derivatives Exchange Ltd (formerly PLUS Stock Exchange plc)	19 July 2007

[1]   As of 1 May 2011 EDX London Ltd was absorbed into Turquoise Global Holdings Limited and is no longer a recognised investment exchange.

Recognised clearing houses	Date of recognition
LCH.Clearnet Ltd	22 November 2001
Euroclear UK & Ireland Ltd	23 November 2001
European Central Counterparty Ltd	27 March 2008
ICE Clear Europe Ltd	15 May 2008
CME Clearing Europe Ltd	15 December 2010

Recognised overseas investment exchanges and clearing houses

The following is a list of overseas investment exchanges and clearing houses recognised under the Financial Services and Markets Act 2000 and able to conduct investment business in the UK.

Recognised overseas investment exchange	Date of recognition
National Association of Securities Dealers Automated Quotations (NASDAQ)	23 November 2001
Australian Securities Exchange Ltd	30 January 2002
The Chicago Mercantile Exchange (CME)	23 November 2001
Chicago Board of Trade (CBOT)	23 November 2001
New York Mercantile Exchange Inc (NYMEX Inc)	23 November 2001
SIX Swiss Exchange AG	23 November 2001
EUREX (Zurich)	23 November 2001
ICE Futures US Inc	17 May 2007
NYSE LIFFE US	29 September 2009
Green Exchange LLC (acquired by CME Group on 3 April 2012)	6 March 2012

Recognised clearing house	Date of recognition
SIX X-Clear	19 August 2004
Eurex Clearing AG	16 January 2007
The Chicago Mercantile Exchange (CME)	11 January 2008
ICE Clear US Inc	25 March 2008
European Multilateral Clearing Facility NV	29 January 2009
Cassa di Compensazione e Garanzia SpA	8 July 2009
LCH SA	18 May 2010

Alternative finance investment bonds

List of recognised stock exchanges designated solely for the purposes of ITA 2007 s 564G, TCGA 1992 s 151N, CTA 2009 s 507.

Recognised stock exchanges	Date of recognition
Abu Dhabi Securities Market	1 April 2007
Bahrain Stock Exchange	1 April 2007
Dubai Financial Market	1 April 2007
NASDAQ Dubai (formerly Dubai International Financial Exchange)	1 April 2007
Labuan International Financial Exchange	1 April 2007
Saudi Stock Exchange (Tadawul)	1 April 2007
Surabaya Stock Exchange	1 April 2007

Applications for clearances and approvals

Clearance application	Address
Transfer of long-term insurance business (TCGA 1992 s 211, TA 1988 s 444AED)	HM Revenue & Customs, CTIAA Corporation Tax and Business Income Tax, Financial Services Team, 3rd Floor, 100 Parliament Street, London SW1A 2BQ
Demergers (CTA 2010 s 1091); Company purchase of own shares (CTA 2010 s 1044); Transactions in securities (CTA 2010 s 748; ITA 2007 s 701); Enterprise Investment Scheme – acquisition of shares by new company (ITA 2007 s 247(1)(f)); Share exchanges (TCGA 1992 s 138) Reconstruction regarding transfer of a business (TCGA 1992 s 139) Transfer of a UK trade between EU member states (TCGA 1992 ss 140B, 140D) Intangible fixed assets (CTA 2009 s 831) Loan relationships transfers/mergers (CTA 2009 ss 426, 427, 438) Derivative contracts transfers/mergers (CTA 2009 ss 677, 686) Schemes converting income to capital (TCGA 1992 ss 184G–H) Assignment of lease granted at under-value (CTA 2009 s 237; ITTOIA 2005 s 300) Transactions in land (CTA 2010 s 831; ITA 2007 s 770)	Clearance and Counteraction Team, Anti-Avoidance Group, SO528, PO Box 194, Bootle, L69 9AA (Applications should be marked "market sensitive" or "non-market sensitive" as appropriate.)[1]
Company migration (TMA 1970 s 109B–F, formerly FA 1988 s 130)	Neil Nagle, HM Revenue & Customs, CTIAA Business International, Transfer Pricing Team, 100 Parliament Street, London SW1A 2BQ
Advance pricing agreements (TIOPA 2010 Part 5)	Maura Parsons, HM Revenue & Customs, CTIAA Business International, Transfer Pricing Team, 100 Parliament Street, London SW1A 2BQ
	For APAs involving oil, gas and mining taxation: Competent Authority, (APAs), Large Business Service Oil & Gas (APAs), 3rd Floor, 22 Kingsway, London WC2B 6NR
Controlled foreign companies (TA 1988 ss 747–756, Schs 24–26)	Mary Sharp, HM Revenue & Customs CTIAA, Business International, 100 Parliament Street, London SW1A 2BQ
Corporate Venturing Schemes (FA 2000 Sch 15)	Small Company Enterprise Centre, HM Revenue & Customs, 1st Floor, Ferrers House, Castle Meadow Road, Nottingham NG2 1BD
Advance thin capitalisation agreements (Statement of Practice 1/12)	The first contact for information about advance thin capitalisation agreements under the Statement of Practice should be the Customer Relationship Manager (CRM) or Customer Contact (CC) of the business concerned, and they will engage the assistance of a transfer pricing specialist. If there is no known CRM or CC, the application may be sent to the local Transfer Pricing team leader Otherwise, enquiries and applications should be addressed through Ashley Culpin at CTIAA Business International
Inward investment (in Statement of Practice 02/07)	HM Revenue & Customs, Business Investment Relief Team S1278, PO Box 202, Bootle, L69 9AL
IHT clearance for business owners	See www.hmrc.gov.uk/cap/clearanceiht.htm

Approval application	Address
Pensions (formerly TA 1988 ss 590, 591)	Registration of a pension scheme from 6 April 2006 must be done online, but HMRC can be contacted at Pension Schemes Services, Fitzroy House, Castle Meadow Road, Nottingham, NG2 1BD
Employee share schemes (ITEPA 2003 Schs 2, 3, 4)	Employee Shares & Securities Unit, HM Revenue & Customs, 1st Floor, Fitzroy House, Castle Meadow Road, Nottingham NG2 1BD Questions on EMI: Small Company Enterprise Centre Admin Team, HM Revenue & Customs, Medvale House, Mote Road, Maidstone, Kent ME15 6AF Questions on share valuation: Shares and Assets Valuation, Ferrers House, PO Box 38, Castle Meadow Road, Nottingham NG2 1BB
Qualifying life assurance policies (TA 1988 Sch 15)	Claire Ritchie, HM Revenue & Customs, CTIAA Corporation Tax and Business Income Tax, Financial Services Team, 3rd Floor, 100 Parliament Street, London SW1A 2BQ
Professional bodies (relief for subscriptions) (ITEPA 2003 s 343)	A list of approved professional bodies and learned societies is available on the HMRC website (at www.hmrc.gov.uk/list3/index.htm)

Confirmation or pre-transaction or general advice	Address
Non-statutory clearances	Large businesses should contact their client relationship manager. All other businesses and their agents should send applications to HMRC Clearances Team, Alexander House, 21 Victoria Avenue, Southend-on-Sea, Essex SS99 1BD[2] or email hmrc.southendteam@hmrc.gsi.gov.uk. Regarding emails see [1]
HMRC advice on non-business activities	See www.hmrc.gov.uk/cap/cap1.htm
General enquiries on IR35	IR35 Customer Service Unit, HM Revenue & Customs, Ground Floor, North Princess House, Cliftonville Road, Northampton, NN1 5AE Telephone 0845 303 3535
CGT post-transaction value checks	Complete form CG34 which must be received by HMRC at least two months before the relevant filing deadline
General advice on specialist technical issues	See www.hmrc.gov.uk/cap/gen-advice.htm
SDLT transactions	See www.hmrc.gov.uk/sdlt/calculate/advance-approval.htm

[1] Where clearance is sought under any one or more of the sections handled by the Clearance and Counteraction Team, clearance applications may be sent in a single letter to the above Bootle address for clearances under those sections. The letter should make clear what clearance(s) is required. HMRC acknowledge only those applications that they do not expect to deal with within a few days of receipt. E-mail applications can be sent to reconstructions@hmrc.gsi.gov.uk and fax applications to 020 7438 4409. Attachments to emails should be no larger than 2MB. Self-extracting zip files should not be sent as HMRC software will block them. Security of emails is not guaranteed. Information about market or price sensitive matters, or well known individuals, should not be sent by email. Phone first before faxing market sensitive information. If the application is faxed no hard copy need be sent. General enquiries can be made on 020 7438 7474.

[2] Non-statutory clearances: Businesses may apply for a non-statutory clearance where there is material uncertainty and the issue is commercially significant. HMRC will provide non-statutory clearances both pre-transaction, where evidence is supplied that the transaction is genuinely contemplated, and post-transaction.

Capital allowances

Rates

Agricultural buildings for periods before April 2011

	Expenditure incurred after	% Rate
Initial allowance	31 October 1992[1]	20
	31 October 1993	Nil
Writing-down allowance	31 March 1986 and before 6 April 2011 (1 April 2011 for companies)	4[2, 3]

[1] Initial allowances were temporarily reintroduced for 1 year in respect of capital expenditure on agricultural buildings or works. The allowances applied to buildings or works constructed under a contract entered into between 1 November 1992 and 31 October 1993, and brought into use for the purposes of the farming trade by 31 December 1994. See CAA 1990 s 124A.

[2] Agricultural buildings allowances are abolished for income tax purposes for 2011–12 onwards and for corporation tax purposes for the financial year beginning 1 April 2011 onwards. (FA 2008, s 84.)

[3] As a transitional measure, writing-down allowances were stepped down over the three financial or tax years prior to abolition. For 2008–09 (for corporation tax, the financial year beginning 1 April 2008) only 75% of the allowance was given. For 2009–10 (or financial year beginning 1 April 2009) only 50% was given and for 2010–11 (or financial year beginning 1 April 2010) only 25%. Where a chargeable period fell in more than one tax or financial year, time apportionment applied to determine the amount of the allowance. (FA 2008, s 85.)

Note: For balancing events on or after 21 March 2007, no election for a balancing adjustment could be made so that the new holder of the relevant interest, in all cases, calculated writing-down allowances based on the previous owner's balance of qualifying expenditure (cost less allowances claimed).

Dredging

	Expenditure incurred after	% Rate
Writing-down allowance	5 November 1962	4

Industrial buildings and structures for periods before April 2011

	Expenditure[1] incurred after	% Rate
Initial allowance		
Generally:	31 October 1992	20
	31 October 1993	Nil
Exception: Enterprise zones	within 10 years of site being included in zone[2]	100
Writing-down allowance		
Generally:	5 April 1946	2
	5 November 1962[3] and before 6 April 2011 (1 April 2011 for companies)[4, 5]	4
Exception: Enterprise zones	within 10 years of site being included in zone[2, 4]	25

[1] The amount qualifying for allowance is the price paid for the relevant interest *minus* (i) the value of the land element and (ii) any value attributable to elements over and above those which would feature in a normal commercial lease negotiated in the open market: FA 1995 s 100 confirming previous practice.

[2] CAA 2001 s 306, 310. Includes expenditure on qualifying hotels. See p 34 for enterprise zones.

[3] Includes expenditure on qualifying hotels (other than in an enterprise zone).
Also includes expenditure on the construction of toll roads incurred for accounting periods or basis periods ending after 5 April 1991.

[4] Industrial buildings allowances and allowances for buildings in enterprise zones are abolished for income tax purposes for 2011–12 onwards and for corporation tax purposes for the financial year beginning 1 April 2011 onwards. (FA 2008, ss 84, 86.)

[5] As a transitional measure, writing-down allowances (other than those on enterprise zones) were stepped down over the three financial or tax years prior to abolition. For 2008–09 (for corporation tax, the financial year beginning 1 April 2008) only 75% of the allowance was given. For 2009–10 (or financial year beginning 1 April 2009) only 50% was given and for 2010–11 (or financial year beginning 1 April 2010) only 25%. Where a chargeable period fell in more than one tax or financial year, time apportionment applied to determine the amount of the allowance. (FA 2008, ss 85, 87.)

Note: For balancing events on or after 21 March 2007, no balancing adjustment arose and the new holder of the relevant interest calculated writing-down allowances based on the previous owner's balance of qualifying expenditure (cost less allowances claimed).

Flat conversions

Initial allowance	Expenditure incurred	% Rate
	10 May 2001 to 1 or 6 April 2013	**100**

Applies to expenditure incurred on renovating or converting vacant or storage space above commercial properties to provide low value flats for rent. A writing-down allowance is given at 25% (on a straight-line basis) on unrelieved expenditure. (CAA 2001 ss 393A–393W; FA 2001 s 67, Sch 19.)
This relief is withdrawn for expenditure incurred on or after 1 April 2013 (corporation tax) and on or after 6 April 2013 (income tax). The entitlement to claim writing down allowance on any outstanding residue of qualifying expenditure also ceased with effect from the same dates (FA 2012 Sch 39).

Know-how

Expenditure incurred after 31 March 1986: annual 25% writing-down allowance (reducing balance basis).

Plant and machinery

	Expenditure incurred after	Expenditure incurred before	Up to pa
Annual investment allowance[1]			
for income tax purposes	**31 December 2012**	**1 January 2015**	**£250,000**
	5 April 2012	1 January 2013	£25,000
	5 April 2010	6 April 2012	£100,000
	5 April 2008	6 April 2010	£50,000
for corporation tax purposes	**31 December 2012**	**1 January 2015**	**£250,000**
	31 March 2012	1 January 2013	£25,000
	31 March 2010	1 April 2012	£100,000
	31 March 2008	1 April 2010	£50,000
First-year allowance (FYA)[13]			
General[12]			**% Rate**
for income tax purposes	5 April 2009	6 April 2010	40
for corporation tax purposes	31 March 2009	1 April 2010	40
Small and medium-sized businesses[2]			
for income tax purposes	1 July 1998	6 April 2008	40
for corporation tax purposes	1 July 1998	1 April 2008	40
	1 July 1997	2 July 1998	50
in Northern Ireland *only*	11 May 1998	12 May 2002	100
Small businesses[3]			
for income tax purposes	5 April 2006	6 April 2008	50
	5 April 2004	6 April 2005	50
for corporation tax purposes	31 March 2006	1 April 2008	50
	31 March 2004	1 April 2005	50
ICT	31 March 2000	1 April 2004	100
Energy-saving plant or machinery[4]	**31 March 2001**		**100**
New low-emission cars and refuelling equipment[5]	**16 April 2002**	**1 April 2015**	**100**
Environmentally beneficial plant or machinery[6]	**31 March 2003**		**100**
Zero-emission goods vehicles[7]			
for income tax purposes	**5 April 2010**	**6 April 2015**	**100**
for corporation tax purposes	**31 March 2010**	**1 April 2015**	**100**
Enterprise zones[18]	**31 March 2012**	**1 April 2017**	**100**
Writing-down allowance (WDA)[8]			
Foreign leased assets[11]	9 March 1982	1 April 2006	10
	Chargeable period beginning on or after		
Long life assets[8, 9]			
for income tax purposes	**6 April 2012**		**8**
for corporation tax purposes	**1 April 2012**		**8**
	Chargeable period ending before		
for income tax purposes	6 April 2012		10
for corporation tax purposes	1 April 2012		10
for income tax purposes	6 April 2008		6

for corporation tax purposes	1 April 2008	6
Integral features[8, 10]	**Chargeable period beginning on or after**	
for income tax purposes	**6 April 2012**	**8**
for corporation tax purposes	**1 April 2012**	**8**
	Chargeable period ending before	
for income tax purposes	6 April 2012	10
for corporation tax purposes	1 April 2012	10
Thermal insulation[8, 15]	**Chargeable period beginning on or after**	
for income tax purposes	**6 April 2012**	**8**
for corporation tax purposes	**1 April 2012**	**8**
	Chargeable period ending before	
for income tax purposes	6 April 2012	10
for corporation tax purposes	1 April 2012	10
Certain cars[8, 14]	**Chargeable period beginning on or after**	
for income tax purposes	**6 April 2012**	**8**
for corporation tax purposes	**1 April 2012**	**8**
	Chargeable period ending before	
for income tax purposes	6 April 2012	10
for corporation tax purposes	1 April 2012	10
Solar panels[8, 17]	**Chargeable period beginning on or after**	
for income tax purposes	**6 April 2012**	**8**
for corporation tax purposes	**1 April 2012**	**8**
Cushion gas[8, 16]	**Chargeable period beginning on or after**	
for income tax purposes	**6 April 2012**	**8**
for corporation tax purposes	**1 April 2012**	**8**
	Chargeable period ending before	
for income tax purposes	6 April 2012	10
for corporation tax purposes	1 April 2012	10
Generally	**Chargeable periods beginning on or after**	
for income tax purposes	**6 April 2012**	**18**
for corporation tax purposes	**1 April 2012**	**18**
	Chargeable period ending before	
for income tax purposes	6 April 2012	20
for corporation tax purposes	1 April 2012	20
for income tax purposes	6 April 2008	25
for corporation tax purposes	1 April 2008	25
	Chargeable periods straddling	
for income tax purposes	**6 April 2012**	**Hybrid rate**[8, 9]
for corporation tax purposes	**1 April 2012**	**Hybrid rate**[8, 9]
for income tax purposes	6 April 2008	Hybrid rate[8, 9]
for corporation tax purposes	1 April 2008	Hybrid rate[8, 9]

[1] **Annual investment allowance:** Applies from April 2008. The first £250,000 (£25,000 for expenditure incurred before 1 January 2013 but after 5 April 2012 (income tax) or after 31 March 2012 (corporation tax)) of qualifying expenditure incurred in a chargeable period qualifies for the annual investment allowance at 100%. Where a chargeable period spans the date of the increase, transitional rules apply. The limit is proportionately increased or decreased where the chargeable period is longer or shorter than a year. A group of companies (defined as for company law purposes) can only receive a single allowance. This restriction also applies to certain related businesses or companies. Expenditure on cars does not qualify. (CAA 2001 ss 38A, 38B, 51A–51N; FA 2011 s 11).

[2] **Small and medium-sized businesses:** The allowance did not apply to certain expenditure including that on plant and machinery for leasing, motor cars, ships, railway assets or long-life assets. After the first year, allowances revert to the normal WDA. The rate of 50% applied only for expenditure incurred during the year ended 1 July 1998 when a 12% FYA applied to long-life assets. (See notes 4 and 11 below.) Small and medium-sized businesses are, broadly, those satisfying any two of the following conditions: (a) turnover £22,800,000 or less (b) assets £11,400,000 or less (c) not more than 250 employees (CAA 1990 ss 22(3C), (6B), 22A, 44, 46–49). For accounting periods ending before 30 January 2004, the thresholds were: (a) turnover £11,200,000 or less (b) assets £5,600,000 or less.

[3] **Small businesses:** See note 2 above for conditions for relief. Small businesses are, broadly, those satisfying any two of the following conditions: (*a*) turnover £5,600,000 or less (*b*) assets £2,800,000 or less (*c*) not more than 50 employees. For accounting periods ending before 30 January 2004, the thresholds were: (*a*) turnover £2,800,000 or less (*b*) assets £1,400,000 or less (FA 2004 s 142).

[4] **Energy-saving plant or machinery:** The allowances are available for investment by *any* business in designated energy-saving plant and machinery in accordance with the Government's Energy Technology Product List. 100% first-year allowances are not available for expenditure incurred on or after 1 April 2012 (corporation tax) or 6 April 2012 (income tax) on plant or machinery to generate renewable electricity or heat where tariff payments are received under either of the renewable energy schemes introduced by the Department of Energy and Climate Change. The restriction applies from April 2014 for combined heat and power equipment (CAA 2001 ss 45A–45C, 46; FA 2001 s 65, Sch 17; SI 2001/2541; SI 2005/1114). The product lists are available at www.eca.gov.uk.

[5] **Low-emission cars:** The allowance is given on (*a*) new cars which are either electrically propelled or emit not more than 95g/km of CO_2 (110g/km for expenditure incurred before 1 April 2013, 120g/km for expenditure incurred before 1 April 2008), registered after 16 April 2002 and (*b*) new plant and machinery to refuel vehicles in a gas refuelling station with natural gas, hydrogen fuels, or (for expenditure on or after 1 April 2008) biogas. For expenditure incurred after 31 March 2013 cars provided for leasing no longer qualify for the FYA (CAA 2001 ss 45D, 45E, 46). **Legislation will be introduced in Finance Bill 2015 to extend the 100% FYA to 31 March 2018. At the same time the qualifying threshold for low emission cars will be reduced to 75g/km.**

[6] **Environmentally beneficial plant or machinery:** Allowances are available for expenditure by *any* business on new and unused designated technologies and products which satisfy the relevant environmental criteria in accordance with the Government's technologies or products lists (CAA 2001 ss 45H–45J, 46; FA 2003 s 167, Sch 30; SI 2003/2076). The product lists are available at www.eca.gov.uk.

[7] **Zero-emission goods vehicles:** The allowance is given on new (and not second hand) vehicles which cannot under any circumstances produce CO_2 emissions when driven and which are of a design primarily suited to the conveyance of goods or burden. The expenditure must be incurred before 1 April 2015 (corporation tax) or 6 April 2015 (income tax) and is limited to expenditure of € 85 million per undertaking (as defined) over the five years. Exclusions apply (CAA 2001 ss 45DA-45DB, 212T).

[8] **WDAs** are calculated on a reducing balance basis. For chargeable periods beginning before 6 April 2012 and ending on or after that date (income tax) or, beginning before 1 April 2012 and ending on or after that date (corporation tax) a hybrid rate of WDAs applies, calculated by time apportionment of the 20% and 18% rates, or, for the special rate expenditure, the 10% and 8% rates. For chargeable periods beginning on or after 6 April 2008 (income tax) or 1 April 2008 (corporation tax), a WDA of up to £1,000 can be claimed in respect of the main pool and/or the special rate pool where the unrelieved expenditure in the pool concerned is £1,000 or less.

[9] **Long-life assets:** Applies to plant or machinery with an expected working life, when new, of 25 years or more. Applies where expenditure on long-life assets in a year is £100,000 or more (in the case of companies the de minimis limit is £100,000 divided by one plus the number of associated companies). Transitional provisions apply to maintain a 25% allowance for expenditure incurred before 1 January 2001 under a contract entered into before 26 November 1996 and to expenditure on second-hand plant or machinery if old rules applied to vendor. It does not apply to plant or machinery in a building used wholly or mainly as, or for purposes ancillary to, a dwelling-house, retail shop, showroom, hotel or office; cars; or sea-going ships and railway assets acquired before 1 January 2011. Expenditure on or after 1 April 2008 (corporation tax) or 6 April 2008 (income tax) qualifies, as special rate expenditure, for a writing down allowance of 8% (10% for periods before 1 or 6 April 2012, see note 8 above) reducing balance. The balance of the long-life asset pool at 1 or 6 April 2008 was also transferred into the special rate pool. The rate applying for chargeable periods beginning before 1 or 6 April 2008 was 6% and a hybrid rate applied for chargeable periods spanning those dates calculated by a time apportionment of the 6% and 10% rates (CAA 2001 ss 90–104, Sch 3 para 20).

[10] **Integral features** of a building are electrical systems (including lighting systems); cold water systems; space or water heating systems, powered ventilation systems, air cooling or purification and any floor or ceiling comprised in such systems; lifts, escalators and moving walkways and external solar shading. Applies to expenditure incurred on or after 1 April 2008 (corporation tax) and 6 April 2008 (income tax). They all fall into the special rate pool and qualify for a 8% (10% for periods before 1 or 6 April 2012, see note 8 above) writing down allowance (CAA 2001 ss 33A, 104A).

[11] **Foreign leased assets:** The relief applies only to leases finalised before 1 April 2006 (CAA 2001 s 109; FA 2006 Sch 9 para 13).

[12] **First-year tax credits:** For expenditure incurred on or after 1 April 2008, a company can surrender a tax loss attributable to first-year allowances for energy-saving or environmentally friendly equipment in exchange for a cash payment from the Government. The cash payment is equal to 19% of the loss surrendered, subject to an upper limit of the greater of £250,000 and the company's PAYE and NIC liability for the period concerned. (CAA 2001 Sch A1). Relief extended to 31 March 2018 by SI 2013/464.

[13] **First year allowances**, where applicable, are available on expenditure over the annual investment allowance level or on which annual investment allowance has not been claimed, which would otherwise qualify for writing down allowance at 18% in the general plant and machinery pool.

[14] **Cars:** For expenditure on and after 1 April 2009 (corporation tax), 6 April 2009 (income tax), cars with CO_2 emissions exceeding 130g/km (160g/km for expenditure incurred before 1 April 2013 (corporation tax) or 6 April 2013 (income tax)) will be allocated to the special rate pool. All other cars will go into the general pool (CAA 2001 ss 104A, 104AA).

[15] **Thermal insulation** Expenditure on thermal insulation incurred on or after 1 April 2008 (corporation tax) and 6 April 2008 (income tax) falls into the special rate pool and qualifies for a 8% (10% for periods before 1 or 6 April 2012, see note 8 above) writing down allowance (CAA 2001 ss 28, 104A).

[16] **Cushion gas** Expenditure on cushion gas incurred on or after 1 April 2010 falls into the special rate pool

and qualifies for a 8% (10% for periods before 1 or 6 April 2012, see note 8 above) writing down allowance (CAA 2001 ss 70J, 104A).

17 **Solar panels** Expenditure on solar panels incurred on or after 1 April 2012 (corporation tax) and 6 April 2012 (income tax) falls into the special rate pool and qualifies for a 8% writing down allowance (CAA 2001 s 104A).

18 **Enterprise zones** For expenditure incurred for the purpose of a qualifying activity in the five-year period from 1 April 2012 to 31 March 2017 inclusive 100% first-year allowances will be available for companies chargeable to corporation tax which invest in unused (not second hand) plant or machinery for use primarily in designated assisted areas within certain enterprise zones. Expenditure must be incurred for the purposes of broadly a new or expanding business carried on by the company, must not be replacement expenditure and is limited to €125 million per single investment project (as defined) over the five years. Exclusions apply. A map of current enterprise zones can be found at http://enterprisezones.communities.gov.uk/enterprise-zone-map/ (CAA 2001 ss 45K–N, 212U).

Cars: Car hire p 79.

Mineral extraction

First-year allowance: 100% FYA is available for certain expenditure incurred after 16 April 2002 wholly for the purposes of a North Sea Oil ring-fence trade or on plant and machinery used in such a trade.

Writing-down allowance: for expenditure incurred after 31 March 1986, 10% for expenditure on the acquisition of a mineral asset and certain pre-trading expenditure, otherwise 25% (on reducing balance basis). (CA 2001 s 418.)

Motor cars

Expenditure on or after 1 April 2009 (corporation tax) or 6 April 2009 (income tax) on cars is allocated to the special rate (currently 8%) plant and machinery pool if the car's CO_2 emissions exceed 130g/km (160g/km for expenditure incurred before 1 April 2013 (corporation tax) or 6 April 2013 (income tax)) and otherwise to the (currently 18%) main pool. (CAA 2001 ss 104AA, 104F, 208A, 268A-268D.) The position for expenditure before 1 April 2009 (for companies) or 6 April 2009 (for unincorporated businesses) is as follows.

		% Rate[1]
Writing-down allowance (WDA)	Chargeable period ending before 1 April 2008 for corporation tax and 5 April 2008 for income tax	25%
	Chargeable period straddling 1 April 2008 for corporation tax and 6 April 2008 for income tax	hybrid rate
	Chargeable period ending before 1 April 2012 for corporation tax or 6 April 2012 income tax	20%
	Chargeable period straddling 1 April 2012 for corporation tax and 6 April 2012 for income tax	hybrid rate
	Chargeable period beginning on or after 1 April 2012 for corporation tax or 6 April 2012 for income tax	18%

1 Restricted to £3,000 for cars costing more than £12,000 and bought outright, on hire purchase or by way of a lease with an option to purchase (CAA 2001 ss 74, 75).
2 Cars that have an element of non-business use will still be dealt with in a single asset pool, but the rate of WDA will depend on the emissions.
3 Expenditure still in a single asset pool for cars costing more than £12,000 on the last day of the first chargeable period ending on or after 31 March 2014 (corporation tax) or 5 April 2014 (income tax) will be carried forward to the main pool (FA 2009 Sch 11 para 31).
4 See also note 5, p 32 and Car hire, p 79.

Patent rights

Writing-down allowance

Expenditure incurred after 31 March 1986: annual 25% writing-down allowance (reducing balance basis). (CAA 2001 s 472.)

Research and development (formerly scientific research)

	Expenditure incurred after	% Rate
Allowance in year 1	5 November 1962	100

Note: Land and houses are excluded from 1 April 1985.

Disadvantaged areas

Renovation of business premises

	Expenditure incurred between	% Rate
First-year allowance	**11 April 2007 and 1 or 6 April 2017**	**100**

The expenditure must be incurred on renovating or converting vacant business properties in Northern Ireland or the designated disadvantaged areas in the UK that have been vacant for at least a year, to bring the property back into business use. Premises refurbished by or used by businesses in the following trades are excluded from the scheme: fisheries and aquaculture, shipbuilding, the coal or steel industries, synthetic fibres, primary production of certain agricultural products and the manufacture of products which imitate or substitute for milk or milk products.) A writing-down allowance is given at 25% (on a straight-line basis) on unrelieved expenditure. (FA 2005 s 92, Sch 6; SI 2012/868)

Enterprise zones

Before 1 April 2011 (corporation tax) or 6 April 2011 (income tax) an initial allowance of 100% was available for expenditure on industrial or commercial building by businesses within enterprise zones. Where the initial allowance was not or was only partially claimed a 25% writing-down allowance on cost, on a straight-line basis, applied to the unclaimed balance. There was no phasing out of the allowance between 2008 and 2011.

For 100% first-year allowances available for companies investing in plant or machinery for use primarily in designated assisted areas within certain Enterprise Zones see under **plant and machinery**.

Capital gains

Annual exemption

(TCGA 1992 s 3)

Individuals[a], personal representatives[b] and certain trusts[c]

[a]   For 2008–09 onwards, an individual who claims to use the remittance basis for a tax year is not entitled to the capital gains tax annual exemption for that year. This does not apply if the individual's unremitted foreign income and gains for the year are less than £2,000 (TCGA 1992 s 3(1A); ITA 2007 s 809D).

[b]   Year of death and following two years (maximum) (TCGA 1992 s 3(7)).

[c]   Trusts for disabled persons as defined. Exemption divided by number of qualifying settlements created (after 9 March 1981) by one settlor, subject to a minimum of one-tenth (TCGA 1992 Sch para 1(1); FA 2005 Sch 1A).

Exempt amount of net gains	2008–09	2009–10	2010–11	2011–12	2012–13	2013–14
	£9,600	£10,100	£10,100	£10,600	£10,600	£10,900

Trusts[a] generally

Exempt amount of net gains	2008–09	2009–10	2010–11	2011–12	2012–13	2013–14
	£4,800	£5,050	£5,050	£5,300	£5,300	£5,450

[a]   Exemption divided by number of qualifying settlements created (after 6 June 1978) by one settlor, subject to a minimum of one-fifth (TCGA 1992 Sch 1 para 1(4)).

Chattel exemption

(TCGA 1992 s 262)

	Disposals exemption	Marginal relief: Maximum chargeable gain
From 1989–90 onwards	£6,000	5/3 excess over £6,000

Rates of tax

(TCGA 1992 s 4)

2013–14	*Individuals*	• to income tax basic rate limit £32,010	**18%**
		• above income tax basic rate limit £32,010	**28%**
	Trusts and personal representatives		**28%**
2012–13	*Individuals*	• to income tax basic rate limit £34,370	18%
		• above income tax basic rate limit £34,370	28%
	Trusts and personal representatives		28%
2011–12	*Individuals*	• to income tax basic rate limit £35,000	18%
		• above income tax basic rate limit £35,000	28%
	Trusts and personal representatives		28%
2010–11	*Individuals*	*gains before 23 June 2010*	18%
		gains on or after 23 June 2010	
		• to income tax basic rate limit £37,400	18%
		• above income tax basic rate limit £37,400	28%
	Trusts and personal representatives		
		gains before 23 June 2010	18%
		gains on or after 23 June 2010	28%
2008–09 to 2009–10	*Individuals, trusts and personal representatives*		18%
2007–08	*Individuals*	• to income tax starting rate limit £2,230	10%
		• from £2,231 to income tax basic rate limit £34,600	20%
		• above income tax basic rate limit £34,600	40%
	Trusts and personal representatives		40%
2006–07	*Individuals*	• to income tax starting rate limit £2,150	10%
		• from £2,151 to income tax basic rate limit £33,300	20%
		• above income tax basic rate limit £33,300	40%
	Trusts and personal representatives		40%

For 2007–08 and earlier years, gains are taxed on individuals as the top slice of income. For gains arising on or after 23 June 2010, the rate of tax for an individual is determined by treating gains as the top slice of income. Also for gains arising on or after 23 June 2010, a rate of 10% applies where entrepreneurs' relief is claimed — see p 38.

Trusts for vulnerable persons: From 2004–05 onwards, gains taxed at beneficiary's rates (on beneficiary if UK resident or on trustees if beneficiary not UK-resident) (FA 2005 ss 30–32).

Indexation allowance – individuals

(TCGA 1992 ss 53–57, 109.)

Indexation allowance is abolished for disposals on or after 6 April 2008 by individuals, trustees and personal representatives (but not companies — see p 43). For disposals before that date by such persons, an indexation allowance is given up to April 1998 and taper relief applies thereafter on disposals made after 5 April 1998 (see below). Indexation allowance is deducted before applying taper relief. The indexation allowance is calculated by multiplying each item of allowable expenditure by:

$$\frac{RD - RI}{RI}$$

where:
    RD is the retail prices index figure for month of disposal;
    RI is the retail prices index for month of expenditure (or March 1982 if later).

See pp 44–59 for indexation allowances applicable for corporation tax and pp 60–61 for RPI values.

For disposals after 31 March 1998 of assets acquired on or before that date the factors below can be used to calculate the indexation allowance available to April 1998 for acquisitions in the month shown.

	Jan	Feb	Mar	Apr	May	Jun	Jul	Aug	Sept	Oct	Nov	Dec
1982	–	–	1·047	1·006	0·992	0·987	0·986	0·985	0·987	0·977	0·967	0·971
1983	0·968	0·960	0·956	0·929	0·921	0·917	0·906	0·898	0·889	0·883	0·876	0·871
1984	0·872	0·865	0·859	0·834	0·828	0·823	0·825	0·808	0·804	0·793	0·788	0·789
1985	0·783	0·769	0·752	0·716	0·708	0·704	0·707	0·703	0·704	0·701	0·695	0·693
1986	0·689	0·683	0·681	0·665	0·662	0·663	0·667	0·662	0·654	0·652	0·638	0·632
1987	0·626	0·620	0·616	0·597	0·596	0·596	0·597	0·593	0·588	0·580	0·573	0·574
1988	0·574	0·568	0·562	0·537	0·531	0·525	0·524	0·507	0·500	0·485	0·478	0·474
1989	0·465	0·454	0·448	0·423	0·414	0·409	0·408	0·404	0·395	0·384	0·372	0·369
1990	0·361	0·353	0·339	0·300	0·288	0·283	0·282	0·269	0·258	0·248	0·251	0·252
1991	0·249	0·242	0·237	0·222	0·218	0·213	0·215	0·213	0·208	0·204	0·199	0·198
1992	0·199	0·193	0·189	0·171	0·167	0·167	0·171	0·171	0·166	0·162	0·164	0·168
1993	0·179	0·171	0·167	0·156	0·152	0·153	0·156	0·151	0·146	0·147	0·148	0·146
1994	0·151	0·144	0·141	0·128	0·124	0·124	0·129	0·124	0·121	0·120	0·119	0·114
1995	0·114	0·107	0·102	0·091	0·087	0·085	0·091	0·085	0·080	0·085	0·085	0·079
1996	0·083	0·078	0·073	0·066	0·063	0·063	0·067	0·062	0·057	0·057	0·057	0·053
1997	0·053	0·049	0·046	0·040	0·036	0·032	0·032	0·026	0·021	0·019	0·019	0·016
1998	0·019	0·014	0·011	–	–	–	–	–	–	–	–	–

Losses. For disposals after 30 November 1993, indexation allowance can only be used to reduce or extinguish a gain. It cannot be used to create or increase a capital loss.

Share identification rules

(TCGA 1992 ss 104–106A; FA 2006 s 74)

For disposals on or after 6 April 2008 by individuals, trustees or personal representatives, shares and securities of the same class in the same company are identified with acquisitions in the following order:
- acquisitions on the same day as the disposal;
- acquisitions[2] within 30 days after the day of disposal[1];
- shares comprised in a single pool incorporating all other shares of the same class, whenever acquired.

For disposals before 6 April 2008 for individuals, trustees and personal representatives, disposals are identified with acquisitions in the following order:
- same day acquisitions (subject to special rules distinguishing shares acquired after 5 April 2002 from approved employee share option schemes from other shares acquired on the same day);
- acquisitions within the following 30 days[1] (thus countering 'bed and breakfasting');
- previous acquisitions after 5 April 1998 on a last in/first out basis;
- shares acquired after 5 April 1982 in the pool at 5 April 1998 (the 'section 104 holding');
- shares acquired before 6 April 1982 (the '1982 holding');
- any shares acquired on or before 6 April 1965 on a last in/first out basis;
- if any shares disposed of are still not fully matched, shares acquired subsequent to the disposal (beyond the above mentioned 30-day period).

For the purposes of corporation tax on chargeable gains, disposals of shares etc are identified with acquisitions in the following order:
- same day acquisitions;
- acquisitions within the previous nine days on a first in/first out basis;
- the pool of shares acquired after 31 March 1982;
- any shares held at 31 March 1982;
- any shares acquired on or before 6 April 1965 on a last in/first out basis;
- (if shares disposed of still not fully matched) subsequent acquisitions.

These rules are modified for disposals of shares before 5 December 2005 if the company acquired shares of the same class within a short period and held not less than 2% of the number issued.

[1] The 30-day matching rule does not apply in relation to acquisitions after 21 March 2006 where the individual making the disposal is not (or is not treated as) resident or ordinarily resident in the UK at the time of the acquisition.

[2] For disposals within the 30-day period on or after 6 April 2013, shares which are not relevant EMI shares are identified before those which are relevant EMI shares. Otherwise shares are identified with relevant EMI shares first on a first in/first out basis and such shares do not form part of the single pool.

Entrepreneurs' relief

(TCGA 1992 ss 169H–169S; FA 2008 s 9, Sch 3)

Entrepreneurs' relief applies to disposals by an individual on or after 6 April 2008 of:
- all or part of a trade carried on alone or in partnership;
- assets of such a trade following cessation; or
- shares or securities in the individual's 'personal trading company' (as defined).

Where a disposal of shares or of an interest in the assets of a partnership qualifies for relief, an associated disposal of assets owned by the individual and used by the company or partnership also qualifies for relief.

Trustees can claim relief where a qualifying beneficiary has an interest in the business concerned.

The relief is available where the relevant conditions are met throughout a period of one year. For gains arising on or after 23 June 2010, the relief operates by charging qualifying net gains to CGT at 10%. Previously, it operated by reducing the amount of qualifying net gains by four-ninths (so that the gains were effectively charged to CGT at 10%). Relief is subject to a lifetime limit of gains of £10 million (£5 million for disposals before 6 April 2011; £2 million for disposals before 23 June 2010; £1 million for disposals before 6 April 2010), but disposals before 6 April 2008 do not count towards the limit. Relief given to trustees counts towards the limit of the qualifying beneficiary.

Transitional rules apply to allow relief to be claimed in certain circumstances where a gain made before 6 April 2008 is deferred and becomes chargeable on or after that date.

Taper relief

(TCGA 1992 s 2A, Sch A1; FA 2000 ss 66, 67; FA 2002 ss 46, 47, Sch 10; FA 2003 s 160)

Taper relief is abolished for gains accruing, or treated as accruing, on or after 6 April 2008. (FA 2008 Sch 2 para 25.) Taper relief was available for disposals made after 5 April 1998 by individuals, trustees and personal representatives. The chargeable gain is reduced according to the number of complete years for which the asset has been held (counting from 6 April 1998). Non-business assets acquired before 17 March 1998 qualify for an addition of one year to the period for which they are held after 5 April 1998. Business assets acquired before 17 March 1998 also qualify for the one-year addition but only if disposed of before 6 April 2000.

Taper relief applies to gains after all deductions and before the annual exemption. Losses are set against pre-tapered gains in the most beneficial way possible. Where applicable, the combined period of holding by spouses is taken into account.

Business assets			
Disposals from 6 April 2002 to 5 April 2008		Disposals from 6 April 2000 to 5 April 2002	
No of complete yrs from 6.4.98 for which asset held	% of gain chargeable	No of complete yrs from 6.4.98 for which asset held	% of gain chargeable
		0	100
0	100	1	87.5
1	50	2	75
2 or more	25	3	50
		4 or more	25

Non-business assets			
No of complete yrs from 6.4.98 for which asset held	% of gain chargeable	No of complete yrs from 6.4.98 for which asset held	% of gain chargeable
0	100	6	80
1	100	7	75
2	100	8	70
3	95	9	65
4	90	10 or more	60
5	85		

Business assets. A 'business asset' is one of the following:
- an asset used for the purposes of a trade carried on (alone or in partnership) by the taxpayer or, after 5 April 2004, any individual, trustee or personal representative; *or*
- an asset used for the purposes of a trade carried on by a 'qualifying company' (alone or, after 4 April 2004, in partnership); *or*
- shares or securities in a 'qualifying company'; *or*
- from 6 April 2000, an asset used for the purpose of any office or employment (full-time or part-time) held by the taxpayer with a person carrying on a trade; or
- before 6 April 2000, an asset held for the purposes of a qualifying office or employment to which the taxpayer is required to devote substantially the whole of his time.

Qualifying company. From 6 April 2000, a *'qualifying company'*, by reference to an individual, is a trading company (or holding company of a trading group), where one or more of the following conditions is met:
- the company is unlisted (including an AIM company); *or*
- the taxpayer is an employee (full-time or part-time) of the company or a fellow group company (in which case the requirement that the company be a trading company etc is dropped, provided the taxpayer's interest in the company, including connected person holdings, is no more than 10%); *or*
- the taxpayer can exercise at least 5% of the voting rights.

Leases

Depreciation table (TCGA 1992 Sch 8 para 1)

Yrs	%	Yrs	%	Yrs	%	Yrs	%
50 (or more)	100	37	93·497	24	79·622	11	50·038
49	99·657	36	92·761	23	78·055	10	46·695
48	99·289	35	91·981	22	76·399	9	43·154
47	98·902	34	91·156	21	74·635	8	39·399
46	98·490	33	90·280	20	72·770	7	35·414
45	98·059	32	89·354	19	70·791	6	31·195
44	97·595	31	88·371	18	68·697	5	26·722
43	97·107	30	87·330	17	66·470	4	21·983
42	96·593	29	86·226	16	64·116	3	16·959
41	96·041	28	85·053	15	61·617	2	11·629
40	95·457	27	83·816	14	58·971	1	5·983
39	94·842	26	82·496	13	56·167	0	0
38	94·189	25	81·100	12	53·191		

Formula: Fraction of expenditure disallowed—

$$\frac{AE - D}{AE}$$

Where:

AE is the percentage for duration of lease at acquisition or expenditure; and
D is the percentage for duration of lease at disposal.

Fractions of years: Add one-twelfth of the difference between the percentage for the whole year and the next higher percentage for each additional month. Odd days under 14 are not counted; 14 odd days or more count as a month.

Short leases: premiums treated as rent (TCGA 1992 Sch 8 para 5; ITTOIA 2005 ss 277–281A; CTA 2009 s 217–221A) Part of premium for grant of a short lease which is chargeable to income tax as property income:

$$P - (2\% \times (n - 1) \times P)$$

Where:

P is the amount of premium;
n is the number of complete years which lease has to run when granted.

Length of lease (complete years)	Amount chargeable to CGT %	Income tax charge %	Length of lease (complete years)	Amount chargeable to CGT %	Income tax charge %	Length of lease (complete years)	Amount chargeable to CGT %	Income tax charge %
Over 50	100	0	34	66	34	17	32	68
50	98	2	33	64	36	16	30	70
49	96	4	32	62	38	15	28	72
48	94	6	31	60	40	14	26	74
47	92	8	30	58	42	13	24	76
46	90	10	29	56	44	12	22	78
45	88	12	28	54	46	11	20	80
44	86	14	27	52	48	10	18	82
43	84	16	26	50	50	9	16	84
42	82	18	25	48	52	8	14	86
41	80	20	24	46	54	7	12	88
40	78	22	23	44	56	6	10	90
39	76	24	22	42	58	5	8	92
38	74	26	21	40	60	4	6	94
37	72	28	20	38	62	3	4	96
36	70	30	19	36	64	2	2	98
35	68	32	18	34	66	1 or less	0	100

Reliefs

The following is a summary of the other main capital gains tax reliefs and exemptions.

Charities

Gains accruing to charities which are both applicable and applied for charitable purposes are exempt. The exemption also applies from 1 April 2002 to Community Amateur Sports Clubs (CASCs).

Individuals

Compensation (injury to person, profession or vocation)	Exempt.
Decorations for valour (acquired otherwise than for money or money's worth)	Gain exempt.
Employee shareholder shares	Gain on disposal of shares which were worth up to £50,000 on acquisition is exempt. Applies from date to be appointed, expected to be 1 September 2013.
Enterprise Investment Scheme (see p 94)	Gain on disposal after relevant three-year period exempt to extent full relief given on shares. Deferral relief is available on gains on assets where the disposal proceeds are reinvested in EIS shares within one year before and three years after the dipsosal.
Entrepreneurs' relief (see p 38)	Gains on specified assets chargeable at 10% rate up to lifetime limit. (Before 23 June 2010, five ninths of qualifying gains chargeable at 18% (an effective rate of 10%) up to lifetime limit.)
Foreign currency acquired for personal expenditure	Gain exempt.
Gifts for public benefit, works of art, historic buildings etc	No chargeable gain/allowable loss.
Gifts of pre-eminent objects	Donors who gift pre-eminent objects to the nation will receive a reduction in their UK tax liability of 30% of the value of the object they are donating. The tax reduction can be against income or capital gains tax and can be spread forward across a period of up to five years starting with the tax year in which the object is offered. The legislation has effect in relation to liabilities for tax years and accounting periods beginning on or after 1 April 2012. The gift must be accepted as pre-eminent by the Arts Council under the Cultural Gifts Scheme. See p 64 for relief applying to companies.
Gilt-edged stock	No chargeable gain/allowable loss.
Hold-over relief for gifts	Restricted to:
	(1) gifts of business assets (including unquoted shares in trading companies and holding companies of trading groups). Relief is not available on the transfer of shares or securities to a company made after 8 November 1999 (other than transfers between 6.4.03 and 20.10.03);
	(2) gifts of heritage property;
	(3) gifts to heritage maintenance funds;
	(4) gifts to political parties; and
	(5) gifts which are chargeable transfers for inheritance tax.
	Where available, transferee's acquisition cost treated as reduced by held-over gain.
Married persons or civil partners living together	No chargeable gain/allowable loss on transfers between spouses or civil partners.
Motor vehicles	Gain exempt.
Principal private residence	Gain exempt.
If residence is partly let, exemption for the let part is limited to the smaller of–	(1) exemption on owner-occupied part; and
	(2) £40,000.
Qualifying corporate bonds	No chargeable gain (for loans made before 17 March 1998, allowable loss in certain cases if all or part of loss is irrecoverable).
Seed enterprise investment scheme (see p 94)	Individuals may claim capital gains reinvestment relief where they realise capital gains on disposals of assets in the tax year 2012–13 or 2013–14 and in the same year make investments that qualify for, and they claim, the main seed enterprise investment scheme (SEIS) relief from income tax. This includes shares treated as issued in 2012–13 or 2013–14 as a result of a carry-back claim. For disposals of assets in 2012–13 the relief applies to the full qualifying reinvested amount. For 2013–14 the relief will apply to half the qualifying re-invested amount. The maximum exemption is £100,000 of gains. A disposal of shares on which SEIS income tax relief has been given and not withdrawn is exempt.

Venture capital trusts (see p 95)	Gain on disposal of shares by original investor exempt if company still a venture capital trust. Exemption applies only to shares acquired up to the permitted maximum of £200,000 per year of assessment (£100,000 for shares acquired before 6 April 2004). Deferral relief was available on gains on assets where the disposal proceeds were reinvested in VCT shares issued before 6 April 2004 and within one year before or after the disposal. This relief is withdrawn for shares issued after that date.

Businesses

Roll-over relief for replacement of business assets

Qualifying assets:

- Buildings and land both occupied and used for the purposes of the trade.
- Fixed plant and machinery.
- Ships, aircraft and hovercraft.
- Satellites, space stations and spacecraft.
- Goodwill*.
- Milk and potato quotas*.
- Ewe and suckler cow premium quotas*.
- Fish quotas (from 29 March 1999)*.
- UK oil licences (from 1 July 1999).
- Payment entitlement under farmers' single payment scheme (from 22 March 2005).

The 'replacement' assets must be acquired within 12 months before or three years after the disposal of the old asset. Both assets must be within any of the above classes. Holdover relief is available where the new asset is a depreciating asset (having a predictable useful life not exceeding 60 years).

Rollover relief on the transfer of a business ("incorporation relief")

On incorporation of a business, the assets of the business are transferred to a company which then carries on the business in succession to the former proprietor. Gains realised on the transfer can be rolled over where the transfer is wholly or partly in consideration for the issue of shares. Relief is automatic (no claim is required).

* From 1 April 2002 onwards, subject to transitional rules, these items are removed from the list for companies only (as they fall within the intangible assets regime from that date (FA 2002 Sch 29 para 132(5)).

Personal representatives

Allowable expenses

Expenses allowable for the costs of establishing title in computing chargeable gains on disposal of assets in a deceased person's estate: deaths occurring after 5 April 2004 (SP 2/04). (HMRC accepts computations based either on the scale or on the actual allowable expenditure incurred.)

Gross value of estate	Allowable expenditure
Up to £50,000	1.8% of the probate value of the assets sold by the personal representatives.
Between £50,001 and £90,000	£900, to be divided between all the assets of the estate in proportion to the probate values and allowed in those proportions on assets sold by the personal representatives.
Between £90,001 and £400,000	1% of the probate value of the assets sold.
Between £400,001 and £500,000	£4,000, to be divided between all the assets of the estate in proportion to the probate values and allowed in those proportions on assets sold by the personal representatives.
Between £500,001 and £1,000,000	0.8% of the probate value of the assets sold.
Between £1,000,001 and £5,000,000	£8,000 to be divided between all the assets of the estate in proportion to the probate values and allowed in those proportions on assets sold by the personal representatives.
Exceeding £5,000,000	0.16% of the probate value of the assets sold subject to a maximum of £10,000.

Trustees

Allowable expenses

Expenses allowable in computing chargeable gains of corporate trustees in the administration of trusts and estates: acquisition, disposals and deemed disposals after 5 April 2004 (SP 2/04). (HMRC accepts computations based either on the scale or on the actual allowable expenditure incurred.)

Transfers of assets to beneficiaries etc	
(a) Quoted stocks and shares	
(i) One beneficiary	£25 per holding.
(ii) More than one beneficiary	£25 per holding, divided equally between the beneficiaries.
(b) Unquoted shares	As (a) above, plus any exceptional expenditure.
(c) Other assets	As (a) above, plus any exceptional expenditure.
Actual disposals and acquisitions	
(a) Quoted stocks and shares	Investment fee as charged by the trustees (where a comprehensive annual management fee is charged, the investment fee is taken to be £0.25 per £100 of the sale or purchase moneys).
(b) Unquoted shares	As (a) above, plus actual valuation costs.
(c) Other assets	Investment fee (as (a) above), subject to a maximum of £75, plus actual valuation costs.
Deemed disposals by trustees	
(a) Quoted stocks and shares	£8 per holding.
(b) Unquoted shares	Actual valuation costs.
(c) Other assets	Actual valuation costs.

Indexation allowance – corporation tax on capital gains

For corporation tax purposes, an indexation allowance is given as a deduction in calculating gains on disposals from the amount realised (or deemed to be realised) on disposal. The indexation allowance is calculated by multiplying each item of allowable expenditure by:

$$\frac{RD - RI}{RI}$$

Where:

    RD is the retail prices index figure for month of disposal;
    RI is the retail prices index for month of expenditure (or March 1982 if later).

See ante for indexation allowances up to April 1998 and taper relief which applies thereafter on disposals made after 5 April 1998 and before 6 April 2008 by individuals, trustees and personal representatives. See post for RPI values. The factors below can be used to calculate the indexation allowance for corporation tax purposes.

MONTH OF DISPOSAL

	2010				2011										
1982	Sept	Oct	Nov	Dec	Jan	Feb	Mar	Apr	May	June	July	Aug	Sept	Oct	Nov
Mar	1·836	1·842	1·855	1·875	1·883	1·912	1·927	1·951	1·961	1·961	1·954	1·972	1·995	1·996	2·002
Apr	1·780	1·786	1·799	1·818	1·826	1·854	1·869	1·892	1·902	1·902	1·896	1·913	1·936	1·937	1·943
May	1·760	1·766	1·779	1·798	1·806	1·834	1·848	1·872	1·882	1·882	1·875	1·893	1·915	1·916	1·922
June	1·753	1·759	1·771	1·790	1·798	1·826	1·841	1·864	1·874	1·874	1·867	1·885	1·907	1·908	1·914
July	1·752	1·758	1·770	1·790	1·797	1·825	1·840	1·863	1·873	1·873	1·867	1·884	1·906	1·907	1·913
Aug	1·751	1·757	1·769	1·789	1·796	1·824	1·839	1·862	1·872	1·872	1·866	1·883	1·905	1·906	1·912
Sept	1·753	1·759	1·771	1·790	1·798	1·826	1·841	1·864	1·874	1·874	1·867	1·885	1·907	1·908	1·914
Oct	1·739	1·745	1·757	1·777	1·784	1·812	1·827	1·850	1·859	1·859	1·853	1·870	1·892	1·893	1·899
Nov	1·726	1·732	1·744	1·763	1·770	1·798	1·813	1·836	1·845	1·845	1·839	1·856	1·878	1·879	1·885
Dec	1·731	1·737	1·749	1·768	1·775	1·803	1·818	1·841	1·851	1·851	1·845	1·861	1·883	1·885	1·891
1983	Sept	Oct	Nov	Dec	Jan	Feb	Mar	Apr	May	June	July	Aug	Sep	Oct	Nov
Jan	1·727	1·733	1·745	1·765	1·772	1·800	1·814	1·837	1·847	1·847	1·841	1·858	1·880	1·881	1·887
Feb	1·176	1·722	1·734	1·753	1·760	1·788	1·802	1·825	1·835	1·835	1·829	1·846	1·867	1·869	1·875
Mar	1·711	1·717	1·729	1·748	1·755	1·783	1·797	1·820	1·830	1·830	1·824	1·841	1·862	1·863	1·869
Apr	1·673	1·679	1·691	1·710	1·717	1·744	1·759	1·781	1·791	1·791	1·785	1·801	1·823	1·824	1·830
May	1·662	1·668	1·680	1·699	1·706	1·733	1·747	1·769	1·779	1·779	1·773	1·790	1·811	1·812	1·818
June	1·656	1·661	1·673	1·692	1·699	1·726	1·740	1·763	1·772	1·772	1·766	1·783	1·804	1·805	1·811
July	1·641	1·647	1·659	1·678	1·685	1·712	1·726	1·748	1·757	1·757	1·752	1·768	1·789	1·790	1·796
Aug	1·630	1·635	1·647	1·666	1·673	1·700	1·714	1·736	1·745	1·745	1·739	1·756	1·777	1·778	1·784
Sept	1·618	1·624	1·635	1·654	1·661	1·688	1·702	1·724	1·733	1·733	1·727	1·743	1·764	1·766	1·771
Oct	1·609	1·615	1·626	1·645	1·652	1·678	1·692	1·714	1·723	1·723	1·718	1·734	1·755	1·756	1·762
Nov	1·600	1·605	1·617	1·635	1·642	1·669	1·683	1·705	1·714	1·714	1·708	1·724	1·745	1·746	1·752
Dec	1·593	1·599	1·610	1·628	1·635	1·662	1·676	1·698	1·707	1·707	1·701	1·717	1·738	1·739	1·745
1984	Sept	Oct	Nov	Dec	Jan	Feb	Mar	Apr	May	June	July	Aug	Sept	Oct	Nov
Jan	1·594	1·600	1·612	1·630	1·637	1·663	1·677	1·699	1·708	1·708	1·703	1·719	1·739	1·741	1·746
Feb	1·584	1·589	1·601	1·619	1·626	1·653	1·666	1·688	1·697	1·697	1·692	1·708	1·728	1·729	1·735
Mar	1·576	1·581	1·593	1·611	1·618	1·644	1·658	1·680	1·689	1·689	1·683	1·699	1·720	1·721	1·726
Apr	1·542	1·547	1·559	1·577	1·583	1·609	1·623	1·644	1·653	1·653	1·648	1·663	1·684	1·685	1·691
May	1·532	1·538	1·549	1·567	1·574	1·600	1·613	1·634	1·643	1·643	1·638	1·654	1·674	1·675	1·681
June	1·526	1·531	1·543	1·560	1·567	1·593	1·606	1·628	1·637	1·637	1·631	1·647	1·667	1·668	1·674
July	1·529	1·534	1·545	1·563	1·570	1·596	1·609	1·631	1·640	1·640	1·634	1·650	1·670	1·671	1·677
Aug	1·505	1·511	1·511	1·540	1·546	1·572	1·585	1·606	1·615	1·615	1·610	1·625	1·645	1·646	1·652
Sept	1·500	1·506	1·517	1·535	1·541	1·567	1·580	1·601	1·610	1·610	1·604	1·620	1·640	1·641	1·647
Oct	1·485	1·490	1·501	1·519	1·526	1·551	1·564	1·585	1·594	1·594	1·588	1·604	1·624	1·625	1·630
Nov	1·477	1·483	1·494	1·511	1·518	1·543	1·556	1·577	1·586	1·586	1·581	1·596	1·616	1·617	1·622
Dec	1·479	1·485	1·496	1·513	1·520	1·545	1·558	1·579	1·588	1·588	1·583	1·598	1·618	1·619	1·624
1985	Sept	Oct	Nov	Dec	Jan	Feb	Mar	Apr	May	June	July	Aug	Sept	Oct	Nov
Jan	1·470	1·476	1·487	1·504	1·511	1·536	1·549	1·570	1·579	1·579	1·573	1·589	1·608	1·610	1·615
Feb	1·451	1·456	1·467	1·484	1·491	1·516	1·529	1·550	1·558	1·558	1·553	1·568	1·588	1·589	1·594
Mar	1·428	1·433	1·444	1·461	1·468	1·492	1·505	1·526	1·534	1·534	1·529	1·544	1·564	1·565	1·570
Apr	1·377	1·382	1·393	1·410	1·416	1·440	1·453	1·473	1·482	1·482	1·476	1·491	1·510	1·511	1·516
May	1·366	1·372	1·382	1·399	1·405	1·429	1·442	1·462	1·470	1·470	1·465	1·480	1·499	1·500	1·505
June	1·361	1·367	1·377	1·394	1·400	1·424	1·437	1·457	1·465	1·465	1·460	1·475	1·493	1·494	1·500
July	1·366	1·371	1·381	1·398	1·405	1·429	1·441	1·461	1·470	1·470	1·464	1·479	1·498	1·499	1·504
Aug	1·359	1·365	1·375	1·392	1·398	1·422	1·435	1·455	1·463	1·463	1·458	1·473	1·491	1·492	1·498
Sept	1·361	1·366	1·376	1·393	1·399	1·424	1·436	1·456	1·464	1·464	1·459	1·474	1·493	1·494	1·499
Oct	1·357	1·362	1·373	1·389	1·396	1·420	1·432	1·452	1·461	1·461	1·455	1·470	1·489	1·490	1·495
Nov	1·349	1·354	1·364	1·381	1·387	1·411	1·424	1·444	1·452	1·452	1·447	1·461	1·480	1·481	1·486
Dec	1·346	1·351	1·361	1·378	1·384	1·408	1·421	1·441	1·449	1·449	1·444	1·458	1·477	1·478	1·483

MONTH OF DISPOSAL

| | 2011 | 2012 | | | | | | | | | | | 2013 | |
	Dec	Jan	Feb	Mar	Apr	May	June	July	Aug	Sept	Oct	Nov	Dec	Jan	Feb
1982															
Mar	2.014	1.996	2.020	2.031	2.053	2.051	2.044	2.047	2.059	2.074	2.092	2.092	2.107	2.094	2.117
Apr	1.954	1.937	1.960	1.971	1.992	1.991	1.984	1.987	1.999	2.013	2.031	2.031	2.045	2.033	2.055
May	1.933	1.916	1.939	1.950	1.971	1.970	1.962	1.966	1.977	1.992	2.009	2.009	2.024	2.011	2.033
June	1.925	1.908	1.931	1.942	1.963	1.961	1.954	1.958	1.969	1.983	2.001	2.001	2.015	2.003	2.025
July	1.924	1.907	1.930	1.941	1.962	1.961	1.953	1.957	1.968	1.983	2.000	2.000	2.014	2.002	2.024
Aug	1.923	1.906	1.929	1.940	1.961	1.960	1.952	1.956	1.967	1.982	1.999	1.999	2.013	2.001	2.023
Sept	1.925	1.908	1.931	1.942	1.963	1.961	1.954	1.958	1.969	1.983	2.001	2.001	2.015	2.003	2.025
Oct	1.910	1.893	1.917	1.927	1.948	1.947	1.940	1.943	1.954	1.969	1.986	1.986	2.000	1.988	2.010
Nov	1.896	1.879	1.902	1.913	1.934	1.932	1.925	1.929	1.940	1.954	1.971	1.971	1.986	1.974	1.995
Dec	1.901	1.885	1.908	1.918	1.939	1.938	1.931	1.934	1.945	1.960	1.977	1.977	1.991	1.979	2.001
1983															
Jan	1.898	1.881	1.904	1.915	1.935	1.934	1.927	1.931	1.942	1.956	1.973	1.973	1.987	1.975	1.997
Feb	1.886	1.869	1.892	1.902	1.923	1.922	1.914	1.918	1.929	1.943	1.960	1.960	1.975	1.963	1.984
Mar	1.880	1.863	1.886	1.897	1.918	1.916	1.909	1.913	1.924	1.938	1.955	1.955	1.969	1.957	1.979
Apr	1.840	1.824	1.846	1.857	1.877	1.876	1.869	1.872	1.883	1.897	1.914	1.914	1.928	1.916	1.938
May	1.828	1.812	1.834	1.845	1.865	1.864	1.857	1.860	1.871	1.885	1.902	1.902	1.916	1.904	1.925
June	1.822	1.805	1.828	1.838	1.858	1.857	1.850	1.854	1.864	1.878	1.895	1.895	1.909	1.897	1.918
July	1.807	1.790	1.812	1.823	1.843	1.842	1.835	1.838	1.849	1.863	1.879	1.879	1.893	1.882	1.903
Aug	1.794	1.778	1.800	1.811	1.830	1.829	1.822	1.826	1.836	1.850	1.867	1.867	1.881	1.869	1.890
Sept	1.782	1.766	1.788	1.798	1.818	1.817	1.810	1.813	1.824	1.838	1.854	1.854	1.868	1.856	1.877
Oct	1.772	1.756	1.778	1.788	1.808	1.807	1.800	1.803	1.814	1.828	1.844	1.844	1.858	1.846	1.867
Nov	1.762	1.746	1.768	1.778	1.798	1.797	1.790	1.793	1.804	1.818	1.834	1.834	1.848	1.836	1.857
Dec	1.755	1.739	1.761	1.771	1.791	1.790	1.783	1.786	1.796	1.810	1.826	1.826	1.840	1.829	1.849
1984															
Jan	1.757	1.741	1.762	1.773	1.792	1.791	1.784	1.788	1.798	1.812	1.828	1.828	1.842	1.830	1.851
Feb	1.745	1.729	1.751	1.762	1.781	1.780	1.773	1.776	1.787	1.800	1.817	1.817	1.830	1.819	1.839
Mar	1.737	1.721	1.742	1.753	1.772	1.771	1.764	1.768	1.778	1.792	1.808	1.808	1.821	1.810	1.830
Apr	1.701	1.685	1.706	1.716	1.736	1.735	1.728	1.731	1.741	1.755	1.771	1.771	1.784	1.773	1.793
May	1.691	1.675	1.696	1.706	1.726	1.724	1.718	1.721	1.731	1.745	1.760	1.760	1.774	1.763	1.783
June	1.684	1.668	1.689	1.700	1.719	1.717	1.711	1.714	1.724	1.738	1.753	1.753	1.767	1.756	1.776
July	1.687	1.671	1.692	1.703	1.722	1.721	1.714	1.717	1.727	1.741	1.756	1.756	1.770	1.759	1.779
Aug	1.662	1.646	1.667	1.677	1.696	1.695	1.689	1.692	1.702	1.715	1.731	1.731	1.744	1.733	1.753
Sept	1.657	1.641	1.662	1.672	1.691	1.690	1.683	1.687	1.697	1.710	1.725	1.725	1.739	1.728	1.748
Oct	1.640	1.625	1.646	1.656	1.674	1.673	1.667	1.670	1.680	1.693	1.709	1.709	1.722	1.711	1.731
Nov	1.632	1.617	1.638	1.648	1.666	1.665	1.659	1.662	1.672	1.685	1.700	1.700	1.714	1.703	1.722
Dec	1.634	1.619	1.640	1.650	1.669	1.667	1.661	1.664	1.674	1.687	1.703	1.703	1.716	1.705	1.725
1985															
Jan	1.625	1.610	1.630	1.640	1.659	1.658	1.651	1.654	1.664	1.678	1.693	1.693	1.706	1.695	1.715
Feb	1.604	1.589	1.609	1.619	1.638	1.637	1.630	1.633	1.643	1.656	1.671	1.671	1.684	1.674	1.693
Mar	1.580	1.565	1.585	1.595	1.613	1.612	1.606	1.609	1.619	1.631	1.647	1.647	1.659	1.649	1.668
Apr	1.526	1.511	1.531	1.541	1.559	1.558	1.551	1.554	1.564	1.577	1.591	1.591	1.604	1.593	1.612
May	1.514	1.500	1.520	1.529	1.547	1.546	1.540	1.543	1.552	1.565	1.580	1.580	1.592	1.582	1.601
June	1.509	1.494	1.514	1.524	1.542	1.541	1.534	1.537	1.547	1.559	1.574	1.574	1.587	1.576	1.595
July	1.514	1.499	1.519	1.528	1.546	1.545	1.539	1.542	1.552	1.564	1.579	1.579	1.591	1.581	1.600
Aug	1.507	1.492	1.512	1.522	1.540	1.539	1.532	1.535	1.545	1.557	1.572	1.572	1.585	1.574	1.593
Sept	1.508	1.494	1.514	1.523	1.541	1.540	1.534	1.537	1.546	1.559	1.573	1.573	1.586	1.576	1.594
Oct	1.504	1.490	1.510	1.519	1.537	1.536	1.530	1.533	1.542	1.555	1.569	1.569	1.582	1.571	1.590
Nov	1.496	1.481	1.501	1.510	1.528	1.527	1.521	1.524	1.533	1.546	1.560	1.560	1.573	1.563	1.581
Dec	1.493	1.478	1.498	1.507	1.525	1.524	1.518	1.521	1.530	1.543	1.557	1.557	1.570	1.559	1.578

MONTH OF DISPOSAL

1986	2010				2011										
	Sept	Oct	Nov	Dec	Jan	Feb	Mar	Apr	May	June	July	Aug	Sept	Oct	Nov
Jan	1·341	1·346	1·346	1·373	1·379	1·403	1·416	1·435	1·444	1·444	1·438	1·453	1·472	1·473	1·478
Feb	1·332	1·337	1·348	1·364	1·371	1·394	1·407	1·426	1·435	1·435	1·430	1·444	1·463	1·464	1·469
Mar	1·329	1·334	1·345	1·361	1·367	1·391	1·404	1·423	1·432	1·432	1·426	1·441	1·459	1·460	1·466
Apr	1·307	1·312	1·322	1·339	1·345	1·368	1·381	1·400	1·408	1·408	1·403	1·417	1·436	1·437	1·442
May	1·303	1·308	1·318	1·334	1·340	1·364	1·376	1·396	1·404	1·404	1·399	1·413	1·431	1·432	1·438
June	1·304	1·309	1·319	1·336	1·342	1·365	1·377	1·397	1·405	1·405	1·400	1·414	1·433	1·434	1·439
July	1·310	1·316	1·326	1·342	1·348	1·372	1·384	1·404	1·412	1·412	1·407	1·421	1·440	1·441	1·446
Aug	1·303	1·308	1·319	1·335	1·341	1·365	1·377	1·396	1·404	1·404	1·399	1·414	1·432	1·433	1·438
Sept	1·292	1·297	1·307	1·323	1·330	1·353	1·365	1·384	1·393	1·393	1·388	1·402	1·420	1·421	1·426
Oct	1·288	1·293	1·304	1·320	1·326	1·349	1·362	1·381	1·389	1·389	1·384	1·398	1·416	1·417	1·422
Nov	1·269	1·274	1·284	1·300	1·306	1·330	1·342	1·361	1·369	1·369	1·364	1·378	1·396	1·397	1·402
Dec	1·262	1·267	1·277	1·293	1·299	1·322	1·334	1·353	1·361	1·361	1·356	1·370	1·388	1·389	1·394

1987	Sept	Oct	Nov	Dec	Jan	Feb	Mar	Apr	May	June	July	Aug	Sept	Oct	Nov
Jan	1·253	1·258	1·268	1·284	1·290	1·313	1·325	1·344	1·352	1·352	1·347	1·361	1·379	1·380	1·385
Feb	1·244	1·249	1·259	1·275	1·281	1·304	1·316	1·335	1·343	1·343	1·338	1·352	1·370	1·371	1·375
Mar	1·240	1·245	1·254	1·270	1·276	1·299	1·311	1·330	1·338	1·338	1·333	1·347	1·365	1·366	1·371
Apr	1·213	1·218	1·228	1·244	1·250	1·272	1·284	1·303	1·310	1·310	1·306	1·319	1·337	1·338	1·343
May	1·211	1·216	1·226	1·241	1·247	1·270	1·282	1·300	1·308	1·308	1·303	1·317	1·335	1·336	1·341
June	1·211	1·216	1·226	1·241	1·247	1·270	1·282	1·300	1·308	1·308	1·303	1·317	1·335	1·336	1·341
July	1·213	1·218	1·228	1·244	1·250	1·272	1·284	1·303	1·310	1·310	1·306	1·319	1·337	1·338	1·343
Aug	1·207	1·212	1·221	1·237	1·243	1·265	1·277	1·296	1·304	1·304	1·299	1·312	1·330	1·331	1·336
Sept	1·200	1·205	1·215	1·230	1·236	1·259	1·271	1·289	1·297	1·297	1·292	1·306	1·323	1·324	1·329
Oct	1·190	1·194	1·204	1·220	1·225	1·248	1·259	1·278	1·286	1·286	1·281	1·294	1·312	1·313	1·318
Nov	1·179	1·184	1·193	1·209	1·215	1·237	1·249	1·267	1·275	1·275	1·270	1·283	1·301	1·302	1·307
Dec	1·181	1·186	1·196	1·211	1·217	1·239	1·251	1·269	1·277	1·277	1·272	1·286	1·303	1·304	1·309

1988	Sept	Oct	Nov	Dec	Jan	Feb	Mar	Apr	May	June	July	Aug	Sept	Oct	Nov
Jan	1·181	1·186	1·196	1·211	1·217	1·239	1·251	1·269	1·277	1·277	1·272	1·286	1·303	1·304	1·309
Feb	1·173	1·177	1·187	1·203	1·208	1·230	1·242	1·260	1·268	1·268	1·263	1·277	1·294	1·295	1·300
Mar	1·164	1·169	1·179	1·194	1·200	1·222	1·233	1·252	1·259	1·259	1·255	1·268	1·285	1·286	1·291
Apr	1·129	1·134	1·144	1·159	1·164	1·186	1·198	1·216	1·223	1·223	1·218	1·232	1·249	1·250	1·254
May	1·121	1·126	1·136	1·151	1·156	1·178	1·189	1·207	1·215	1·215	1·210	1·223	1·240	1·241	1·246
June	1·114	1·118	1·128	1·143	1·148	1·170	1·181	1·199	1·206	1·206	1·202	1·215	1·232	1·233	1·237
July	1·112	1·116	1·126	1·141	1·146	1·168	1·179	1·197	1·204	1·204	1·200	1·213	1·230	1·231	1·235
Aug	1·088	1·093	1·102	1·117	1·122	1·144	1·155	1·172	1·180	1·180	1·175	1·188	1·205	1·206	1·210
Sept	1·078	1·083	1·092	1·107	1·113	1·134	1·145	1·162	1·170	1·170	1·165	1·178	1·195	1·196	1·200
Oct	1.058	1.062	1.071	1.086	1.091	1.112	1.123	1.141	1.148	1.148	1.143	1.156	1.173	1.174	1.178
Nov	1.048	1.053	1.062	1.076	1.082	1.103	1.114	1.131	1.138	1.138	1.134	1.146	1.163	1.164	1.168
Dec	1.043	1.047	1.056	1.071	1.076	1.097	1.108	1.125	1.132	1.132	1.128	1.141	1.157	1.158	1.162

1989	Sept	Oct	Nov	Dec	Jan	Feb	Mar	Apr	May	June	July	Aug	Sept	Oct	Nov
Jan	1.030	1.034	1.043	1.058	1.063	1.084	1.095	1.112	1.119	1.119	1.114	1.127	1.143	1.144	1.149
Feb	1.015	1.020	1.029	1.043	1.048	1.069	1.080	1.097	1.104	1.104	1.099	1.112	1.128	1.129	1.133
Mar	1.006	1.011	1.020	1.034	1.039	1.060	1.070	1.087	1.094	1.094	1.090	1.102	1.118	1.119	1.124
Apr	·971	·976	·984	·998	1.003	1.024	1.034	1.051	1.058	1.058	1.053	1.066	1.081	1.082	1.087
May	·959	·963	·972	·986	·991	1·011	1·022	1·038	1·045	1·045	1·041	1·053	1·069	1·070	1·074
June	·952	·957	·965	·979	·984	1·004	1·015	1·031	1·038	1·038	1·034	1·046	1·062	1·062	1·067
July	·951	·955	·964	·977	·983	1·003	1·013	1·029	1·036	1·036	1·032	1·044	1·060	1·061	1·065
Aug	·946	·950	·959	·972	·978	·997	1·008	1·024	1·031	1·031	1·027	1·039	1·054	1·055	1·060
Sept	·932	·937	·945	·959	·964	·984	·994	1.010	1.017	1.017	1.013	1.025	1.040	1.041	1.045
Oct	·917	·922	·930	·944	·949	·969	·979	·995	1·002	1·002	·997	1·009	1·025	1·026	1·030
Nov	·901	·905	·914	·927	·932	·952	·962	·978	·985	·985	·981	·992	1·008	1·008	1·013
Dec	·896	·901	·909	·923	·928	·947	·957	·973	·980	·980	·976	·987	1·003	1·003	1·008

MONTH OF DISPOSAL

1986	2011 Dec	2012 Jan	Feb	Mar	Apr	May	June	July	Aug	Sept	Oct	Nov	Dec	2013 Jan	Feb
Jan	1·487	1·473	1·493	1·502	1·520	1·518	1·512	1·515	1·525	1·537	1·552	1·552	1·564	1.554	1.573
Feb	1·478	1·464	1·483	1·493	1·510	1·509	1·503	1·506	1·515	1·528	1·542	1·542	1·555	1.544	1.563
Mar	1·475	1·460	1·480	1·489	1·507	1·506	1·500	1·503	1·512	1·525	1·539	1·539	1·551	1.541	1.560
Apr	1·451	1·437	1·456	1·465	1·483	1·482	1·476	1·479	1·488	1·500	1·515	1·515	1·527	1.517	1.535
May	1·447	1·432	1·452	1·461	1·478	1·477	1·471	1·474	1·484	1·496	1·510	1·510	1·522	1.512	1.531
June	1·448	1·434	1·453	1·462	1·480	1·479	1·473	1·476	1·485	1·497	1·511	1·511	1·524	1.513	1.532
July	1·455	1·441	1·460	1·469	1·487	1·486	1·480	1·483	1·492	1·504	1·519	1·519	1·531	1.521	1.539
Aug	1·447	1·433	1·452	1·462	1·479	1·478	1·472	1·475	1·484	1·496	1·511	1·511	1·523	1.513	1.531
Sept	1·435	1·421	1·440	1·450	1·467	1·466	1·460	1·463	1·472	1·484	1·498	1·498	1·511	1.500	1.519
Oct	1·432	1·417	1·437	1·446	1·463	1·462	1·456	1·459	1·468	1·480	1·495	1·495	1·507	1.497	1.515
Nov	1·411	1·397	1·416	1·425	1·442	1·441	1·435	1·438	1·447	1·459	1·474	1·474	1·486	1.476	1.494
Dec	1·403	1·389	1·408	1·417	1·434	1·433	1·427	1·430	1·439	1·451	1·465	1·465	1·477	1.467	1.485

1987	Dec	Jan	Feb	Mar	Apr	May	June	July	Aug	Sept	Oct	Nov	Dec	Jan	Feb
Jan	1·394	1·380	1·399	1·408	1·425	1·424	1·418	1·421	1·430	1·442	1·456	1·456	1·468	1.458	1.476
Feb	1·384	1·371	1·389	1·398	1·415	1·414	1·408	1·411	1·420	1·432	1·446	1·446	1·458	1.448	1.466
Mar	1·380	1·366	1·385	1·394	1·411	1·410	1·404	1·407	1·416	1·427	1·441	1·441	1·453	1.443	1.461
Apr	1·352	1·338	1·357	1·365	1·382	1·381	1·375	1·378	1·387	1·399	1·413	1·413	1·424	1.415	1.432
May	1·349	1·336	1·354	1·363	1·380	1·379	1·373	1·376	1·385	1·396	1·410	1·410	1·422	1.412	1.430
June	1·349	1·336	1·354	1·363	1·380	1·379	1·373	1·376	1·385	1·396	1·410	1·410	1·422	1.412	1.430
July	1·352	1·338	1·357	1·365	1·382	1·381	1·375	1·378	1·387	1·399	1·413	1·413	1·424	1.415	1.432
Aug	1·345	1·331	1·350	1·358	1·375	1·374	1·368	1·371	1·380	1·392	1·405	1·405	1·417	1.407	1.425
Sept	1·338	1·324	1·343	1·352	1·368	1·367	1·361	1·364	1·373	1·385	1·398	1·398	1·410	1.400	1.418
Oct	1·327	1·313	1·331	1·340	1·357	1·356	1·350	1·353	1·362	1·373	1·387	1·387	1·398	1.389	1.406
Nov	1·315	1·302	1·320	1·329	1·345	1·344	1·338	1·341	1·350	1·362	1·375	1·375	1·387	1.377	1.395
Dec	1·010	1·004	1·022	1·001	1·040	1·047	1·041	1·044	1·052	1·064	1·070	1·070	1·000	1.070	1.007

1988	Dec	Jan	Feb	Mar	Apr	May	June	July	Aug	Sept	Oct	Nov	Dec	Jan	Feb
Jan	1·318	1·304	1·322	1·331	1·348	1·347	1·341	1·344	1·352	1·364	1·378	1·378	1·389	1.379	1.397
Feb	1·309	1·295	1·313	1·322	1·338	1·338	1·332	1·335	1·343	1·355	1·368	1·368	1·380	1.370	1.388
Mar	1·300	1·286	1·305	1·313	1.329	1.329	1·323	1·326	1·334	1·346	1·359	1·359	1·371	1.361	1.378
Apr	1.263	1.250	1.267	1.276	1.292	1.291	1.285	1.288	1.297	1.308	1.321	1.321	1.333	1.323	1.340
May	1.254	1.241	1.259	1.267	1.283	1.282	1.277	1.280	1.288	1.299	1.313	1.313	1.324	1.315	1.331
June	1.246	1.233	1.250	1.259	1.275	1.274	1.268	1.271	1.280	1.291	1.304	1.304	1.315	1.306	1.323
July	1.244	1.231	1.248	1.257	1.273	1.272	1.266	1.269	1.277	1.289	1.302	1.302	1.313	1.304	1.321
Aug	1·219	1·206	1·223	1·232	1·247	1·247	1·241	1·244	1·252	1·263	1·276	1·276	1·287	1.278	1.295
Sept	1·208	1·196	1·213	1·221	1·237	1·236	1·231	1·233	1·242	1·253	1·266	1·266	1·277	1.268	1.284
Oct	1.186	1.174	1.191	1.199	1.215	1.214	1.208	1.211	1.219	1.230	1.243	1.243	1.254	1.245	1.261
Nov	1.176	1.164	1.181	1.189	1.205	1.204	1.198	1.201	1.209	1.220	1.233	1.233	1.244	1.235	1.251
Dec	1.170	1.158	1.175	1.183	1.199	1.198	1.192	1.195	1.203	1.214	1.227	1.227	1.238	1.228	1.245

1989	Dec	Jan	Feb	Mar	Apr	May	June	July	Aug	Sept	Oct	Nov	Dec	Jan	Feb
Jan	1.157	1.144	1.161	1.169	1.185	1.184	1.178	1.181	1.189	1.200	1.213	1.213	1.223	1.214	1.231
Feb	1.141	1.129	1.146	1.154	1.169	1.168	1.163	1.165	1.174	1.184	1.197	1.197	1.208	1.199	1.215
Mar	1.132	1.119	1.136	1.144	1.159	1.159	1.153	1.156	1.164	1.175	1.187	1.187	1.198	1.189	1.205
Apr	1.094	1.082	1.099	1.107	1.122	1.121	1.115	1.118	1.126	1.136	1.149	1.149	1.159	1.150	1.166
May	1·082	1·070	1·086	1·094	1·109	1·108	1·103	1·105	1·113	1·123	1·136	1·136	1·146	1.137	1.153
June	1·075	1·062	1·079	1·087	1·101	1·101	1·095	1·098	1·106	1·116	1·128	1·128	1·139	1.130	1.146
July	1·073	1·061	1·077	1·085	1·100	1·099	1·094	1·096	1·104	1·114	1·126	1·126	1·137	1.128	1.144
Aug	1·067	1·055	1·072	1·079	1·094	1·093	1·088	1·091	1·098	1·109	1·121	1·121	1·131	1.123	1.138
Sept	1·053	1·041	1·057	1·065	1·080	1·079	1·074	1·076	1·084	1·094	1·106	1·106	1·117	1.108	1.123
Oct	1·037	1·026	1·042	1·049	1·064	1·063	1·058	1·060	1·068	1·078	1·090	1·090	1·100	1.092	1.107
Nov	1·020	1·008	1·024	1·032	1·046	1·046	1·041	1·043	1·051	1·061	1·073	1·073	1·083	1.074	1.089
Dec	1·015	1·003	1·019	1·027	1·041	1·040	1·035	1·038	1·045	1·056	1·067	1·067	1·077	1.069	1.084

MONTH OF DISPOSAL

	2010				2011										
1990	Sept	Oct	Nov	Dec	Jan	Feb	Mar	Apr	May	June	July	Aug	Sept	Oct	Nov
Jan	·885	·890	·898	·911	·916	·936	·946	·962	·968	·968	·964	·976	·991	·992	·996
Feb	·874	·879	·887	·900	·905	·924	·934	·950	·957	·957	·953	·964	·979	·980	·984
Mar	·856	·860	·868	·881	·886	·905	·915	·931	·937	·937	·933	·945	·960	·960	·965
Apr	·801	·805	·813	·826	·831	·849	·859	·874	·880	·880	·876	·887	·902	·902	·906
May	·785	·789	·797	·810	·815	·833	·842	·857	·864	·864	·860	·871	·885	·886	·890
June	·778	·782	·790	·803	·807	·826	·835	·850	·856	·856	·852	·863	·878	·878	·882
July	·777	·781	·789	·801	·806	·824	·834	·849	·855	·855	·851	·862	·876	·877	·881
Aug	·759	·763	·770	·783	·788	·806	·815	·830	·836	·836	·832	·843	·857	·858	·862
Sept	·742	·746	·754	·766	·771	·789	·798	·813	·819	·819	·815	·826	·840	·841	·845
Oct	·729	·733	·741	·753	·757	·775	·784	·799	·805	·805	·801	·812	·826	·827	·830
Nov	·733	·737	·745	·757	·762	·779	·788	·803	·809	·809	·805	·816	·830	·831	·835
Dec	·734	·738	·746	·758	·763	·781	·790	·804	·811	·811	·807	·818	·831	·832	·836
1991	Sept	Oct	Nov	Dec	Jan	Feb	Mar	Apr	May	June	July	Aug	Sept	Oct	Nov
Jan	·730	·734	·742	·754	·759	·776	·786	·800	·806	·806	·803	·813	·827	·828	·832
Feb	·721	·725	·733	·745	·749	·767	·776	·791	·797	·797	·793	·804	·817	·818	·822
Mar	·715	·718	·726	·738	·743	·760	·769	·784	·790	·790	·786	·797	·811	·811	·815
Apr	·693	·696	·704	·716	·721	·738	·747	·761	·767	·767	·763	·774	·787	·788	·792
May	·688	·691	·699	·711	·715	·733	·742	·756	·762	·762	·758	·769	·782	·783	·787
June	·680	·684	·691	·703	·708	·725	·734	·748	·754	·754	·750	·761	·774	·775	·779
July	·684	·688	·695	·707	·712	·729	·738	·752	·758	·758	·754	·765	·778	·779	·783
Aug	·680	·684	·691	·703	·708	·725	·734	·748	·754	·754	·750	·761	·774	·775	·779
Sept	·674	·678	·685	·697	·701	·718	·727	·741	·747	·747	·744	·754	·767	·768	·772
Oct	·668	·671	·679	·691	·695	·712	·721	·735	·741	·741	·737	·748	·761	·762	·765
Nov	·662	·665	·673	·684	·689	·706	·715	·729	·735	·735	·731	·741	·754	·755	·759
Dec	·660	·664	·671	·683	·688	·704	·713	·727	·733	·733	·730	·740	·753	·754	·758
1992	Sept	Oct	Nov	Dec	Jan	Feb	Mar	Apr	May	June	July	Aug	Sept	Oct	Nov
Jan	·662	·665	·673	·684	·689	·706	·715	·729	·735	·735	·731	·741	·754	·755	·759
Feb	·653	·657	·664	·676	·680	·697	·706	·720	·726	·726	·722	·732	·745	·746	·750
Mar	·648	·652	·659	·671	·675	·692	·701	·715	·721	·721	·717	·727	·740	·741	·745
Apr	·623	·627	·634	·646	·650	·666	·675	·689	·695	·695	·691	·701	·714	·715	·718
May	·617	·621	·628	·640	·644	·660	·669	·683	·688	·688	·685	·695	·708	·709	·712
June	·617	·621	·628	·640	·644	·660	·669	·683	·688	·688	·685	·695	·708	·709	·712
July	·623	·627	·634	·646	·650	·666	·675	·689	·695	·695	·691	·701	·714	·715	·718
Aug	·622	·626	·633	·644	·649	·665	·674	·688	·693	·693	·690	·700	·713	·713	·717
Sept	·616	·620	·627	·638	·643	·659	·668	·681	·687	·687	·684	·694	·707	·707	·711
Oct	·610	·614	·621	·633	·637	·653	·662	·675	·681	·681	·678	·688	·701	·701	·705
Nov	.613	.616	.623	.635	.639	.656	.664	.678	.684	.684	.680	.690	.703	.704	.707
Dec	·619	·622	·629	·641	·645	·662	·670	·684	·690	·690	·686	·696	·709	·710	·713
1993	Sept	Oct	Nov	Dec	Jan	Feb	Mar	Apr	May	June	July	Aug	Sept	Oct	Nov
Jan	·634	·637	·645	·656	·661	·677	·686	·700	·706	·706	·702	·712	·725	·726	·730
Feb	·623	·627	·634	·646	·650	·666	·675	·689	·695	·695	·691	·701	·714	·715	·718
Mar	·617	·621	·628	·640	·644	·660	·669	·683	·688	·688	·685	·695	·708	·709	·712
Apr	·602	·606	·613	·624	·629	·645	·654	·667	·673	·673	·669	·679	·692	·693	·696
May	·597	·600	·607	·619	·623	·639	·648	·661	·667	·667	·663	·673	·686	·687	·690
June	·598	·601	·609	·620	·624	·640	·649	·662	·668	·668	·665	·674	·687	·688	·691
July	·601	·605	·612	·623	·628	·644	·652	·666	·672	·672	·668	·678	·691	·692	·695
Aug	·594	·598	·605	·616	·621	·637	·645	·659	·665	·665	·661	·671	·684	·684	·688
Sept	·588	·591	·598	·610	·614	·630	·638	·652	·658	·658	·654	·664	·677	·677	·681
Oct	·589	·592	·599	·611	·615	·631	·640	·653	·659	·659	·655	·665	·678	·678	·682
Nov	·591	·595	·602	·613	·617	·633	·642	·655	·661	·661	·657	·667	·680	·681	·684
Dec	·588	·591	·598	·610	·614	·630	·638	·652	·658	·658	·654	·664	·677	·677	·681

MONTH OF DISPOSAL

	2011	2012												2013	
1990	Dec	Jan	Feb	Mar	Apr	May	June	July	Aug	Sept	Oct	Nov	Dec	Jan	Feb
Jan	1·003	·992	1·008	1·015	1·029	1·028	1·023	1·026	1·033	1·044	1·055	1·055	1·065	1.057	1.072
Feb	·992	·980	·996	1·003	1·017	1·017	1·012	1·014	1·022	1·032	1·043	1·043	1·053	1.045	1.060
Mar	·972	·960	·976	·984	·998	·997	·992	·994	1·002	1·012	1·023	1·023	1·033	1.025	1.040
Apr	·914	·902	·918	·925	·938	·938	·933	·935	·942	·952	·963	·963	·973	.965	.979
May	·897	·886	·901	·908	·922	·921	·916	·918	·926	·935	·946	·946	·956	.948	.962
June	·890	·878	·893	·901	·914	·913	·908	·911	·918	·927	·938	·938	·948	.940	.954
July	·888	·877	·892	·899	·912	·912	·907	·909	·916	·926	·937	·937	·946	.938	.953
Aug	·869	·858	·873	·880	·893	·892	·888	·890	·897	·906	·917	·917	·927	.919	.933
Sept	·852	·841	·855	·862	·875	·875	·870	·872	·879	·889	·899	·899	·909	.901	.915
Oct	·837	·827	·841	·848	·861	·860	·856	·858	·865	·874	·885	·885	·894	.886	.900
Nov	·842	·831	·845	·852	·865	·865	·860	·862	·869	·878	·889	·889	·898	.891	.905
Dec	·843	·832	·847	·854	·867	·866	·861	·864	·871	·880	·891	·891	·900	.892	.906
1991	Dec	Jan	Feb	Mar	Apr	May	June	July	Aug	Sept	Oct	Nov	Dec	Jan	Feb
Jan	·839	·828	·843	·849	·863	·862	·857	·859	·866	·876	·886	·886	·896	.888	.902
Feb	·829	·818	·833	·840	·853	·852	·847	·850	·856	·866	·876	·876	·885	.878	.892
Mar	·822	·811	·826	·833	·846	·845	·840	·842	·849	·858	·869	·869	·878	.871	.884
Apr	·799	·788	·802	·809	·822	·821	·817	·819	·826	·835	·845	·845	·854	.847	.860
May	·793	·783	·797	·804	·816	·816	·811	·813	·820	·829	·840	·840	·849	.841	.855
June	·785	·775	·789	·796	·808	·808	·803	·805	·812	·821	·831	·831	·840	.833	.846
July	·789	·779	·793	·800	·812	·812	·807	·809	·816	·825	·836	·836	·845	.837	.851
Aug	·785	·775	·789	·796	·808	·808	·803	·805	·812	·821	·831	·831	·840	.833	.846
Sept	·779	·768	·782	·789	·802	·801	·796	·799	·805	·814	·825	·825	·834	.826	.840
Oct	·772	·762	·776	·782	·795	·794	·790	·792	·799	·808	·818	·818	·827	.819	.833
Nov	·765	·755	·769	·776	·788	·788	·783	·785	·792	·801	·811	·811	·820	.813	.826
Dec	·764	·754	·768	·775	·787	·786	·782	·784	·791	·800	·810	·810	·819	.811	.825
1992	Dec	Jan	Feb	Mar	Apr	May	June	July	Aug	Sept	Oct	Nov	Dec	Jan	Feb
Jan	·765	·755	·769	·776	·788	·788	·783	·785	·792	·801	·811	·811	·820	.813	.826
Feb	·756	·746	·760	·767	·779	·778	·774	·776	·783	·792	·802	·802	·811	.803	.817
Mar	·751	·741	·755	·762	·774	·773	·769	·771	·778	·786	·797	·797	·805	.798	.811
Apr	·725	·715	·728	·735	·747	·746	·742	·744	·751	·759	·769	·769	·778	.771	.784
May	·719	·709	·722	·729	·741	·740	·736	·738	·744	·753	·763	·763	·772	.765	.777
June	·719	·709	·722	·729	·741	·740	·736	·738	·744	·753	·763	·763	·772	.765	.777
July	·725	·715	·728	·735	·747	·746	·742	·744	·751	·759	·769	·769	·778	.771	.784
Aug	·724	·713	·727	·734	·746	·745	·741	·743	·749	·758	·768	·768	·777	.770	.783
Sept	·717	·707	·721	·727	·740	·739	·735	·737	·743	·752	·762	·762	·770	.763	.776
Oct	·711	·701	·715	·721	·733	·733	·728	·731	·737	·746	·756	·756	·764	.757	.770
Nov	·714	·704	·717	·724	·736	·735	·731	·733	·739	·748	·758	·758	·767	.759	.772
Dec	·720	·710	·723	·730	·742	·741	·737	·739	·746	·754	·764	·764	·773	.766	.779
1993	Dec	Jan	Feb	Mar	Apr	May	June	July	Aug	Sept	Oct	Nov	Dec	Jan	Feb
Jan	·736	·726	·740	·746	·759	·758	·753	·756	·762	·771	·781	·781	·790	.782	.796
Feb	·725	·715	·728	·735	·747	·746	·742	·744	·751	·759	·769	·769	·778	.771	.784
Mar	·719	·709	·722	·729	·741	·740	·736	·738	·744	·753	·763	·763	·772	.765	.777
Apr	·703	·693	·706	·713	·725	·724	·720	·722	·728	·737	·747	·747	·755	.748	.761
May	·697	·687	·700	·707	·719	·718	·714	·716	·722	·731	·741	·741	·749	.742	.755
June	·698	·688	·701	·708	·720	·719	·715	·717	·723	·732	·742	·742	·750	.743	.756
July	·701	·692	·705	·711	·724	·723	·719	·721	·727	·736	·746	·746	·754	747	760
Aug	·694	·684	·698	·704	·716	·715	·711	·713	·720	·728	·738	·738	·747	.740	.752
Sept	·687	·677	·691	·697	·709	·708	·704	·706	·712	·721	·731	·731	·739	.732	.745
Oct	·688	·678	·692	·698	·710	·709	·705	·707	·714	·722	·732	·732	·740	.733	.746
Nov	·691	·681	·694	·701	·713	·712	·708	·710	·716	·725	·734	·734	·743	.736	.749
Dec	·687	·677	·691	·697	·709	·708	·704	·706	·712	·721	·731	·731	·739	.732	.745

	2010				2011										
1994	Sept	Oct	Nov	Dec	Jan	Feb	Mar	Apr	May	June	July	Aug	Sept	Oct	Nov
Jan	·594	·598	·605	·616	·621	·637	·645	·659	·665	·665	·661	·671	·684	·684	·688
Feb	·586	·589	·596	·607	·612	·628	·636	·650	·655	·655	·652	·662	·674	·675	·678
Mar	·581	·585	·592	·603	·607	·623	·632	·645	·651	·651	·647	·657	·669	·670	·674
Apr	·562	·566	·573	·584	·588	·604	·612	·626	·631	·631	·628	·637	·650	·650	·654
May	·557	·560	·567	·578	·583	·598	·607	·620	·625	·625	·622	·632	·644	·645	·648
June	·557	·560	·567	·578	·583	·598	·607	·620	·625	·625	·622	·632	·644	·645	·648
July	·565	·568	·575	·586	·590	·606	·615	·628	·633	·633	·630	·640	·652	·653	·656
Aug	·557	·560	·567	·578	·583	·598	·607	·620	·625	·625	·622	·632	·644	·645	·648
Sept	·554	·557	·564	·575	·579	·595	·603	·617	·622	·622	·619	·628	·641	·641	·645
Oct	·552	·555	·562	·573	·577	·593	·601	·614	·620	·620	·616	·626	·638	·639	·643
Nov	·551	·554	·561	·572	·576	·592	·600	·613	·619	·619	·615	·625	·637	·638	·641
Dec	·543	·547	·553	·564	·568	·584	·592	·605	·611	·611	·608	·617	·629	·630	·634
1995	Sept	Oct	Nov	Dec	Jan	Feb	Mar	Apr	May	June	July	Aug	Sept	Oct	Nov
Jan	·543	·547	·553	·564	·568	·584	·592	·605	·611	·611	·608	·617	·629	·630	·634
Feb	·534	·537	·544	·555	·559	·575	·583	·596	·601	·601	·598	·607	·619	·620	·624
Mar	·527	·531	·538	·548	·553	·568	·576	·589	·595	·595	·591	·601	·613	·614	·617
Apr	·512	·515	·522	·533	·537	·552	·560	·573	·579	·579	·575	·585	·597	·597	·601
May	·506	·509	·516	·527	·531	·546	·554	·567	·572	·572	·569	·578	·590	·591	·594
June	·504	·507	·514	·525	·529	·544	·552	·565	·570	·570	·567	·576	·588	·589	·592
July	·511	·514	·521	·532	·536	·551	·559	·572	·577	·577	·574	·584	·596	·596	·600
Aug	·503	·506	·513	·524	·528	·543	·551	·564	·569	·569	·566	·575	·587	·588	·591
Sept	·496	·499	·506	·517	·521	·536	·544	·556	·562	·562	·558	·568	·580	·580	·584
Oct	·504	·507	·514	·525	·529	·544	·552	·565	·570	·570	·567	·576	·588	·589	·592
Nov	·504	·507	·514	·525	·529	·544	·552	·565	·570	·570	·567	·576	·588	·589	·592
Dec	·495	·498	·505	·516	·520	·535	·543	·555	·561	·561	·557	·567	·579	·579	·583
1996	Sept	Oct	Nov	Dec	Jan	Feb	Mar	Apr	May	June	July	Aug	Sept	Oct	Nov
Jan	·500	·503	·510	·521	·525	·540	·548	·561	·566	·566	·563	·572	·584	·585	·588
Feb	·493	·496	·503	·514	·518	·533	·541	·553	·559	·559	·555	·565	·577	·577	·581
Mar	·487	·490	·497	·508	·512	·527	·535	·547	·552	·552	·549	·558	·570	·571	·574
Apr	·476	·480	·486	·497	·501	·516	·524	·536	·541	·541	·538	·547	·559	·560	·563
May	·474	·477	·483	·494	·498	·513	·521	·533	·538	·538	·535	·544	·556	·557	·560
June	·473	·476	·482	·493	·497	·512	·520	·532	·537	·537	·534	·543	·555	·556	·559
July	·478	·482	·488	·499	·503	·518	·526	·538	·543	·543	·540	·549	·561	·562	·565
Aug	·472	·475	·481	·492	·496	·511	·519	·531	·536	·536	·533	·542	·554	·555	·558
Sept	·465	·468	·475	·485	·489	·504	·512	·524	·529	·529	·526	·535	·547	·547	·551
Oct	·465	·468	·475	·485	·489	·504	·512	·524	·529	·529	·526	·535	·547	·547	·551
Nov	·464	·467	·474	·484	·488	·503	·511	·523	·528	·528	·525	·534	·546	·546	·550
Dec	·459	·462	·469	·479	·483	·498	·506	·523	·523	·523	·520	·529	·541	·541	·545
1997	Sept	Oct	Nov	Dec	Jan	Feb	Mar	Apr	May	June	July	Aug	Sept	Oct	Nov
Jan	·459	·462	·469	·479	·483	·498	·506	·518	·523	·523	·520	·529	·541	·541	·545
Feb	·454	·457	·463	·474	·477	·492	·500	·512	·517	·517	·514	·523	·535	·535	·539
Mar	·450	·453	·459	·470	·474	·488	·496	·508	·514	·514	·510	·519	·531	·532	·535
Apr	·441	·445	·451	·461	·465	·480	·488	·500	·505	·505	·502	·511	·522	·523	·526
May	·436	·439	·446	·456	·460	·474	·482	·494	·499	·499	·496	·505	·516	·517	·520
June	·430	·434	·440	·450	·454	·469	·476	·488	·493	·493	·490	·499	·510	·511	·514
July	·430	·434	·440	·450	·454	·469	·476	·488	·493	·493	·490	·499	·510	·511	·514
Aug	·421	·425	·431	·441	·445	·459	·467	·479	·484	·484	·481	·490	·501	·502	·505
Sept	·414	·417	·424	·434	·438	·452	·460	·471	·476	·476	·473	·482	·493	·494	·497
Oct	·413	·416	·422	·432	·436	·450	·458	·470	·475	·475	·471	·480	·492	·492	·495
Nov	·412	·415	·421	·431	·435	·449	·457	·469	·474	·474	·471	·479	·491	·491	·494
Dec	·408	·411	·418	·428	·431	·446	·453	·465	·470	·470	·467	·476	·487	·488	·491

MONTH OF DISPOSAL

	2011	2012												2013	
1994	Dec	Jan	Feb	Mar	Apr	May	June	July	Aug	Sept	Oct	Nov	Dec	Jan	Feb
Jan	·694	·684	·698	·704	·716	·715	·711	·713	·720	·728	·738	·738	·747	.740	.752
Feb	·685	·675	·688	·695	·707	·706	·702	·704	·710	·719	·728	·728	·737	.730	.742
Mar	·680	·670	·684	·690	·702	·701	·697	·699	·705	·714	·724	·724	·732	.725	.738
Apr	·660	·650	·664	·670	·682	·681	·677	·679	·685	·693	·703	·703	·712	.705	.717
May	·654	·645	·658	·664	·676	·675	·671	·673	·679	·688	·697	·697	·706	.699	.711
June	·654	·645	·658	·664	·676	·675	·671	·673	·679	·688	·697	·697	·706	.699	.711
July	·663	·653	·666	·672	·684	·683	·679	·681	·688	·696	·706	·706	·714	.707	.719
Aug	·654	·645	·658	·664	·676	·675	·671	·673	·679	·688	·697	·697	·706	.699	.711
Sept	·651	·641	·654	·661	·672	·672	·668	·670	·676	·684	·694	·694	·702	.695	.708
Oct	·649	·639	·652	·658	·670	·669	·665	·667	·674	·682	·691	·691	·700	.693	.705
Nov	·648	·638	·651	·657	·669	·668	·664	·666	·672	·681	·690	·690	·699	.692	.704
Dec	·640	·630	·643	·649	·661	·660	·656	·658	·664	·673	·682	·682	·690	.684	.696
1995	Dec	Jan	Feb	Mar	Apr	May	June	July	Aug	Sept	Oct	Nov	Dec	Jan	Feb
Jan	·640	·630	·643	·649	·661	·660	·656	·658	·664	·673	·682	·682	·690	.684	.696
Feb	·630	·620	·633	·639	·651	·650	·646	·648	·654	·662	·672	·672	·680	.673	.686
Mar	·623	·614	·626	·633	·644	·643	·639	·641	·647	·656	·665	·665	·673	.666	.679
Apr	·607	·597	·610	·616	·628	·627	·623	·625	·631	·639	·648	·648	·656	.650	.662
May	·600	·591	·604	·610	·621	·620	·616	·618	·624	·632	·642	·642	·650	.643	.655
June	·598	·589	·601	·607	·619	·618	·614	·616	·622	·630	·640	·640	·648	.641	.653
July	·606	·596	·609	·615	·626	·626	·622	·624	·630	·638	·647	·647	·655	.649	.661
Aug	·597	·588	·600	·606	·618	·617	·613	·615	·621	·629	·638	·638	·646	.640	.652
Sept	·590	·580	·593	·599	·610	·610	·606	·608	·614	·622	·631	·631	·639	.632	.644
Oct	·598	·589	·601	·607	·619	·618	·614	·616	·622	·630	·640	·640	·648	.641	.653
Nov	·598	·589	·601	·607	·619	·618	·614	·616	·622	·630	·640	·640	·648	.641	.653
Dec	·600	·570	·602	·608	·600	·608	·606	·607	·613	·620	·630	·630	·638	.631	.643
1996	Dec	Jan	Feb	Mar	Apr	May	June	July	Aug	Sept	Oct	Nov	Dec	Jan	Feb
Jan	·594	·585	·597	·603	·615	·614	·610	·612	·618	·626	·635	·635	·643	.636	.648
Feb	·586	·577	·590	·596	·607	·606	·602	·604	·610	·618	·628	·628	·636	.629	.641
Mar	·580	·571	·583	·589	·601	·600	·596	·598	·604	·612	·621	·621	·629	.622	.634
Apr	·569	·560	·572	·578	·589	·588	·585	·587	·592	·600	·609	·609	·617	.611	.623
May	·566	·557	·569	·575	·586	·585	·581	·583	·589	·597	·606	·606	·614	.608	.619
June	·565	·556	·568	·574	·585	·584	·580	·582	·588	·596	·605	·605	·613	.607	.618
July	·571	·562	·574	·580	·591	·591	·587	·589	·594	·602	·612	·612	·619	.613	.625
Aug	·564	·555	·567	·573	·584	·583	·579	·581	·587	·595	·604	·604	·612	.605	.617
Sept	·557	·547	·560	·566	·577	·576	·572	·574	·580	·588	·597	·597	·605	.598	.610
Oct	·557	·547	·560	·566	·577	·576	·572	·574	·580	·588	·597	·597	·605	.598	.610
Nov	·556	·546	·559	·565	·576	·575	·571	·573	·579	·587	·596	·596	·604	.597	.609
Dec	·551	·541	·554	·560	·571	·570	·566	·568	·574	·582	·591	·591	·598	.592	.604
1997	Dec	Jan	Feb	Mar	Apr	May	June	July	Aug	Sept	Oct	Nov	Dec	Jan	Feb
Jan	·551	·541	·554	·560	·571	·570	·566	·568	·574	·582	·591	·591	·598	.592	.604
Feb	·545	·535	·548	·554	·565	·564	·560	·562	·568	·575	·585	·585	·592	.586	.597
Mar	·541	·532	·544	·550	·560	·560	·556	·558	·564	·571	·580	·580	·588	.582	.593
Apr	·532	·523	·535	·541	·552	·551	·547	·549	·555	·562	·571	·571	·579	.573	.584
May	·526	·517	·529	·535	·546	·545	·541	·543	·549	·556	·565	·565	·573	.567	.578
June	·520	·511	·523	·529	·540	·539	·535	·537	·543	·550	·559	·559	·567	.561	.572
July	·520	·511	·523	·529	·540	·539	·535	·537	·543	·550	·559	·559	·567	.561	.572
Aug	·510	·502	·514	·519	·530	·529	·526	·527	·533	·541	·550	·550	·557	.551	.562
Sept	·503	·494	·506	·512	·522	·522	·518	·520	·525	·533	·542	·542	·549	.543	.554
Oct	·501	·492	·504	·510	·520	·520	·516	·518	·524	·531	·540	·540	·547	.541	.552
Nov	·500	·491	·503	·509	·519	·519	·515	·517	·523	·530	·539	·539	·546	.540	.551
Dec	·496	·488	·499	·505	·516	·515	·511	·513	·519	·526	·535	·535	·543	.536	.548

MONTH OF DISPOSAL

	2010				2011										
1998	Sept	Oct	Nov	Dec	Jan	Feb	Mar	Apr	May	June	July	Aug	Sept	Oct	Nov
Jan	·413	·416	·422	·432	·436	·450	·458	·470	·475	·475	·471	·480	·492	·492	·495
Feb	·405	·409	·415	·425	·429	·443	·450	·462	·467	·467	·464	·473	·484	·485	·488
Mar	·401	·404	·410	·420	·424	·438	·446	·458	·463	·463	·460	·468	·479	·480	·483
Apr	·386	·389	·395	·405	·408	·423	·430	·442	·446	·446	·443	·452	·463	·464	·467
May	·378	·381	·387	·397	·401	·415	·422	·434	·439	·439	·435	·444	·455	·456	·459
June	·379	·382	·388	·398	·401	·416	·423	·435	·439	·439	·436	·445	·456	·457	·460
July	·382	·385	·391	·401	·405	·419	·426	·438	·443	·443	·440	·448	·460	·460	·463
Aug	·376	·379	·385	·395	·399	·413	·420	·432	·437	·437	·434	·442	·453	·454	·457
Sept	·370	·373	·380	·389	·393	·407	·414	·426	·431	·431	·428	·436	·447	·448	·451
Oct	·370	·373	·379	·388	·392	·406	·413	·425	·430	·430	·427	·435	·446	·447	·450
Nov	·370	·373	·380	·389	·393	·407	·414	·426	·431	·431	·428	·436	·447	·448	·451
Dec	·370	·373	·380	·389	·393	·407	·414	·426	·431	·431	·428	·436	·447	·448	·451
1999	Sept	Oct	Nov	Dec	Jan	Feb	Mar	Apr	May	June	July	Aug	Sept	Oct	Nov
Jan	·379	·382	·388	·398	·401	·416	·423	·435	·439	·439	·436	·445	·456	·457	·460
Feb	·376	·379	·385	·395	·399	·413	·420	·432	·437	·437	·434	·442	·453	·454	·457
Mar	·373	·376	·382	·392	·395	·410	·417	·428	·433	·433	·430	·439	·450	·450	·453
Apr	·364	·367	·373	·383	·386	·400	·407	·419	·424	·424	·421	·429	·440	·441	·444
May	·361	·364	·370	·379	·383	·397	·404	·415	·420	·420	·417	·426	·437	·437	·440
June	·361	·364	·370	·379	·383	·397	·404	·415	·420	·420	·417	·426	·437	·437	·440
July	·365	·368	·374	·383	·387	·401	·408	·420	·425	·425	·422	·430	·441	·442	·445
Aug	·361	·364	·370	·380	·384	·398	·405	·416	·421	·421	·418	·427	·437	·438	·441
Sept	·356	·359	·365	·374	·378	·392	·399	·410	·415	·415	·412	·421	·431	·432	·435
Oct	·353	·356	·362	·372	·375	·389	·396	·408	·413	·413	·410	·418	·429	·429	·432
Nov	·352	·355	·361	·370	·374	·388	·395	·406	·411	·411	·408	·416	·427	·428	·431
Dec	·347	·350	·356	·365	·369	·383	·390	·401	·406	·406	·403	·411	·422	·423	·426
2000	Sept	Oct	Nov	Dec	Jan	Feb	Mar	Apr	May	June	July	Aug	Sept	Oct	Nov
Jan	·352	·355	·361	·371	·375	·388	·396	·407	·412	·412	·409	·417	·428	·429	·432
Feb	·345	·348	·354	·364	·367	·381	·388	·399	·404	·404	·401	·410	·420	·421	·424
Mar	·338	·341	·347	·356	·360	·374	·381	·392	·397	·397	·394	·402	·413	·413	·416
Apr	·325	·327	·333	·343	·346	·360	·367	·378	·383	·383	·380	·388	·399	·399	·402
May	·320	·323	·329	·338	·342	·355	·362	·373	·378	·378	·375	·383	·394	·394	·397
June	·317	·320	·326	·335	·338	·352	·359	·370	·375	·375	·372	·380	·390	·391	·394
July	·321	·324	·330	·340	·343	·357	·364	·375	·379	·379	·377	·385	·395	·396	·399
Aug	·321	·324	·330	·340	·343	·357	·364	·375	·379	·379	·377	·385	·395	·395	·399
Sept	·312	·315	·321	·330	·334	·347	·354	·365	·370	·370	·367	·375	·386	·386	·389
Oct	·313	·316	·322	·331	·334	·348	·355	·366	·371	·371	·368	·376	·386	·387	·390
Nov	·309	·312	·318	·327	·331	·344	·351	·362	·367	·367	·364	·372	·382	·383	·386
Dec	·308	·311	·317	·326	·330	·343	·350	·361	·366	·366	·363	·371	·382	·382	·385
2001	Sept	Oct	Nov	Dec	Jan	Feb	Mar	Apr	May	June	July	Aug	Sept	Oct	Nov
Jan	·317	·320	·326	·335	·338	·352	·359	·370	·375	·375	·372	·380	·390	·391	·394
Feb	·310	·313	·319	·328	·331	·345	·352	·363	·367	·367	·365	·373	·383	·384	·387
Mar	·308	·311	·317	·326	·330	·343	·350	·361	·366	·366	·363	·371	·382	·382	·385
Apr	·302	·304	·310	·319	·323	·336	·343	·354	·359	·359	·356	·364	·374	·375	·378
May	·293	·296	·302	·311	·315	·328	·335	·346	·350	·350	·347	·355	·366	·366	·369
June	·292	·295	·300	·310	·313	·326	·333	·344	·349	·349	·346	·354	·364	·365	·368
July	·300	·303	·309	·318	·321	·335	·342	·353	·357	·357	·354	·362	·373	·373	·376
Aug	·295	·298	·303	·313	·316	·329	·336	·347	·352	·352	·349	·357	·367	·368	·371
Sept	·290	·293	·299	·308	·312	·325	·332	·342	·347	·347	·344	·352	·363	·363	·366
Oct	·293	·295	·301	·310	·314	·327	·334	·345	·349	·349	·347	·355	·365	·365	·368
Nov	·298	·301	·306	·316	·319	·332	·339	·350	·355	·355	·352	·360	·370	·371	·374
Dec	·299	·302	·308	·317	·321	·334	·341	·352	·356	·356	·354	·362	·372	·373	·375

MONTH OF DISPOSAL

	2011	2012												2013	
1998	Dec	Jan	Feb	Mar	Apr	May	June	July	Aug	Sept	Oct	Nov	Dec	Jan	Feb
Jan	·501	·492	·504	·510	·520	·520	·516	·518	·524	·531	·540	·540	·547	.541	.552
Feb	·493	·485	·497	·502	·513	·512	·508	·510	·516	·523	·532	·532	·540	.533	.545
Mar	·489	·480	·492	·498	·508	·507	·504	·506	·511	·519	·527	·527	·535	.529	.540
Apr	·472	·464	·475	·481	·491	·491	·487	·489	·494	·502	·510	·510	·518	.512	.523
May	·464	·456	·467	·473	·483	·483	·479	·481	·486	·494	·502	·502	·509	.503	.514
June	·465	·457	·468	·474	·484	·483	·480	·482	·487	·494	·503	·503	·510	.504	.515
July	·469	·460	·472	·477	·488	·487	·483	·485	·491	·498	·507	·507	·514	.508	.519
Aug	·462	·454	·465	·471	·481	·481	·477	·479	·484	·492	·500	·500	·508	.502	.513
Sept	·456	·448	·459	·465	·475	·474	·471	·473	·478	·485	·494	·494	·501	.495	.506
Oct	·455	·447	·458	·464	·474	·474	·470	·472	·477	·484	·493	·493	·500	.494	.505
Nov	·456	·448	·459	·465	·475	·474	·471	·473	·478	·485	·494	·494	·501	.495	.506
Dec	·456	·448	·459	·465	·475	·474	·471	·473	·478	·485	·494	·494	·501	.495	.506
1999	Dec	Jan	Feb	Mar	Apr	May	June	July	Aug	Sept	Oct	Nov	Dec	Jan	Feb
Jan	·465	·457	·468	·474	·484	·483	·480	·482	·487	·494	·503	·503	·510	.504	.515
Feb	·462	·454	·465	·471	·481	·481	·477	·479	·484	·492	·500	·500	·508	.502	.513
Mar	·459	·450	·462	·467	·478	·477	·473	·475	·481	·488	·497	·497	·504	.498	.509
Apr	·449	·441	·452	·458	·468	·467	·464	·465	·471	·478	·487	·487	·494	.488	.499
May	·446	·437	·449	·454	·464	·464	·460	·462	·467	·475	·483	·483	·490	.484	.495
June	·446	·437	·449	·454	·464	·464	·460	·462	·467	·475	·483	·483	·490	.484	.495
July	·450	·442	·453	·459	·469	·468	·465	·466	·472	·479	·488	·488	·495	.489	.500
Aug	·447	·438	·450	·455	·465	·465	·461	·463	·468	·476	·484	·484	·491	.485	.496
Sept	·440	·432	·443	·449	·459	·458	·455	·457	·462	·469	·478	·478	·485	.479	.490
Oct	·438	·429	·441	·446	·456	·456	·452	·454	·459	·467	·475	·475	·482	.476	.487
Nov	·436	·428	·439	·445	·455	·454	·451	·452	·458	·465	·473	·473	·481	.475	.485
Dec	·431	·423	·434	·439	·449	·449	·445	·447	·452	·460	·468	·468	·475	.469	.480
2000	Dec	Jan	Feb	Mar	Apr	May	June	July	Aug	Sept	Oct	Nov	Dec	Jan	Feb
Jan	·437	·429	·440	·445	·456	·455	·451	·453	·459	·466	·474	·474	·481	.475	.486
Feb	·429	·421	·432	·438	·448	·447	·444	·445	·451	·458	·466	·466	·473	.467	.478
Mar	·422	·413	·425	·430	·440	·439	·436	·438	·443	·450	·458	·458	·466	.460	.470
Apr	·407	·399	·410	·416	·426	·425	·422	·423	·429	·436	·444	·444	·451	.445	.456
May	·402	·394	·405	·411	·421	·420	·417	·418	·424	·431	·439	·439	·446	.440	.450
June	·399	·391	·402	·407	·417	·417	·413	·415	·420	·427	·435	·435	·442	.437	.447
July	·404	·396	·407	·412	·422	·422	·418	·420	·425	·432	·440	·440	·448	.442	.452
Aug	·404	·396	·407	·412	·422	·422	·418	·420	·425	·432	·440	·440	·448	.442	.452
Sept	·394	·386	·397	·402	·412	·412	·408	·410	·415	·422	·430	·430	·437	.432	.442
Oct	·395	·387	·398	·403	·413	·413	·409	·411	·416	·423	·431	·431	·438	.432	.443
Nov	·391	·383	·394	·399	·409	·408	·405	·407	·412	·419	·427	·427	·434	.428	.439
Dec	·390	·382	·393	·398	·408	·408	·404	·406	·411	·418	·426	·426	·433	.427	.438
2001	Dec	Jan	Feb	Mar	Apr	May	June	July	Aug	Sept	Oct	Nov	Dec	Jan	Feb
Jan	·399	·391	·402	·407	·417	·417	·413	·415	·420	·427	·435	·435	·442	.437	.447
Feb	·392	·384	·395	·400	·410	·409	·406	·408	·413	·420	·428	·428	·435	.429	.440
Mar	·390	·382	·393	·398	·408	·408	·404	·406	·411	·418	·426	·426	·433	.420	.430
Apr	·383	·375	·386	·391	·401	·400	·397	·399	·404	·411	·419	·419	·426	.420	.430
May	·374	·366	·377	·382	·392	·392	·388	·390	·395	·402	·410	·410	·417	.411	.421
June	·373	·365	·376	·381	·390	·390	·386	·388	·393	·400	·408	·408	·415	.409	.420
July	·381	·373	·384	·389	·399	·399	·395	·397	·402	·409	·417	·417	·424	.418	.429
Aug	·376	·368	·379	·384	·394	·393	·390	·391	·397	·403	·411	·411	·418	.413	.423
Sept	·371	·363	·374	·379	·389	·388	·385	·387	·392	·399	·407	·407	·414	.408	.418
Oct	·373	·365	·376	·382	·391	·391	·387	·389	·394	·401	·409	·409	·416	.410	.421
Nov	·379	·371	·382	·387	·397	·396	·393	·395	·400	·407	·415	·415	·422	.416	.426
Dec	·381	·373	·384	·389	·399	·398	·394	·396	·401	·408	·416	·416	·423	.418	.428

MONTH OF DISPOSAL

	2010				2011										
2002	Sept	Oct	Nov	Dec	Jan	Feb	Mar	Apr	May	June	July	Aug	Sept	Oct	Nov
Jan	·300	·303	·309	·318	·321	·335	·342	·353	·357	·357	·354	·362	·373	·373	·376
Feb	·296	·299	·305	·314	·318	·331	·338	·349	·353	·353	·350	·358	·369	·369	·372
Mar	·291	·294	·300	·309	·312	·326	·332	·343	·348	·348	·345	·353	·363	·364	·367
Apr	·282	·285	·291	·300	·303	·316	·323	·334	·339	·339	·336	·344	·354	·355	·357
May	·279	·281	·287	·296	·300	·313	·320	·330	·335	·335	·332	·340	·350	·351	·354
June	·279	·281	·287	·296	·300	·313	·320	·330	·335	·335	·332	·340	·350	·351	·354
July	·281	·284	·289	·298	·302	·315	·322	·333	·337	·337	·334	·342	·352	·353	·356
Aug	·277	·280	·286	·295	·298	·311	·318	·329	·333	·333	·330	·338	·349	·349	·352
Sept	·269	·271	·277	·286	·289	·302	·309	·320	·324	·324	·322	·329	·340	·340	·343
Oct	·266	·269	·275	·284	·287	·300	·307	·318	·322	·322	·319	·327	·337	·338	·341
Nov	·264	·267	·273	·282	·285	·298	·305	·315	·320	·320	·317	·325	·335	·336	·338
Dec	·262	·265	·271	·280	·283	·296	·303	·313	·318	·318	·315	·323	·333	·333	·336
2003	Sept	Oct	Nov	Dec	Jan	Feb	Mar	Apr	May	June	July	Aug	Sept	Oct	Nov
Jan	·263	·266	·271	·280	·284	·297	·303	·314	·318	·318	·316	·323	·334	·334	·337
Feb	·257	·259	·265	·274	·277	·290	·297	·307	·312	·312	·309	·317	·327	·327	·330
Mar	·252	·255	·261	·270	·273	·286	·292	·303	·307	·307	·305	·312	·322	·323	·326
Apr	·243	·246	·252	·260	·264	·276	·283	·294	·298	·298	·295	·303	·313	·313	·316
May	·241	·244	·250	·258	·262	·274	·281	·291	·296	·296	·293	·301	·311	·311	·314
June	·243	·245	·251	·260	·263	·276	·282	·293	·297	·297	·295	·302	·312	·313	·315
July	·243	·245	·251	·260	·263	·276	·282	·293	·297	·297	·295	·302	·312	·313	·315
Aug	·241	·243	·249	·258	·261	·274	·280	·291	·295	·295	·292	·300	·310	·311	·313
Sept	·235	·237	·243	·252	·255	·267	·274	·284	·289	·289	·286	·294	·304	·304	·307
Oct	·234	·237	·242	·251	·254	·267	·273	·284	·288	·288	·285	·293	·303	·303	·306
Nov	·233	·236	·241	·250	·253	·266	·273	·283	·287	·287	·285	·292	·302	·303	·305
Dec	·228	·231	·236	·245	·248	·260	·267	·277	·282	·282	·279	·287	·296	·297	·300
2004	Sept	Oct	Nov	Dec	Jan	Feb	Mar	Apr	May	June	July	Aug	Sept	Oct	Nov
Jan	·230	·233	·239	·247	·251	·263	·270	·280	·285	·285	·282	·289	·299	·300	·303
Feb	·226	·229	·234	·243	·246	·258	·265	·275	·280	·280	·277	·285	·294	·295	·298
Mar	·220	·223	·229	·237	·241	·253	·259	·270	·274	·274	·271	·279	·289	·289	·292
Apr	·213	·216	·221	·230	·233	·246	·252	·262	·267	·267	·264	·271	·281	·282	·284
May	·208	·211	·216	·225	·228	·240	·247	·257	·261	·261	·258	·266	·276	·276	·279
June	·206	·209	·214	·223	·226	·238	·245	·255	·259	·259	·256	·264	·274	·274	·277
July	·206	·209	·214	·223	·226	·238	·245	·255	·259	·259	·256	·264	·274	·274	·277
Aug	·202	·205	·210	·219	·222	·234	·241	·251	·255	·255	·252	·260	·269	·270	·273
Sept	·198	·200	·206	·214	·217	·230	·236	·246	·250	·250	·248	·255	·265	·265	·268
Oct	·195	·197	·203	·211	·214	·226	·233	·243	·247	·247	·244	·252	·261	·262	·265
Nov	·192	·195	·200	·208	·212	·224	·230	·240	·244	·244	·242	·249	·259	·259	·262
Dec	·186	·189	·194	·203	·206	·218	·224	·234	·239	·239	·236	·243	·253	·253	·256
2005	Sept	Oct	Nov	Dec	Jan	Feb	Mar	Apr	May	June	July	Aug	Sept	Oct	Nov
Jan	·193	·195	·201	·209	·212	·224	·231	·241	·245	·245	·242	·250	·259	·260	·263
Feb	·188	·191	·196	·205	·208	·220	·226	·236	·241	·241	·238	·245	·255	·255	·258
Mar	·183	·185	·191	·199	·202	·214	·220	·230	·235	·235	·232	·239	·249	·249	·252
Apr	·176	·178	·184	·192	·195	·207	·213	·223	·228	·228	·225	·232	·242	·242	·245
May	·173	·176	·181	·190	·193	·205	·211	·221	·225	·225	·222	·230	·239	·240	·242
June	·172	·175	·180	·188	·191	·203	·210	·220	·224	·224	·221	·228	·238	·238	·241
July	·172	·175	·180	·188	·191	·203	·210	·220	·224	·224	·221	·228	·238	·238	·241
Aug	·170	·172	·178	·186	·189	·201	·207	·217	·221	·221	·219	·226	·235	·236	·238
Sept	·167	·169	·175	·183	·186	·198	·204	·214	·218	·218	·215	·223	·232	·233	·235
Oct	·166	·168	·173	·182	·185	·197	·203	·213	·217	·217	·214	·221	·231	·231	·234
Nov	·164	·166	·171	·180	·183	·195	·201	·211	·215	·215	·212	·220	·229	·229	·232
Dec	·161	·163	·168	·177	·180	·192	·198	·208	·212	·212	·209	·216	·226	·226	·229

MONTH OF DISPOSAL

	2011	2012												2013	
2002	Dec	Jan	Feb	Mar	Apr	May	June	July	Aug	Sept	Oct	Nov	Dec	Jan	Feb
Jan	·381	·373	·384	·389	·399	·399	·395	·397	·402	·409	·417	·417	·424	.418	.429
Feb	·377	·369	·380	·386	·395	·395	·391	·393	·398	·405	·413	·413	·420	.414	.425
Mar	·372	·364	·375	·380	·390	·389	·386	·387	·393	·399	·407	·407	·414	.409	.419
Apr	·363	·355	·365	·371	·380	·380	·376	·378	·383	·390	·398	·398	·405	.399	.409
May	·359	·351	·362	·367	·376	·376	·372	·374	·379	·386	·394	·394	·401	.395	.405
June	·359	·351	·362	·367	·376	·376	·372	·374	·379	·386	·394	·394	·401	.395	.405
July	·361	·353	·364	·369	·379	·378	·375	·376	·381	·388	·396	·396	·403	.397	.408
Aug	·357	·349	·360	·365	·375	·374	·371	·372	·378	·384	·392	·392	·399	.393	.404
Sept	·348	·340	·351	·356	·365	·365	·361	·363	·368	·375	·383	·383	·390	.384	.394
Oct	·346	·338	·349	·354	·363	·363	·359	·361	·366	·373	·381	·381	·387	.382	.392
Nov	·343	·336	·346	·351	·361	·360	·357	·359	·364	·370	·378	·378	·385	.379	.389
Dec	·341	·333	·344	·349	·359	·358	·355	·356	·361	·368	·376	·376	·383	.377	.387
2003	Dec	Jan	Feb	Mar	Apr	May	June	July	Aug	Sept	Oct	Nov	Dec	Jan	Feb
Jan	·342	·334	·345	·350	·359	·359	·355	·357	·362	·369	·377	·377	·383	.378	.388
Feb	·335	·327	·338	·343	·352	·352	·349	·350	·355	·362	·370	·370	·376	.371	.381
Mar	·331	·323	·334	·339	·348	·347	·344	·346	·351	·357	·365	·365	·372	.366	.376
Apr	·321	·313	·324	·329	·338	·338	·334	·336	·341	·348	·355	·355	·362	.357	.366
May	·319	·311	·322	·327	·336	·336	·332	·334	·339	·345	·353	·353	·360	.354	.364
June	·320	·313	·323	·328	·338	·337	·334	·335	·340	·347	·355	·355	·361	.356	.366
July	·320	·313	·323	·328	·338	·337	·334	·335	·340	·347	·355	·355	·361	.356	.366
Aug	·318	·311	·321	·326	·335	·335	·331	·333	·338	·345	·352	·352	·359	.354	.363
Sept	·312	·304	·315	·319	·329	·328	·325	·327	·332	·338	·346	·346	·352	.347	.357
Oct	·311	·303	·314	·319	·328	·327	·324	·326	·331	·337	·345	·345	·352	.346	.356
Nov	·310	·303	·313	·318	·327	·327	·323	·325	·330	·337	·344	·344	·351	.345	.355
Dec	·305	·297	·307	·312	·322	·321	·318	·319	·324	·331	·338	·338	·345	.340	.349
2004	Dec	Jan	Feb	Mar	Apr	May	June	July	Aug	Sept	Oct	Nov	Dec	Jan	Feb
Jan	·307	·300	·310	·315	·324	·324	·321	·322	·327	·334	·341	·341	·348	.342	.352
Feb	·303	·295	·305	·310	·319	·319	·316	·317	·322	·329	·336	·336	·343	.337	.347
Mar	·297	·289	·300	·304	·314	·313	·310	·311	·316	·323	·330	·330	·337	.332	.341
Apr	·289	·282	·292	·297	·306	·305	·302	·304	·309	·315	·323	·323	·329	.324	.333
May	·284	·276	·286	·291	·300	·300	·297	·298	·303	·309	·317	·317	·323	.318	.328
June	·282	·274	·284	·289	·298	·298	·294	·296	·301	·307	·315	·315	·321	.316	.325
July	·282	·274	·284	·289	·298	·298	·294	·296	·301	·307	·315	·315	·321	.316	.325
Aug	·277	·270	·280	·285	·294	·293	·290	·292	·297	·303	·311	·311	·317	.312	.321
Sept	·273	·265	·275	·280	·289	·289	·285	·287	·292	·298	·306	·306	·312	.307	.316
Oct	·269	·262	·272	·277	·286	·285	·282	·284	·288	·295	·302	·302	·309	.303	.313
Nov	·267	·259	·269	·274	·283	·283	·279	·281	·286	·292	·299	·299	·306	.301	.310
Dec	·261	·253	·263	·268	·277	·276	·273	·275	·280	·286	·293	·293	·300	.294	.304
2005	Dec	Jan	Feb	Mar	Apr	May	June	July	Aug	Sept	Oct	Nov	Dec	Jan	Feb
Jan	·267	·260	·270	·275	·284	·283	·280	·282	·286	·293	·300	·300	·307	.301	.311
Feb	·263	·255	·265	·270	·279	·278	·275	·277	·282	·288	·295	·295	·302	.296	.306
Mar	·257	·249	·259	·264	·273	·272	·269	·271	·276	·282	·289	·289	·296	.290	.300
Apr	·249	·242	·252	·257	·266	·265	·262	·264	·268	·275	·282	·282	·288	.283	.292
May	·247	·240	·249	·254	·263	·263	·259	·261	·266	·272	·279	·279	·285	.280	.290
June	·246	·238	·248	·253	·262	·261	·258	·260	·264	·271	·278	·278	·284	.279	.288
July	·246	·238	·248	·253	·262	·261	·258	·260	·264	·271	·278	·278	·284	.279	.288
Aug	·243	·236	·246	·250	·259	·259	·255	·257	·262	·268	·275	·275	·281	.276	.286
Sept	·240	·233	·242	·247	·256	·255	·252	·254	·258	·265	·272	·272	·278	.273	.282
Oct	·238	·231	·241	·246	·255	·254	·251	·252	·257	·263	·271	·271	·277	.272	.281
Nov	·237	·229	·239	·244	·253	·252	·249	·251	·255	·261	·269	·269	·275	.270	.279
Dec	·233	·226	·236	·241	·249	·249	·246	·247	·252	·258	·265	·265	·272	.266	.276

	2010				2011										
2006	Sept	Oct	Nov	Dec	Jan	Feb	Mar	Apr	May	June	July	Aug	Sept	Oct	Nov
Jan	·165	·168	·173	·181	·184	·196	·202	·212	·216	·216	·214	·221	·230	·231	·233
Feb	·160	·163	·168	·176	·179	·191	·197	·207	·211	·211	·209	·216	·225	·226	·228
Mar	·155	·158	·163	·171	·174	·186	·192	·202	·206	·206	·204	·211	·220	·221	·223
Apr	·147	·149	·154	·162	·165	·177	·183	·193	·197	·197	·194	·202	·211	·211	·214
May	·140	·142	·147	·155	·158	·170	·176	·186	·190	·190	·187	·194	·203	·204	·206
June	·135	·138	·143	·151	·154	·165	·171	·181	·185	·185	·182	·189	·198	·199	·202
July	·135	·138	·143	·151	·154	·165	·171	·181	·185	·185	·182	·189	·198	·199	·202
Aug	·131	·134	·139	·147	·150	·161	·167	·177	·181	·181	·178	·185	·194	·195	·197
Sept	·126	·128	·133	·141	·144	·156	·162	·171	·175	·175	·173	·180	·189	·189	·192
Oct	·124	·127	·132	·140	·143	·154	·160	·170	·174	·174	·171	·178	·187	·188	·190
Nov	·120	·123	·128	·136	·139	·150	·156	·166	·170	·170	·167	·174	·183	·183	·186
Dec	·111	·114	·119	·127	·130	·141	·147	·156	·160	·160	·158	·165	·174	·174	·177
2007	Sept	Oct	Nov	Dec	Jan	Feb	Mar	Apr	May	June	July	Aug	Sept	Oct	Nov
Jan	·118	·120	·125	·133	·136	·147	·153	·163	·167	·167	·164	·171	·180	·181	·183
Feb	·109	·112	·117	·125	·128	·139	·145	·154	·158	·158	·156	·162	·171	·172	·174
Mar	·102	·105	·110	·117	·120	·132	·137	·147	·151	·151	·148	·155	·164	·164	·167
Apr	·097	·099	·104	·112	·115	·126	·132	·141	·145	·145	·143	·149	·158	·159	·161
May	·093	·095	·100	·108	·111	·122	·128	·137	·141	·141	·138	·145	·154	·154	·157
June	·087	·089	·094	·102	·105	·116	·122	·131	·135	·135	·132	·139	·148	·148	·151
July	·093	·096	·100	·108	·111	·122	·128	·137	·141	·141	·139	·146	·154	·155	·157
Aug	·087	·089	·094	·102	·105	·116	·122	·131	·135	·135	·132	·139	·148	·148	·151
Sept	·083	·086	·090	·098	·101	·112	·118	·127	·131	·131	·128	·135	·144	·144	·147
Oct	·079	·081	·086	·093	·096	·107	·113	·122	·126	·126	·124	·130	·139	·139	·142
Nov	·074	·077	·082	·089	·092	·103	·109	·118	·122	·122	·119	·126	·134	·135	·137
Dec	·068	·071	·075	·083	·086	·097	·102	·111	·115	·115	·113	·119	·128	·128	·131
2008	Sept	Oct	Nov	Dec	Jan	Feb	Mar	Apr	May	June	July	Aug	Sept	Oct	Nov
Jan	·074	·076	·081	·089	·092	·102	·108	·117	·121	·121	·119	·125	·134	·134	·137
Feb	·066	·068	·073	·080	·083	·094	·100	·109	·113	·113	·110	·117	·125	·126	·128
Mar	·062	·065	·069	·077	·080	·091	·096	·105	·109	·109	·107	·113	·122	·122	·124
Apr	·053	·055	·060	·067	·070	·081	·086	·095	·099	·099	·097	·103	·112	·112	·114
May	·047	·050	·054	·062	·065	·075	·081	·090	·093	·093	·091	·098	·106	·106	·109
June	·039	·042	·046	·054	·056	·067	·072	·081	·085	·085	·083	·089	·097	·098	·100
July	·041	·043	·048	·055	·058	·068	·074	·083	·086	·086	·084	·091	·099	·099	·102
Aug	·037	·040	·044	·052	·054	·065	·070	·079	·083	·083	·081	·087	·095	·096	·098
Sept	·032	·034	·038	·046	·049	·059	·065	·073	·077	·077	·075	·081	·089	·090	·092
Oct	·035	·037	·042	·049	·052	·062	·068	·077	·080	·080	·078	·085	·093	·093	·096
Nov	·043	·045	·050	·057	·060	·071	·076	·085	·089	·089	·087	·093	·101	·102	·104
Dec	·058	·061	·065	·073	·076	·086	·092	·101	·105	·105	·102	·109	·117	·118	·120
2009	Sept	Oct	Nov	Dec	Jan	Feb	Mar	Apr	May	June	July	Aug	Sept	Oct	Nov
Jan	·072	·075	·079	·087	·090	·101	·107	·116	·119	·119	·117	·124	·132	·133	·135
Feb	·066	·068	·073	·080	·083	·094	·100	·109	·113	·113	·110	·117	·125	·126	·128
Mar	·066	·069	·073	·081	·084	·095	·100	·109	·113	·113	·111	·117	·126	·126	·129
Apr	·065	·068	·072	·080	·083	·094	·099	·108	·112	·112	·110	·116	·125	·125	·128
May	·059	·061	·066	·073	·076	·087	·093	·102	·105	·105	·103	·109	·118	·118	·121
June	·056	·058	·063	·070	·073	·084	·090	·098	·102	·102	·100	·106	·115	·115	·118
July	·056	·058	·063	·070	·073	·084	·090	·098	·102	·102	·100	·106	·115	·115	·118
Aug	·051	·053	·058	·065	·068	·079	·084	·093	·097	·097	·095	·101	·110	·110	·112
Sept	·046	·049	·053	·061	·064	·074	·080	·089	·092	·092	·090	·097	·105	·105	·108
Oct	·043	·045	·050	·057	·060	·071	·076	·085	·089	·089	·087	·093	·101	·102	·104
Nov	·040	·042	·047	·054	·057	·068	·073	·082	·086	·086	·084	·090	·098	·099	·101
Dec	·033	·036	·040	·048	·050	·061	·067	·075	·079	·079	·077	·083	·091	·092	·094

MONTH OF DISPOSAL

	2011	2012												2013	
2006	Dec	Jan	Feb	Mar	Apr	May	June	July	Aug	Sept	Oct	Nov	Dec	Jan	Feb
Jan	·238	·231	·240	·245	·254	·253	·250	·252	·256	·263	·270	·270	·276	.271	.280
Feb	·233	·226	·235	·240	·249	·248	·245	·247	·251	·257	·265	·265	·271	.266	.275
Mar	·228	·221	·230	·235	·244	·243	·240	·242	·246	·252	·259	·259	·266	.261	.270
Apr	·218	·211	·221	·225	·234	·234	·231	·232	·237	·243	·250	·250	·256	.251	.260
May	·211	·204	·213	·218	·227	·226	·223	·225	·229	·235	·242	·242	·248	.243	.252
June	·206	·199	·209	·213	·222	·221	·218	·220	·224	·230	·237	·237	·243	.238	.247
July	·206	·199	·209	·213	·222	·221	·218	·220	·224	·230	·237	·237	·243	.238	.247
Aug	·202	·195	·204	·209	·217	·217	·214	·215	·220	·226	·233	·233	·239	.234	.243
Sept	·196	·189	·199	·203	·212	·211	·208	·210	·214	·220	·227	·227	·233	.228	.237
Oct	·195	·188	·197	·202	·210	·210	·207	·208	·213	·219	·226	·226	·232	.227	.236
Nov	·190	·183	·193	·197	·206	·205	·202	·204	·208	·214	·221	·221	·227	.222	.231
Dec	·181	·174	·184	·188	·196	·196	·193	·194	·199	·205	·212	·212	·218	.213	.222
2007	Dec	Jan	Feb	Mar	Apr	May	June	July	Aug	Sept	Oct	Nov	Dec	Jan	Feb
Jan	·188	·181	·190	·194	·203	·202	·199	·201	·205	·211	·218	·218	·224	.219	.228
Feb	·179	·172	·181	·186	·194	·194	·191	·192	·196	·202	·209	·209	·215	.210	.219
Mar	·171	·164	·174	·178	·186	·186	·183	·184	·189	·195	·202	·202	·207	.203	.211
Apr	·166	·159	·168	·172	·181	·180	·177	·179	·183	·189	·196	·196	·202	.197	.205
May	·161	·154	·163	·168	·176	·176	·173	·174	·178	·184	·191	·191	·197	.192	.201
June	·155	·148	·157	·162	·170	·169	·166	·168	·172	·178	·185	·185	·191	.186	.194
July	·162	·155	·164	·168	·177	·176	·173	·175	·179	·185	·192	·192	·197	.193	.201
Aug	·155	·148	·157	·162	·170	·169	·166	·168	·172	·178	·185	·185	·191	.186	.194
Sept	·151	·144	·153	·158	·166	·165	·163	·164	·168	·174	·181	·181	·187	.182	.190
Oct	·146	·139	·148	·153	·161	·160	·157	·159	·163	·169	·176	·176	·181	.177	.185
Nov	·142	·135	·144	·148	·156	·156	·153	·155	·159	·165	·171	·171	·177	.172	.181
Dec	·135	·128	·138	·142	·150	·149	·147	·148	·152	·158	·165	·165	·170	.165	.174
2008	Dec	Jan	Feb	Mar	Apr	May	June	July	Aug	Sept	Oct	Nov	Dec	Jan	Feb
Jan	·141	·134	·143	·148	·156	·155	·153	·154	·158	·164	·171	·171	·176	.172	.180
Feb	·132	·126	·135	·139	·147	·147	·144	·145	·149	·155	·162	·162	·167	.163	.171
Mar	·129	·122	·131	·135	·143	·143	·140	·141	·146	·151	·158	·158	·164	.159	.167
Apr	·119	·112	·121	·125	·133	·133	·130	·131	·136	·141	·148	·148	·153	.149	.157
May	·113	·106	·115	·119	·127	·127	·124	·126	·130	·135	·142	·142	·147	.143	.151
June	·104	·098	·107	·111	·119	·118	·115	·117	·121	·126	·133	·133	·138	.134	.142
July	·106	·099	·108	·112	·120	·120	·117	·118	·122	·128	·134	·134	·140	.135	.144
Aug	·102	·096	·105	·109	·116	·116	·113	·115	·119	·124	·131	·131	·136	.132	.140
Sept	·096	·090	·098	·103	·110	·110	·107	·109	·113	·118	·125	·125	·130	.125	.134
Oct	·100	·093	·102	·106	·114	·113	·111	·112	·116	·122	·128	·128	·134	.129	.137
Nov	·108	·102	·111	·115	·123	·122	·119	·121	·125	·131	·137	·137	·143	.138	.146
Dec	·124	·118	·127	·131	·139	·139	·137	·137	·141	·147	·154	·154	·159	.155	.163
2009	Dec	Jan	Feb	Mar	Apr	May	June	July	Aug	Sept	Oct	Nov	Dec	Jan	Feb
Jan	·139	·133	·142	·146	·154	·154	·151	·152	·157	·162	·169	·169	·175	.170	.178
Feb	·132	·126	·135	·139	·147	·147	·144	·145	·149	·155	·162	·162	·167	.163	.171
Mar	·133	·126	·135	·140	·148	·147	·144	·146	·150	·156	·162	·162	·168	.163	.172
Apr	·132	·125	·134	·139	·147	·146	·143	·145	·149	·155	·161	·161	·167	.162	.171
May	·125	·118	·127	·132	·140	·139	·136	·138	·142	·148	·154	·154	·160	.155	.164
June	·122	·115	·124	·128	·136	·136	·133	·134	·139	·144	·151	·151	·157	.152	.160
July	·122	·115	·124	·128	·136	·136	·133	·134	·139	·144	·151	·151	·157	.152	.160
Aug	·117	·110	·119	·123	·131	·131	·128	·129	·133	139	140	146	151	.146	.155
Sept	·112	·105	·114	·118	·126	·126	·123	·124	·129	·134	·141	·141	·146	.142	.150
Oct	·108	·102	·111	·115	·123	·122	·119	·121	·125	·131	·137	·137	·143	.138	.146
Nov	·105	·099	·108	·112	·120	·119	·116	·118	·122	·127	·134	·134	·139	.135	.143
Dec	·098	·092	·100	·105	·112	·112	·109	·111	·115	·120	·127	·127	·132	.128	.136

MONTH OF DISPOSAL

	2010				2011										
2010	Sept	Oct	Nov	Dec	Jan	Feb	Mar	Apr	May	June	July	Aug	Sept	Oct	Nov
Jan	·034	·036	·041	·048	·051	·061	·067	·076	·079	·079	·077	·084	·092	·092	·095
Feb	·028	·030	·035	·042	·045	·055	·061	·069	·073	·073	·071	·077	·085	·086	·088
Mar	·021	·023	·028	·035	·038	·048	·053	·062	·066	·066	·063	·070	·078	·078	·081
Apr	·011	·013	·018	·025	·028	·038	·044	·052	·056	·056	·053	·060	·068	·068	·070
May	·008	·010	·014	·021	·024	·034	·040	·048	·052	·052	·050	·056	·064	·064	·067
June	·005	·008	·012	·019	·022	·032	·037	·046	·050	·050	·047	·054	·062	·062	·064
July	·008	·010	·014	·021	·024	·034	·040	·048	·052	·052	·050	·056	·064	·064	·067
Aug	·004	·006	·010	·017	·020	·030	·036	·044	·048	·048	·045	·052	·060	·060	·062
Sept	—	·002	·007	·014	·016	·027	·032	·040	·044	·044	·042	·048	·056	·056	·059
Oct	—	—	·004	·012	·014	·024	·030	·038	·042	·042	·039	·046	·054	·054	·056
Nov	—	—	—	·007	·010	·020	·025	·034	·037	·037	·035	·041	·049	·049	·052
Dec	—	—	—	—	·003	·013	·018	·026	·030	·030	·028	·034	·042	·042	·044
2011	Sept	Oct	Nov	Dec	Jan	Feb	Mar	Apr	May	June	July	Aug	Sept	Oct	Nov
Jan	—	—	—	—	—	·010	·015	·024	·027	·027	·025	·031	·039	·039	·041
Feb	—	—	—	—	—	—	·005	·013	·017	·017	·015	·021	·029	·029	·031
Mar	—	—	—	—	—	—	—	·008	·012	·012	·009	·015	·023	·024	·026
Apr	—	—	—	—	—	—	—	—	·003	·003	·001	·007	·015	·015	·017
May	—	—	—	—	—	—	—	—	—	.000	.000	·004	·011	·012	·014
Jun	—	—	—	—	—	—	—	—	—	—	.000	·004	·011	·012	·014
July	—	—	—	—	—	—	—	—	—	—	—	·006	·014	·014	·016
Aug	—	—	—	—	—	—	—	—	—	—	—	—	·008	·008	·010
Sept	—	—	—	—	—	—	—	—	—	—	—	—	—	·000	·003
Oct	—	—	—	—	—	—	—	—	—	—	—	—	—	—	·002
Nov	—	—	—	—	—	—	—	—	—	—	—	—	—	—	—
Dec	—	—	—	—	—	—	—	—	—	—	—	—	—	—	—
2012	Sept	Oct	Nov	Dec	Jan	Feb	Mar	Apr	May	June	July	Aug	Sept	Oct	Nov
Jan	—	—	—	—	—	—	—	—	—	—	—	—	—	—	—
Feb	—	—	—	—	—	—	—	—	—	—	—	—	—	—	—
Mar	—	—	—	—	—	—	—	—	—	—	—	—	—	—	—
Apr	—	—	—	—	—	—	—	—	—	—	—	—	—	—	—
May	—	—	—	—	—	—	—	—	—	—	—	—	—	—	—
June	—	—	—	—	—	—	—	—	—	—	—	—	—	—	—
July	—	—	—	—	—	—	—	—	—	—	—	—	—	—	—
Aug	—	—	—	—	—	—	—	—	—	—	—	—	—	—	—
Sept	—	—	—	—	—	—	—	—	—	—	—	—	—	—	—
Oct	—	—	—	—	—	—	—	—	—	—	—	—	—	—	—
Nov	—	—	—	—	—	—	—	—	—	—	—	—	—	—	—
Dec	—	—	—	—	—	—	—	—	—	—	—	—	—	—	—
2012	Sept	Oct	Nov	Dec	Jan	Feb	Mar	Apr	May	June	July	Aug	Sept	Oct	Nov
Jan	—	—	—	—	—	—	—	—	—	—	—	—	—	—	—
Feb	—	—	—	—	—	—	—	—	—	—	—	—	—	—	—

MONTH OF DISPOSAL

	2011	2012												2013	
2010	Dec	Jan	Feb	Mar	Apr	May	June	July	Aug	Sept	Oct	Nov	Dec	Jan	Feb
Jan	·099	·092	·101	·105	·113	·112	·110	·111	·115	·121	·127	·127	·133	.128	.136
Feb	·092	·086	·094	·099	·106	·106	·103	·104	·109	·114	·120	·120	·126	.121	.130
Mar	·085	·078	·087	·091	·099	·098	·096	·097	·101	·106	·113	·113	·118	.114	.122
Apr	·075	·068	·077	·081	·088	·088	·085	·087	·091	·096	·102	·102	·108	.103	.111
May	·071	·064	·073	·077	·085	·084	·081	·083	·087	·092	·098	·098	·104	.099	.107
June	·068	·062	·071	·075	·082	·082	·079	·080	·084	·090	·096	·096	·101	.097	.105
July	·071	·064	·073	·077	·085	·084	·081	·083	·087	·092	·098	·098	·104	.099	.107
Aug	·066	·060	·069	·073	·080	·080	·077	·078	·082	·088	·094	·094	·099	.095	.103
Sept	·063	·056	·065	·069	·076	·076	·073	·075	·079	·084	·090	·090	·095	.091	.099
Oct	·060	·054	·062	·066	·074	·074	·071	·072	·076	·081	·088	·088	·093	.089	.097
Nov	·056	·049	·058	·062	·069	·069	·066	·067	·071	·077	·083	·083	·088	.084	.092
Dec	·048	·042	·050	·054	·062	·061	·059	·060	·064	·069	·075	·075	·081	.076	.084
2011	Dec	Jan	Feb	Mar	Apr	May	June	July	Aug	Sept	Oct	Nov	Dec	Jan	Feb
Jan	·045	·039	·048	·052	·059	·059	·056	·057	·061	·066	·072	·072	·078	.073	.081
Feb	·035	·029	·037	·041	·048	·048	·045	·047	·051	·056	·062	·062	·067	.063	.070
Mar	·030	·024	·032	·036	·043	·043	·040	·041	·045	·050	·056	·056	·062	.057	.065
Apr	·021	·015	·023	·027	·035	·034	·032	·033	·037	·042	·048	·048	·053	.049	.056
May	·018	·012	·020	·024	·031	·031	·028	·029	·033	·038	·044	·044	·049	.045	.053
June	·018	·012	·020	·024	·031	·031	·028	·029	·033	·038	·044	·044	·049	.045	.053
July	·020	·014	·022	·026	·033	·033	·030	·032	·035	·040	·046	·046	·052	.047	.055
Aug	·014	·008	·016	·020	·027	·027	·024	·025	·029	·034	·040	·040	·045	.041	.049
Sept	·006	·000	·008	·012	·019	·019	·016	·018	·021	·026	·032	·032	·037	.033	.041
Oct	·006	·000	·008	·012	·019	·018	·016	·017	·021	·026	·032	·032	·037	.033	.040
Nov	·004	·000	·006	·010	·017	·016	·014	·015	·019	·024	·030	·030	·035	.031	.038
Dec	—	·000	·002	·006	·013	·013	·010	·011	·015	·020	·026	·026	·031	.027	.034
2012	Dec	Jan	Feb	Mar	Apr	May	June	July	Aug	Sept	Oct	Nov	Dec	Jan	Feb
Jan	—	—	·008	·012	·019	·018	·016	·017	·021	·026	·032	·032	·037	.033	.040
Feb	—	—	—	·004	·011	·010	·008	·009	·013	·018	·024	·024	·029	.025	.032
Mar	—	—	—	—	·007	·007	·004	·005	·009	·014	·020	·020	·025	.021	.028
Apr	—	—	—	—	—	·000	·000	·000	·002	·007	·013	·013	·018	.014	.021
May	—	—	—	—	—	—	·000	·000	·002	·007	·013	·013	·018	.014	.021
June	—	—	—	—	—	—	—	·001	·005	·010	·016	·016	·021	.017	.024
July	—	—	—	—	—	—	—	—	·004	·005	·011	·011	·016	.012	.019
Aug	—	—	—	—	—	—	—	—	—	·005	·011	·011	·016	.012	.019
Sept	—	—	—	—	—	—	—	—	—	—	·006	·006	·011	.007	.014
Oct	—	—	—	—	—	—	—	—	—	—	—	·000	·005	.001	.008
Nov	—	—	—	—	—	—	—	—	—	—	—	—	·005	.001	.008
Dec	—	—	—	—	—	—	—	—	—	—	—	—	—	.000	.003
2013	Dec	Jan	Feb	Mar	Apr	May	June	July	Aug	Sept	Oct	Nov	Dec	Jan	Feb
Jan	—	—	—	—	—	—	—	—	—	—	—	—	—	—	.007
Feb	—	—	—	—	—	—	—	—	—	—	—	—	—	—	—

Retail prices index

	Jan	Feb	Mar	Apr	May	Jun
1982	78·73	78·76	79·44	81·04	81·62	81·85
1983	82·61	82·97	83·12	84·28	84·64	84·84
1984	86·84	87·20	87·48	88·64	88·97	89·20
1985	91·20	91·94	92·80	94·78	95·21	95·41
1986	96·25	96·60	96·73	97·67	97·85	97·79
1987	100·00	100·40	100·60	101·80	101·90	101·90
1988	103·30	103·70	104·10	105·80	106·20	106·60
1989	111·00	111·80	112·30	114·30	115·00	115·40
1990	119·50	120·20	121·40	125·10	126·20	126·70
1991	130·20	130·90	131·40	133·10	133·50	134·10
1992	135·60	136·30	136·70	138·80	139·30	139·30
1993	137·90	138·80	139·30	140·60	141·10	141·00
1994	141·30	142·10	142·50	144·20	144·70	144·70
1995	146·00	146·90	147·50	149·00	149·60	149·80
1996	150·20	150·90	151·50	152·60	152·90	153·00
1997	154·40	155·00	155·40	156·30	156·90	157·50
1998	159·50	160·30	160·80	162·60	163·50	163·40
1999	163·40	163·70	164·10	165·20	165·60	165·60
2000	166·60	167·50	168·40	170·10	170·70	171·10
2001	171·10	172·00	172·20	173·10	174·20	174·40
2002	173·30	173·80	174·50	175·70	176·20	176·20
2003	178·40	179·30	179·90	181·20	181·50	181·30
2004	183·10	183·80	184·60	185·70	186·50	186·80
2005	188·90	189·60	190·50	191·60	192·00	192·20
2006	193·40	194·20	195·00	196·50	197·70	198·50
2007	201·60	203·10	204·40	205·40	206·20	207·30
2008	209·80	211·40	212·10	214·00	215·10	216·80
2009	210·10	211·40	211·30	211·50	212·80	213·40
2010	218·00	219·20	220·70	222·80	223·60	224·10
2011	229·00	231·30	232·50	234·40	235·20	235·20
2012	238·00	239·90	240·80	242·50	242·40	241·80
2013	245.80	247.60				

Retail prices index, cont.

	Jul	Aug	Sep	Oct	Nov	Dec
1982	81·88	81·90	81·85	82·26	82·66	82·51
1983	85·30	85·68	86·06	86·36	86·67	86·89
1984	89·10	89·94	90·11	90·67	90·95	90·87
1985	95·23	95·49	95·44	95·59	95·92	96·05
1986	97·52	97·82	98·30	98·45	99·29	99·62
1987	101·80	102·10	102·40	102·90	103·40	103·30
1988	106·70	107·90	108·40	109·50	110·00	110·30
1989	115·50	115·80	116·60	117·50	118·50	118·80
1990	126·80	128·10	129·30	130·30	130·00	129·90
1991	133·80	134·10	134·60	135·10	135·60	135·70
1992	138·80	138·90	139·40	139·90	139·70	139·20
1993	140·70	141·30	141·90	141·80	141·60	141·90
1994	144·00	144·70	145·00	145·20	145·30	146·00
1995	149·10	149·90	150·60	149·80	149·80	150·70
1996	152·40	153·10	153·80	153·80	153·90	154·40
1997	157·50	158·50	159·30	159·50	159·60	160·00
1998	163·00	163·70	164·40	164·50	164·40	164·40
1999	165·10	165·50	166·20	166·50	166·70	167·30
2000	170·50	170·50	171·70	171·60	172·10	172·20
2001	173·30	174·00	174·60	174·30	173·60	173·40
2002	175·90	176·40	177·60	177·90	178·20	178·50
2003	181·30	181·60	182·50	182·60	182·70	183·50
2004	186·80	187·40	188·10	188·60	189·00	189·90
2005	192·20	192·60	193·10	193·30	193·60	194·10
2006	198·50	199·20	200·10	200·40	201·10	202·70
2007	206·10	207·30	208·00	208·90	209·70	210·90
2008	216·50	217·20	218·40	217·70	216·00	212·90
2009	213·40	214.40	215.30	216.00	216·60	218·00
2010	223.60	224.50	225.30	225.80	226.80	228.40
2011	234.70	236.10	237.90	238.00	238.50	239.40
2012	242.10	243.00	244.20	245.60	245.60	246.80

Corporation tax

Rates

Financial year	2008	2009	2010	2011	2012	2013
Full rate	28%	28%	28%	26%	24%	**23%**
Small profits rate[2]	21%	21%	21%	20%	20%	**20%**
lower limit[1]	£300,000	£300,000	£300,000	£300,000	£300,000	**£300,000**
upper limit[1]	£1.5m	£1.5m	£1.5m	£1.5m	£1.5m	**£1.5m**
marginal relief fraction	7/400	7/400	7/400	3/200	1/100	**3/400**
effective marginal rate	29.75%	29.75%	29.75%	27.5%	25%	**23.75%**
Tax credit: from 6 April	10%	10%	10%	10%	10%	**10%**

[1] Reduced proportionally for accounting periods of less than 12 months. The limits are divided by the number of associated companies (including the company in question).

[2] For ring fenced trades, the small profits rate remains at 19% for financial years 2007 to 2013 and the main rate of corporation tax remains at 30% for those years. The marginal relief ring fenced fraction is 11/400.

[3] The full rate of corporation tax will be 21% for financial year 2014 and 20% for 2015.

Marginal relief The small profits rate applies to total taxable profits where augmented profits (see below) do not exceed the lower limit. Where a company's profits exceed the lower limit but do not exceed the upper limit, the charge to corporation tax on the company's taxable total profits is reduced by an amount calculated in accordance with a statutory formula—

$$F \times (U - A) \times \frac{N}{A}$$

where—

F is the marginal relief fraction;
U is the upper limit;
N is the amount of the taxable total profits;
A is the amount of the augmented profits—its adjusted taxable total profits plus franked investment income (other than from UK companies in the same group or owned by a consortium of which the recipient is a member). A company's adjusted taxable total profits exclude amounts which are chargeable to capital gains tax under TCGA 1992 s 2B (capital gains tax charge on certain high value disposals by companies) instead of corporation tax (see p 65).

Reliefs

Corporate Venturing Scheme

(FA 2000 s 63, Schs 15, 16; FA 2001 s 64, Sch 16; FA 2004 s 95, Sch 20; FA 2006 s 91, Sch 14)

In relation to shares issued between 1 April 2000 and 31 March 2010, an investing company can obtain 20% CT relief on amounts subscribed for ordinary shares in small higher-risk unquoted trading companies which are held for at least three years. The investor must not own or be entitled to acquire more than 30% of the ordinary shares in the investee company. At least 20% must be owned by independent individuals. Chargeable gains on share disposals can be deferred by reinvestment in another shareholding. Allowable losses (net of 20% relief) can be set against income if not deducted from chargeable gains.

Research and development

(CTA 2009 ss 1039–1142; FA 2000 ss 68, 69, Schs 19–21; FA 2002 s 53, Sch 12; FA 2003 s 168, Sch 31; FA 2007 s 50; FA 2011 s 43; FA 2012 Sch 3)

Existing scheme

An 'SME' incurring R&D expenditure (of at least £10,000 for accounting periods ending before 1 April 2012, though this minimum expenditure requirement is now removed) in a 12-month accounting period can obtain relief for 225% (applying from 1 April 2012) of that expenditure (200% for expenditure incurred between 1 April 2011 and 1 April 2012; 175% for expenditure incurred between 1 August 2008 and 1 April 2011; 150% for expenditure incurred before 1 August 2008). Large companies incurring R&D expenditure (of at least £10,000 for accounting periods ending before 1 April 2012) can obtain relief for 130% of that expenditure (125% for expenditure incurred before 1 April 2008). SMEs not yet in profit or which have not yet started to trade can claim relief upfront as a cash payment (R&D tax credit).

An 'SME' is a company with less than 500 employees (250 before 1 August 2008) and either annual turnover of €100m or less (€50m before 1 August 2008; €40m for accounting periods ending before 1 January 2005) or annual balance sheet total of €86m or less (€43m before 1 August 2008; €27m for accounting periods ending before 1 January 2005). Large companies incurring R&D expenditure (of at least £10,000 for accounting periods ending before 1 April 2012) can generally deduct 125% of the expenditure for SMEs.

Large companies can claim a similar relief to that for SMEs above, including tax credits, for expenditure incurred on certain vaccines research. The relief was previously also available to SMEs but is withdrawn for them from April 2012.

'Above the line' credit scheme for large companies

This new scheme applies from 1 April 2013. Large companies (and certain SMEs with sub-contracted or subsidised R&D) can claim R&D relief as a taxable above the line (ATL) credit to the value of 10% of their qualifying R&D expenditure. The credit will be fully payable, net of tax, to companies with no corporation tax liability. The scheme will initially be optional. Companies that do not elect to claim the ATL credit will be able to continue claiming R&D relief under the current large company scheme (see above) until 31 March 2016. The ATL credit will become mandatory on 1 April 2016.

Real Estate Investment Trusts (REITs)

(CTA 2010 ss 518–609; FA 2006 ss 103–145, Schs 16, 17)

From 1 January 2007, qualifying rental income from and gains on disposals of investment properties by UK companies within the REIT scheme are exempt from corporation tax.

Gifts of pre-eminent objects

(FA 2012 Sch 14)

Companies which gift pre-eminent objects to the nation will receive a reduction in their UK tax liability of 20% of the value of the object they are donating. The legislation has effect in relation to liabilities for tax years and accounting periods beginning on or after 1 April 2012. The gift must be accepted as pre-eminent by the Arts Council under the Cultural Gifts Scheme.

Patent box

(CTA 2010 Pt 8A)

The patent box allows companies to elect to apply a 10% corporation tax rate to a proportion of profits attributable to qualifying patents, whether paid separately as royalties or embedded in the sales price of products, and to certain other qualifying intellectual property rights such as regulatory data protection (also called 'data exclusivity'), supplementary protection certificates and plant variety rights from 1 April 2013. In the first year the proportion of profits qualifying for the 10% rate is 60% and this will increase annually to 100% from April 2017.

Disincorporation relief

With effect for disincorporations between 1 April 2013 and 31 March 2018 inclusive, joint claims may be made by a company and its shareholders to allow goodwill or interests in land not held as trading stock to be transferred at a reduced value so that no corporation tax will be payable by the company on the transfer. Relief will be restricted to cases where the market value of the assets allowed for disincorporation relief does not exceed £100,000. Joint claims must be made to HMRC within two years of the date of the transfer and other eligibility criteria will also apply. Shareholders to whom the assets are transferred will inherit the transfer value for the purpose of capital gains tax.

Annual tax on enveloped dwellings

From 1 April 2013 a charge is imposed on certain non-natural persons (NNPs), ie companies, partnerships with at least one company member, and collective investment schemes which hold UK residential dwellings valued at greater than £2 million on specified valuation dates. Payment will be due by 31 October 2013 for 2013–14, and on or before 30 April each year subsequently. If the payer is not chargeable for the full year, a later repayment claim can be made. Various reliefs from the charge apply. **A charge to capital gains tax** at 28% also applies to the disposal of such properties, whether by UK resident or non-resident NNPs. See also p 131 regarding the 15% **stamp duty land tax** which can apply to acquisitions of such properties.

Property value[1]	Annual tax 2013–14
More than £2 million to £5 million	£15,000
More than £5 million to £10 million	£35,000
More than £10 million to £20 million	£70,000
More than £20 million	£140,000

[1] The valuation date is the first day of the chargeable period if the chargeable person is within the charge on that day, otherwise the first day in the chargeable period on which he is first within the charge.

Environmental taxes and other levies

Aggregates levy

(FA 2001 ss 16–49, Schs 4–10; SI 2004/1959; SI 2010/2598)

Levy on commercial exploitation of aggregates including rock, gravel or sand together with any other substance incorporated or naturally occurring with it. Applies to all aggregate (not recycled) extracted in the UK or territorial waters unless exempt. It does not apply to quarried or mined products such as clay, shale, slate, metal and metal ores, gemstones, semi-precious gemstones and industrial minerals. It was charged at 20% of the full rate for aggregate processed in Northern Ireland until 30 November 2010. From 1 December 2010 operators in Northern Ireland have to pay the full aggregate levy.

From 1 April 2009	£2.00 per tonne
1 April 2008 to 31 March 2009	£1.95 per tonne
1 April 2002 to 31 March 2008	£1.60 per tonne

Air passenger duty

(FA 1994 s 30, Sch 5A; FA 2008 s 153; FA 2009 s 17, Sch 5; FA 2010, s 14; FA 2012 Sch 23)

APD is extended to smaller aircraft and business jets (reducing the de minimis weight limit from 10 tonnes to 5.7 tonnes) from 1.4.13 and passengers on 'luxury' business jets (20 tonnes or more and fewer than 19 seats) will pay APD at twice the standard rate. From 1.11.11 to 31.12.12 the band A rates apply to all direct long haul flights departing from Northern Ireland. The rates for all direct long haul flights departing from Northern Ireland from 1.1.13 are devolved to the Northern Ireland Assembly and set at £0.

Band and distance of capital city of destination country from UK in miles	Reduced rate (lowest class of travel)			Standard rate (all classes other than lowest class)[2]			Higher rate[3]
	1.11.10–31.3.12	1.4.12–31.3.13	On & after 1.4.13	1.11.10–31.3.12	1.4.12–31.3.13	On & after 1.4.13	On & after 1.4.13
Band A[1] (0–2,000)	£12	£13	£13	£24	£26	£26	£52
Band B (2,001–4,000)	£60	£65	£67	£120	£130	£134	£268
Band C (4,001–6,000)	£75	£81	£83	£150	£162	£166	£332
Band D (over 6,000)	£85	£92	£94	£170	£184	£188	£376

[1] Applies to all direct long haul flights from Northern Ireland from 1 November 2011 to 31 December 2012.
[2] From 1 November 2008, if a class of travel provides a seat pitch in excess of 1.016 metres (40 inches) the standard rate is the minimum rate that applies, even if it is the lowest or only class of travel.
[3] The higher rate applies to flights aboard aircraft of 20 tonnes and above with fewer than 19 seats.
[4] From April 2014 the reduced rate in bands B and C will increase by £2 and in band D by £3. The standard rate in bands B and C will increase by £4 and in band D by £6.

The following specifies which countries come into which bands.

Band A territories — 0–2,000 miles from London		
Albania	Greenland	Morocco
Algeria	Guernsey	Netherlands
Andorra	Hungary	Norway (including Svalbard)
Austria	Iceland	Poland
Azores	Republic of Ireland	Portugal (including Madeira)
Belarus	Isle of Man	Romania
Belgium	Italy (including Sicily and Sardinia)	Russian Federation (west of the Urals)
Bosnia and Herzegovina	Jersey	San Marino
Bulgaria	Republic of Kosovo	Serbia
Croatia	Latvia	Slovak Republic
Cyprus	Libya	Slovenia
Czech Republic	Liechtenstein	Spain (including the Balearic Islands and the Canary Islands)
Denmark (including the Faroe Islands)	Lithuania	Sweden
Estonia	Luxembourg	Switzerland
Finland	former Yugoslav Republic of Macedonia	Tunisia
France (including Corsica)	Malta	Turkey
Germany	Moldova	Ukraine
Gibraltar	Monaco	Western Sahara (*HMRC Notice 550 Appendix 1 (updated March 2013) does not include Western Sahara.*)
Greece	Montenegro	

Band B territories — 2,001–4,000 miles from London

Afghanistan	Gambia	Pakistan
Armenia	Georgia	Qatar
Azerbaijan	Ghana	Russian Federation (east of the Urals)
Bahrain	Guinea	Saint Pierre and Miquelon
Benin	Guinea-Bissau	Sao Tome and Principe
Bermuda	Iran	Saudi Arabia
Burkina Faso	Iraq	Senegal
Cameroon	Israel & Occupied Palestinian Territories	Sierra Leone
Canada	Ivory Coast	Sudan
Cape Verde	Jordan	Syria
Central African Republic	Kazakhstan	Tajikistan
Chad	Kuwait	Togo
Democratic Republic of Congo	Kyrgyzstan	Turkmenistan
Republic of Congo	Lebanon	Uganda
Djibouti	Liberia	United Arab Emirates
Egypt	Mali	United States of America
Equatorial Guinea	Mauritania	Uzbekistan
Eritrea	Niger	Yemen
Ethiopia	Nigeria	
Gabon	Oman	

Band C territories — 4,001–6,000 miles from London

Angola	Grenada	Nepal
Anguilla	Guadelope	former Netherlands Antilles[1]
Antigua and Barbuda	Guatemala	Nicaragua
Aruba	Guyana	Panama
Ascension Island	Haiti	Puerto Rico
Bahamas	Honduras	Reunion
Bangladesh	Hong Kong SAR	Rwanda
Barbados	India	Saint Barthelemy
Belize	Jamaica	Saint Christopher and Nevis (St Kitts and Nevis)
Bhutan	Japan	Saint Helena
Botswana	Kenya	Saint Lucia
Brazil	North Korea	Saint Martin
British Indian Ocean Territory	South Korea	Saint Vincent and the Grenadines
British Virgin Islands	Laos	Seychelles
Burma	Lesotho	Somalia
Burundi	Macao SAR	South Africa
Cayman Islands	Madagascar	Sri Lanka
China	Malawi	Suriname
Colombia	Maldives	Swaziland
Comoros	Martinique	Tanzania
Costa Rica	Mauritius	Thailand
Cuba	Mayotte	Trinidad and Tobago
Dominica	Mexico	Turks and Caicos Islands
Dominican Republic	Mongolia	Venezuela
Ecuador	Montserrat	Vietnam
El Salvador	Mozambique	Virgin Islands
French Guiana	Namibia	Zambia
		Zimbabwe

[1]   Now known as Curaçao, Sint Maarten and BES Islands.

Band D — journey ends in any other place.

Bank levy

(FA 2011 Sch 19 para 6; FA 2012 s 211)

From 1 January 2011 a bank levy is charged based on the total chargeable equity and liabilities reported in the relevant balance sheets of affected banks, banking and building society groups at the end of the chargeable period. It is payable through the existing corporation tax self assessment system. It is not charged on the first £20 billion of chargeable liabilities.

	1.1.11 – 28.2.11	1.3.11 – 30.4.11	1.5.11 – 31.12.11	1.1.12– 31.12.12	1.1.13– 31.12.13	From 1.1.14
Short-term chargeable liabilities	0.05%	0.1%	0.075%	0.088%	**0.130%**	0.142%
Long-term chargeable equity and liabilities	0.025%	0.05%	0.0375%	0.044%	**0.065%**	0.071%

Climate change levy

(FA 2000 s 30, Sch 6; FA 2006 ss 171, 172; FA 2007 s 13; FA 2008 s 19; FA 2010 ss 17, 18; FA 2011 ss 23, 78; FA 2012 Schs 30–32)

Levy on supply for industrial or commercial purposes of energy, from 1.4.01, in the form of electricity, gas, petroleum and hydrocarbon gas supplied in a liquid state, coal and lignite, coke and semi coke of coal or lignite and petroleum coke.

Taxable commodity supplied	Rate[1]				
	1.4.09–31.3.11	1.4.11–31.3.12	1.4.12–31.3.13	**1.4.13–31.3.14**	From 1 April 2014
Electricity	0.47p per kWh	0.485p per kWh	0.509p per kWh	**0.524p per kWh**	0.541p per kWh
Gas supplied by a gas utility or any gas supplied in a gaseous state that is of a kind supplied by a gas utility	0.164p per kWh	0.169p per kWh	0.177p per kWh	**0.182p per kWh**	0.188p per kWh
Gas supplied as above in Northern Ireland	Exempt	0.059p per kWh	0.062p per kWh	**0.064p per kWh until 31.10.13 then main rate applies**	See aside
Any petroleum gas, or other gaseous hydrocarbon supplied in a liquid state	1.05p per kg	1.083p per kg	1.137p per kg	**1.172p per kg**	1.210p per kg
Any other taxable commodity	1.281p per kg	1.321p per kg	1.387p per kg	**1.429p per kg**	1.476p per kg

[1] Rate at which payable if supply is not a reduced-rate supply. The levy is charged at 35% (20% for supplies treated as taking place before 1 April 2011) of the full rate for facilities covered by a climate change agreement. It is charged at 20% from 1 April 2012 for supplies of taxable commodities used in recycling of steel and aluminium (previously exempt) and 10% from 1 April 2013 for electricity supplies. It was charged at half the full rate for horticultural producers until 31.3.06. Horticultural businesses which sign climate change agreements can pay the same 35% of full rate outlined above in exchange for meeting specific energy efficiency targets. It is proposed to introduce exemptions for energy used in metallurgical and mineralogical processes from 1 April 2014.

Carbon price support rates for climate change levy and fuel duty

The carbon price floor is introduced from 1 April 2013. Supplies of solid fossil fuels, gas and liquefied petroleum gas used in most forms of electricity generation are liable to the CPS rates of CCL, which differs from the main CCL rates (see above) levied on consumers' use of these commodities (and electricity). Subject to state aid approval, the carbon price floor does not apply to Northern Ireland. The CPS rate is reduced by the carbon capture percentage where there is a supply of fossil fuels to an electricity generator who uses carbon capture and storage (CCS) technology.

Supplies of commodity		
	1.4.13–31.3.14	1.4.14–31.3.15
Gas supplied by a gas utility or any gas supplied in a gaseous state that is of a kind supplied by a gas utility	0.091p per kWh	0.175p per kWh
Any petroleum gas, or other gaseous hydrocarbon supplied in a liquid state	1.460p per kg	2.822p per kg
Coal and other taxable solid fossil fuels	44.264p per gross gigajoule	85.489p per gross gigajoule
Gas oil; rebated bioblend	1.365p per litre	2.642p per litre
Fuel oil; other heavy oil; rebated light oil	1.568p per litre	3.011p per litre

Fuel duty

(FA 2010 ss 12, 13; FA 2011 s 20; FA 2012 s 188; SI 2011/2935)

A Rural Fuel Duty relief scheme for retailers of road fuel on the Inner and Outer Hebrides, the Northern Isles, the Islands of the Clyde and the Isles of Scilly was introduced on 1 January 2012. Retailers of road fuel within these areas will be eligible to register with HMRC to claim back five pence per litre relief on unleaded petrol and diesel for retail sale within the eligible areas. The retailers will have 60 days following registration for the scheme to reduce the cost of every litre of road fuel sold by the equivalent amount of the relief claimed. (HMRC Brief 40/11)

	Petrol/diesel	Biodiesel or bioethanol	LPG used as road fuel	Natural gas used as road fuel	Red diesel	Fuel oil
from 6pm 23 March 2011 to 31 August 2014	57.95p per litre	57.95p per litre	31.61p per kg	24.70p per kg	11.14p per litre	10.70p per litre
from 1 January 2011 to 6pm 23 March 2011	58.95p per litre	58.95p per litre	33.04p per kg	26.15p per kg	11.33p per litre	10.88p per litre
from 1 October 2010 to 31 December 2010	58.19p per litre	58.19p per litre	31.95p per kg	25.05p per kg	11.18p per litre	10.74p per litre
from 1 April 2010 to 30 September 2010	57.19p per litre	57.19p per litre	30.53p per kg	23.60p per kg	10.99p per litre	10.55p per litre
from 1 September 2009 to 31 March 2010	56.19p per litre	36.19p per litre	27.67p per kg	22.16p per kg	10.80p per litre	10.37p per litre
from 1 April 2009 to 31 August 2009	54.19p per litre	34.19p per litre	24.82p per kg	19.26p per kg	10.42p per litre	10.00p per litre
from 1 December 2008 to 31 March 2009	52.35p per litre	32.35 per litre	20.77p per kg	16.60p per kg	10.07p per litre	9.66p per litre
from 1 October 2007 to 30 November 2008	50.35 per litre	30.35 per litre	16.49p per kg	13.70p per kg	9.69p per litre	9.29p per litre

Insurance premium tax

(FA 1994 ss 48–74, Schs 6A, 7, 7A; F(No 2)A 2010 s 4)

IPT is a tax on premiums received under insurance contracts other than those which are specifically exempt.

	Standard rate	Higher rate[1]
From 4.1.11	6.0%	20.0%
1.7.99–3.1.11	5.0%	17.5%
1.4.97–30.6.99	4.0%	17.5%
1.10.94–31.3.97	2.5%	–

[1] The higher rate applies to sales of motor cars, light vans and motorcycles, electrical or mechanical domestic appliances, and travel insurance.

Landfill tax

(FA 1996 ss 39–71, 197, Sch 5; SI 1996/1527; SI 1996/1528, FA 2011 s 25; FA 2012 ss 205–206; Notice LFT 1 para 4.5)

Tax on disposal of waste imposed on operators of landfill sites calculated by reference to the weight and type of waste deposited. Exemption applies to mining and quarrying waste, dredging waste, pet cemeteries, disposals of NATO waste, inert waste used to fill working and old quarries and (before 1 September 2009) inert waste used to restore landfill sites. An exemption for waste from reclamation of contaminated land was abolished with effect from 30 November 2008 although some exemption certificates remained valid until 31 March 2012. Legislation introduced in Finance Act 2012 brought landfill tax legislation in Scotland into line with the rest of the UK and had retrospective effect back to 21 March 2000.

Period	Active waste per tonne	Inert waste per tonne[2]	Maximum credit[1]
From 1 April 2014	£80	£2.50	TBA
1.4.13–31.3.14	**£72**	**£2.50**	**6.8%**
1.4.12–31.3.13	£64	£2.50	5.6%
1.4.11–31.3.12	£56	£2.50	6.2%
1.4.10–31.3.11	£48	£2.50	5.5%
1.4.09–31.3.10	£40	£2.50	6%
1.4.08–31.3.09	£32	£2.50	6%
1.4.07–31.3.08	£24	£2	6.6%
1.4.06–31.3.07	£21	£2	6.7%
1.4.05–31.3.06	£18	£2	6.0%
1.4.04–31.3.05	£15	£2	6.8%
1.4.03–31.3.04	£14	£2	6.5%
1.4.02–31.3.03	£13	£2	20.0%
1.4.01–31.3.02	£12	£2	20.0%

[1] Tax credits are available to operators who make donations to environmental trusts of 90% of the donation to the maximum percentage above of the tax payable in a 12-month period.

[2] For details of waste materials liable at the lower rate see SI 2011/1017 as amended by SI 2012/940 and HMRC Briefs 15/2012 and 18/2012.

Vehicle excise duty

(FA 2009 ss 13, 14; FA 2010 s 11; FA 2011, s 21; FA 2012 s 195)

Vehicle tax, or 'road tax' is charged according to CO_2 emissions, as follows:

Standard rates

Band	CO_2 (g/km)	2011–12	2012–13	2013–14
A	Up to 100	£0	£0	£0
B	101–110	£20	£20	£20
C	111–120	£30	£30	£30
D	121–130	£95	£100	£105
E	131–140	£115	£120	£125
F	141–150	£130	£135	£140
G	151–165	£165	£170	£175
H	166–175	£190	£195	£200
I	176–185	£210	£215	£220
J	186–200	£245	£250	£260
K	201–225	£260	£270	£280
L	226–255	£445	£460	£475
M	Over 255	£460	£475	£490

There is an alternative fuel discount of £10 for all cars from 2010–11 onwards. From 1 April 2010, a different rate of tax applies in the year of purchase of a new vehicle. In later years, the standard rate applies.

First-year rates

Band	CO_2 (g/km)	2011–12 first-year rate	2012–13 first-year rate	2013–14 first-year rate
A	Up to 100	£0	£0	£0
B	101–110	£0	£0	£0
C	111–120	£0	£0	£0
D	121–130	£0	£0	£0
E	131–140	£115	£120	£125
F	141–150	£130	£135	£140
G	151–165	£165	£170	£175
H	166–175	£265	£275	£285
I	176–185	£315	£325	£335
J	186–200	£445	£460	£475
K	201–225	£580	£600	£620
L	226–255	£790	£815	£840
M	Over 255	£1,000	£1,030	£1,065

Light goods vehicle rates

Tax class	2011–12	2012–13	2013–14
Light goods vehicle[1]	£210	£215	£220
Euro 4 & 5 LGV	£130	£135	£140

[1]   Registered on or after 1 March 2001.

Motorcycle rates

VED band	2011–12	2012–13	2013–14
Up to 150 cc	£16	£16	£17
151–400 cc	£35	£36	£37
401–600 cc	£53	£55	£57
Over 600 cc	£74	£76	£78

Income tax

Starting, basic, higher and additional rates

Band of taxable income	Band	Rate	Tax	Cumulative tax
£	£	%	£	£
2013–14				
0–32,010	32,010	20	6,402	6,402
32,011–150,000	117,990	40	47,196	53,598
Over 150,000	–	45	–	–
2012–13				
0–34,370	34,370	20	6,874	6,874
34,371–150,000	115,630	40	46,252	53,126
Over 150,000	–	50	–	–
2011–12				
0–35,000	35,000	20	7,000	7,000
35,001–150,000	115,000	40	46,000	53,000
Over 150,000	–	50	–	–
2010–11				
0–37,400	37,400	20	7,480	7,480
37,401–150,000	112,600	40	45,040	52,520
Over 150,000	–	50	–	–
2009–10				
0–37,400	37,400	20	7,480	7,480
Over 37,400	–	40	–	–
2008–09				
0–34,800	34,800	20	6,960	6,960
Over £34,800	–	40	–	–

2014–15 rates For 2014–15 the basic rate limit will be £31,865.

Child benefit income tax charge Where an individual or their partner is in receipt of child benefit a high income child benefit charge can arise from 7 January 2013. The charge is applied to the higher earner. Taxpayers with adjusted net income between £50,000 and £60,000 are subject to an income tax charge of 1% of the amount of child benefit for every £100 of income that exceeds £50,000. For taxpayers with income above £60,000, the amount of the charge will equal the amount of child benefit received. Alternatively, a taxpayer with expected income over £60,000 can elect not to receive any child benefit. The election has effect for weeks beginning after it is made. It can be revoked at any time to restore payment of child benefit, and, where the election was made in the erroneous belief that the charge would arise, it may be revoked up to two years after the end of the tax year to which it relates in order for child benefit to be paid for the period. (ITEPA 2003 ss 681B–H; Social Security Administration Act 1992, s 13A).

Taxation of savings: For 2007–08 and earlier years, savings income is chargeable at the rates of 10% (if within the starting rate band), 20% and/or 40% (TA 1988 s 1A; FA 2000 s 32). From 2008–09 onwards the starting rate band is abolished. A new starting rate for savings band for individuals is introduced. For 2008–09 the band is £2,320, for 2009–10 and 2010–11 it is £2,440, for 2011–12 it is £2,560, for 2012–13 it is £2,710, and for 2013–14 it is £2,790. Where an individual's non-savings income is less than the starting rate limit for savings, the savings income is taxable at the 10% starting rate for savings up to the limit. Where non-savings income exceeds the limit, the starting rate for savings does not apply. Savings income includes interest from banks and building societies, interest distributions from authorised unit trusts, interest on gilts and other securities including corporate bonds, purchased life annuities and discounts. Where income does not exceed the basic rate limit, there will be no further tax to pay on savings income from which the 20% tax rate has been deducted, and any tax over-deducted is repayable. Higher rate taxpayers are liable to pay tax at 40% on that part of their savings income falling above the higher rate limit. From 2010–11 to 2012–13 additional rate taxpayers are liable to pay tax at 50% on that part of their savings income falling above the additional rate limit. From 2013–14 that rate is reduced to 45%. Savings income is generally treated as the second top slice of income behind dividends. Non-taxpayers may apply to have interest paid without deduction of tax where their total income is expected to be covered by personal allowances. Taxpayers who are entitled to a refund of tax deducted from interest can claim the refund using form R40. For HMRC advice regarding repayments see: www.hmrc.gov.uk/incometax/refund-reclaim.htm.

Taxation of dividends: UK and foreign dividends (except those foreign dividends taxed under the remittance basis) form the top slice of taxable income. Where income does not exceed the basic rate limit the rate is 10% (applied to the dividend grossed-up by a tax credit of $^1/_9$) so that the liability is met by the tax credit. Higher rate taxpayers are liable to pay tax at 32.5% on that part of their dividend income falling above the higher rate limit. From 2010–11 to 2012–13 additional rate taxpayers are liable to pay tax at 42.5% on that part of their dividend income falling above the additional rate limit. From 2013–14 additional rate taxpayers are liable at 37.5%. See ITA 2007 s 13. A non-payable tax credit of one-ninth of the dividend was extended to individuals in receipt of dividends from non-UK resident companies where they had a holding of less than 10% and the company is not an offshore fund, by ITTOIA 2005 s 397A on or after 6 April 2008. The tax credit is extended to taxpayers with a holding of 10% or more and to distributions from offshore funds with effect on or after 22 April 2009.

Construction industry sub-contractors rate of deduction at source from 6 April 2007 (SI 2007/46)			
Registered sub-contractors	**20%**	Unregistered sub-contractors	**30%**

Taxation of trusts

	Trust rate	Dividend trust rate
2013–14 onwards	**45%**	**37.5%**
2010–11 to 2012–13	50%	42.5%
2004–05 to 2009–10	40%	32.5%

From 2005–06 onwards: The first £1,000 for 2006–07 onwards and £500 for 2005–06 of income arising to a trust chargeable at the trust rate or the dividend trust rate is instead chargeable at the basic, savings or dividend rate.

Vulnerable beneficiaries: From 2004–05 onwards, trustees can be taxed (on election) on trust income as if it were income of the vulnerable beneficiary taking into account the beneficiary's personal allowances, starting and basic rate bands (FA 2005 ss 23–45).

Table of income tax reliefs

	2013–14	2012–13
	£	£
Personal allowance[5] born after 5.4.1948 / age under 65	9,440	8,105
Total income limit	100,000	100,000
Not beneficial if individual's		
total income exceeds	118,880	116,210
Age allowance[1]		
Total income limit	26,100	25,400
Personal allowance born after 5.4.1938 but before 6.4.1948 / age 65–74	10,500	10,500
Not beneficial if individual's		
total income exceeds	28,220	30,190
Personal allowance born before 6.4.1938 / age 75 and over	10,660	10,660
Not beneficial if individual's		
total income exceeds	28,540	30,510
Married couple's allowance[2,4]		
Elder partner 65 before 6.4.2000		
Basic allowance	3,040	2,960
Age allowance[3,4]		
Total income limit	26,100	25,400
Neither partner aged 75 or over	N/A	N/A
Not beneficial if relevant partner[3]		
under 65 and his total income exceeds	N/A	N/A
65–74 and his total income exceeds	N/A	N/A
Either partner aged 75 and over and born before 6 April 1935	7,915	7,705
Not beneficial if relevant partner[3]		
born after 5.4.1948 / under 65 and his total income exceeds	35,850	34,890
born after 5.4.1938 but before 6.4.1948 / 65–74 and his total income exceeds	37,970	39,680
born before 6.4.1938 / 75 or over and his total income exceeds	38,290	40,000
Blind person's allowance[6]	2,160	2,100

[1]   The higher age allowances are available if the claimant's adjusted net income does not exceed the statutory income limit.
Where the adjusted net income exceeds the statutory limit, the maximum allowance is reduced by one-half of the excess until it is reduced to the ordinary personal allowance. The allowances will be frozen at the 2013–14 levels. From 2013–14 the differing levels of personal allowances apply based on specified dates of birth. For 2012–13 and earlier years they applied to those under age 65, those age 65–74 and those age over 75.

[2]   The universal married couple's allowance was withdrawn for 2000–01 onwards but continues to be available to any married couple or, from 2005–06, civil partnership where at least one spouse or partner was born before 6 April 1935.
The relief is given as a reduction in income tax liability restricted to the lower of 10% of the amount of the allowance or the claimant's total income tax liability.

[3]   The higher age allowances are available if the claimant's adjusted net income does not exceed the statutory income limit (subject to relief given as a reduction in tax liability as in note 2 above).
Where the adjusted net income exceeds the statutory limit, the maximum allowance is reduced by one-half of the excess (less any reduction made in the personal age allowance as in note 1 above) but it cannot be reduced to less than the basic couple's allowance.

National insurance contributions – self-employed

		2013–14	2012–13
Class 2	Flat rate per week	£2.70	£2.65
	Small earnings exception	£5,725	5,595
Class 4	Band	7,755–41,450	7,605–42,475
	Rate	33,695@ 9%	34,870@ 9%
	Amount payable to upper limit	3,032.55	3,138.30
	Charge on profits above the limit	2%	2%

Table of income tax reliefs (cont.)

2011–12	2010–11	2009–10	2008–09	2007–08
£	£	£	£	£
7,475	6,475	6,475	6,035	5,225
100,000	100,000	N/A	N/A	N/A
114,950	112,950	N/A	N/A	N/A
24,000	22,900	22,900	21,800	20,900
9,940	9,490	9,490	9,030	7,550
28,930	28,930	28,930	27,790	25,550
10,090	9,640	9,640	9,180	7,690
29,230	29,230	29,230	28,090	25,830
2,800	2,670	2,670	2,540	2,440
24,000	22,900	22,900	21,800	20,900
N/A	N/A	N/A	6,535	6,285
N/A	N/A	N/A	29,790	28,590
N/A	N/A	N/A	35,780	33,240
7,295	6,965	6,965	6,625	6,365
32,990	31,490	31,490	29,790	28,750
37,920	37,520	37,520	35,960	33,400
38,220	37,820	37,820	36,260	33,680
1,980	1,890	1,890	1,800	1,730

[4] For marriages entered into before 5 December 2005, married couple's allowance is given to the husband (subject to right of transfer to the wife), the amount of the allowance being determined by the level of the husband's income. For marriages and civil partnerships entered into on or after that date, the allowance is given to whichever of the two partners has the higher total income for the tax year in question, the amount of the allowance being determined by the level of that partner's income (subject to the right to transfer half or all of the basic allowance or excess allowances to the partner). Couples married before 5 December 2005 may make a joint election to be brought within the above rules for couples marrying on or after that date. The election must be made before the start of the first tax year for which it is to have effect. It will continue to have effect for all subsequent tax years and is irrevocable.

[5] From 2010–11, the basic personal allowance for income tax is gradually reduced to nil for individuals with adjusted net incomes in excess of £100,000. The reduction is £1 for every £2 of income over the limit. From 2013–14 the differing levels of personal allowances apply based on specified dates of birth. For 2012–13 and earlier years they applied to those under age 65, those age 65–74 and those age over 75. For 2014–15 the basic personal allowance will be £10,000 for individuals born after 5 April 1948.

[6] The allowance is available for persons who are registered blind but not for persons registered partially-sighted.

National insurance contributions – self-employed (cont.)

£2.50	£2.40	£2.40	£2.30	£2.20
5,315	5,075	5,075	4,825	4,635
7,225–42,475	5,715–43,875	5,715–43,875	5,435–40,040	5,225–34,840
35,250@ 9%	38,160@ 8%	38,160@ 8%	34,605@ 8%	29,615@ 8%
3,172.50	3,052.80	3,052.80	2,768.40	2,369.20
2%	1%	1%	1%	1%

Cars, vans and related benefits

Cars

From 6 April 2002: The income tax charge is based on a percentage of the car's price graduated according to the level of the car's carbon dioxide measured in grams per kilometre (g/km). (ITEPA 2003 ss 114–148, 169.)

CO_2 emissions (g/km)[1]						% of list price	
2005–06–2007–08	2008–09–2009–10	2010–11	2011–12	2012–13	2013–14	Petrol	Diesel[1]
N/A	N/A	75[1]	75[1]	75[1]	75[1]	5%	8%
N/A	120[1]	120[1]	120[1]	99[1]	94[1]	10%	13%
N/A	N/A	N/A	N/A	100	95	11%	14%
N/A	N/A	N/A	N/A	105	100	12%	15%
N/A	N/A	N/A	N/A	110	105	13%	16%
N/A	N/A	N/A	N/A	115	110	14%	17%
140	135	130	125	120	115	15%	18%
145	140	135	130	125	120	16%	19%
150	145	140	135	130	125	17%	20%
155	150	145	140	135	130	18%	21%
160	155	150	145	140	135	19%	22%
165	160	155	150	145	140	20%	23%
170	165	160	155	150	145	21%	24%
175	170	165	160	155	150	22%	25%
180	175	170	165	160	155	23%	26%
185	180	175	170	165	160	24%	27%
190	185	180	175	170	165	25%	28%
195	190	185	180	175	170	26%	29%
200	195	190	185	180	175	27%	30%
205	200	195	190	185	180	28%	31%
210	205	200	195	190	185	29%	32%
215	210	205	200	195	190	30%	33%
220	215	210	205	200	195	31%	34%
225	220	215	210	205	200	32%	35%
230	225	220	215	210	205	33%	35%
235	230	225	220	215	210	34%	35%
240	235	230	225	220	215	35%	35%

[1] Where a car's CO_2 figure is not a multiple of 5, it is rounded down to the nearest 5. However, to qualify for the 10/13% rate a car's emissions figure must be exactly 120g/km or less for 2008–09 to 2011–12, 99g/km or less for 2012–13 and 94g/km or less for 2013–14. From 2010–11 the emissions must be exactly 75g/km or less to qualify for the 5/8% rate.

For 2008–09 to 2010–11: For cars registered on or after 1.1.98 which are constructed to be capable of being propelled by bioethanol or E85 fuel, the percentage chargeable was reduced by 2%.

For 2010–11 to 2014–15: No benefit applies to cars which are incapable of producing carbon dioxide when driven.

For 2014–15: The relevant threshold will remain at 95g/km but the percentage applying at that threshold (the threshold percentage) will be increased from 11/14% to 12/15%. The 11%/14% rate will then apply to cars with CO_2 emissions of 76g/km to 94g/km

Cars registered after 28 February 2001

For cars registered on or after 1.3.01, the definitive CO_2 emissions figure is recorded on the vehicle registration document. For cars first registered between 1.1.98 and 28.2.01, the Vehicle Certification Agency supply relevant information on their website at carfueldata.direct.gov.uk/ and in their free, twice-yearly edition of the 'New Car Fuel Consumption & Emission Figures' booklet.

Cars registered on or after 1 January 1998 with no CO_2 emission figures

Cylinder capacity of car[3]	Appropriate percentage[1, 2]
1,400cc or less	15%
Over 1,400cc up to 2,000cc	25%
Over 2,000cc	35%
Before 6 April 2010: Electrically propelled vehicle	15%
From 6 April 2010 to 5 April 2015: Cars incapable of producing CO_2 when driven	0%

[1] **Diesel cars:** A 3% supplement applies to diesel cars up to a maximum of 35%. The supplement does not apply before 5.4.06 to diesel cars meeting the Euro IV emissions standards. For 2006–07 to 2010–11 it does not apply to such cars registered before 1 January 2006.

[2] **Discounts:** Special discounts applied to cars, with or without CO_2 emission figures, registered on or after 1.1.98: 6% for electrically propelled vehicles (before 2010–11 only), 3% for hybrid electric vehicles (before 2011–12 only, 2% before 2006–07) and 2% for gas or bi-fuel cars with CO_2 emission figures for gas (before 2011–12 only, 1% before 2006–07).

[3] **No cylinder capacity:** For a car with no cylinder capacity 35% applies.

Cars registered before 1.1.98: Tax is charged on 15% of the list price for engines to 1,400cc, 22% for engines of 1,401 to 2,000cc and 32% for engines above 2,000cc. Cars without a cylinder capacity are taxed on 32% of the list price.

Automatic cars for disabled drivers: CO_2 figure reduced to equivalent for manual car (ITEPA 2003 s 138).

Car unavailable for part of year: Value of the benefit is reduced proportionately (ITEPA 2003 s 143).

National Insurance: Also used to calculate the national insurance contributions payable by employers on the benefit of cars they provide for the private use of their employees, see p 109.

The cash equivalent is reduced proportionately where the car is not available for the whole tax year. The amount (as so reduced) is reduced by any payments made by the employee for private use.

List price of car:
(1) Includes qualifying accessories, excluding accessories provided after car made available if its list price was less than £100. Accessories designed for use only by disabled people also excluded. From 6 April 2011 accessories do not include certain security enhancements provided to meet the threat to an employee's personal physical security arising from the nature of the employment. Where a car is manufactured so as to be capable of running on road fuel gas, its price is proportionately reduced by so much of that price as is reasonably attributable to it being manufactured in that way. Where a new car is converted to run on road fuel gas, the equipment is not regarded as an accessory. With effect from 6 April 2009 disabled drivers of automatic cars who hold a disabled person's badge can use the list price of an equivalent manual car.
(2) Reduced by capital contributions made by employee up to £5,000.
(3) For 2010–11 and earlier years the list price as adjusted was capped at £80,000.
(4) Classic cars (aged 15 years or more and with a market value of £15,000 or more at end of tax year): substitute market value at end of tax year if higher than adjusted list price. Reduction for capital contributions (and for earlier years the £80,000 cap) applies.

(ITEPA 2003 ss 120–132)

Vans and fuel for vans

(ITEPA 2003 ss 114–119, 154–164, 168, 169A, 170)

Van benefit	Van's age at end of tax year	
	Under 4 years	4 years or more
2007–08 onwards		
Vehicle weight up to 3,500kg	**£3,000**	**£3,000**
1993–94 to 2006–07		
Vehicle weight up to 3,500kg	£500	£350

From 6 April 2005: no charge applies to employees who have to take their van home and private use is restricted other than for ordinary commuting (insignificant use is disregarded).

For 2010–11 to 2014–15: No benefit applies to vans which are incapable of producing CO_2 when driven.

Van fuel benefit	
2013–14	**£564**
2010–11 to 2012–13	£550
2007–08 to 2009–10	£500

From 6 April 2007: the fuel charge applies where the van benefit charge applies & fuel is provided for private use.

Related benefits

Parking facilities: No taxable benefit for work place provision of car parking spaces, or parking for bicycles or motorcycles or, from 6 April 2005, vans (ITEPA 2003 s 237).

Cycles and cyclist's safety equipment: No taxable benefit in respect of the provision to employees of bicycles or cycling safety equipment for travel to and from work (ITEPA 2003 s 244) nor, from 6 April 2005, for subsequent transfer to the employee at market value (ITEPA 2003 s 206).

On-call emergency vehicles: From 6 April 2004 onwards no tax or NIC charge where emergency service workers have private use of their emergency vehicle when on call (ITEPA 2003 s 248A).

Bus services: From 6 April 2002 onwards no taxable benefit in respect of the provision of works buses with a seating capacity of 9 or more provided to employees (or their children) to travel to & from work (ITEPA 2003 s 242).

Car and motorcycle hire: restricted allowances

(ITTOIA 2005 ss 48–50B; CTA 2009 ss 56–58B)

Before April 2009, if a car with a retail price when new of more than £12,000 is acquired under a rental lease the maximum allowable deduction in computing trading profits is restricted to:

$$\frac{£12,000 + P}{2P} \times R$$

P = retail price of car when new. R = annual rental.

From April 2009, the disallowance is a flat rate of 15%. This applies only to cars with CO_2 emissions exceeding 130g/km (160g/km before 1 April 2013 (corporation tax) or 6 April 2013 (income tax)).

Capital allowances see p 33.

Car fuel: company cars

(ITEPA 2003 ss 149–153)

For 2003–04 onwards, the same percentage figures on p 75 used to calculate the car benefit charge for the company car, which are directly linked to the car's CO_2 emissions, are used to calculate the benefit charge for fuel provided for private motoring. The relevant percentage figure is multiplied by £14,400 for 2003–04 to 2007–08, by £16,900 for 2008–09 and 2009–10, by £18,000 for 2010–11, by £18,800 for 2011–12, by £20,200 for 2012–13, and by £21,100 for 2013–14.

CO_2 emissions (g/km)	Petrol	Diesel
2013–14	£	£
75	1,055	1,688
94	2,110	2,743
95	2,321	2,954
100	2,532	3,165
105	2,743	3,376
110	2,954	3,587
115	3,165	3,798
120	3,376	4,009
125	3,587	4,220
130	3,798	4,431
135	4,009	4,642
140	4,220	4,853
145	4,431	5,064
150	4,642	5,275
155	4,853	5,486
160	5,064	5,697
165	5,275	5,908
170	5,486	6,119
175	5,697	6,330
180	5,908	6,541
185	6,119	6,752
190	6,330	6,963
195	6,541	7,174
200	6,752	7,385
205	6,963	7,385
210	7,174	7,385
215	7,385	7,385

CO_2 emissions (g/km)	Petrol	Diesel
2012–13	£	£
75	1,010	1,616
99	2,020	2,626
100	2,222	2,828
105	2,424	3,030
110	2,626	3,232
115	2,828	3,434
120	3,030	3,636
125	3,232	3,838
130	3,434	4,040
135	3,636	4,242
140	3,838	4,444
145	4,040	4,646
150	4,242	4,848
155	4,444	5,050
160	4,646	5,252
165	4,848	5,454
170	5,050	5,656
175	5,252	5,858
180	5,454	6,060
185	5,656	6,262
190	5,858	6,464
195	6,060	6,666
200	6,262	6,868
205	6,464	7,070
210	6,666	7,070
215	6,868	7,070
220	7,070	7,070

CO_2 emissions (g/km)	Petrol	Diesel
2011–12	£	£
75	940	1,504
120	1,880	2,444
125	2,820	3,384
130	3,008	3,572
135	3,196	3,760
140	3,384	3,948
145	3,572	4,136
150	3,760	4,324
155	3,948	4,512
160	4,136	4,700
165	4,324	4,888
170	4,512	5,076
175	4,700	5,264
180	4,888	5,452
185	5,076	5,640
190	5,264	5,828
195	5,452	6,016
200	5,640	6,204
205	5,828	6,392
210	6,016	6,580
215	6,204	6,580
220	6,392	6,580
225	6,580	6,580

CO_2 emissions (g/km)	Petrol	Diesel
2010–11	£	£
75	900	1,440
120	1,800	2,340
130	2,700	3,240
135	2,880	3,420
140	3,060	3,600
145	3,240	3,780
150	3,420	3,960
155	3,600	4,140
160	3,780	4,320
165	3,960	4,500
170	4,140	4,680
175	4,320	4,860
180	4,500	5,040
185	4,680	5,220
190	4,860	5,400
195	5,040	5,580
200	5,220	5,760
205	5,400	5,940
210	5,580	6,120
215	5,760	6,300
220	5,940	6,300
225	6,120	6,300
230	6,300	6,300

CO_2 emissions (g/km)	Petrol	Diesel
2008–09– 2009–2010	£	£
120	1,690	2,197
135	2,535	3,042
140	2,704	3,211
145	2,873	3,380
150	3,042	3,549
155	3,211	3,718
160	3,380	3,887
165	3,549	4,056
170	3,718	4,225
175	3,887	4,394
180	4,056	4,563
185	4,225	4,732
190	4,394	4,901
195	4,563	5,070
200	4,732	5,239
205	4,901	5,408
210	5,070	5,577
215	5,239	5,746
220	5,408	5,915
225	5,577	5,915
230	5,746	5,915
235	5,915	5,915

CO$_2$ emissions (g/km)			Petrol	Diesel
2003–04	**2004–05**	**2005–06– 2007–08**	£	£
155	145	**140**	2,160	2,592
160	150	**145**	2,304	2,736
165	155	**150**	2,448	2,880
170	160	**155**	2,592	3,024
175	165	**160**	2,736	3,168
180	170	**165**	2,880	3,312
185	175	**170**	3,024	3,456
190	180	**175**	3,168	3,600
195	185	**180**	3,312	3,744
200	190	**185**	3,456	3,888
205	195	**190**	3,600	4,032
210	200	**195**	3,744	4,176
215	205	**200**	3,888	4,320
220	210	**205**	4,032	4,464
225	215	**210**	4,176	4,608
230	220	**215**	4,320	4,752
235	225	**220**	4,464	4,896
240	230	**225**	4,608	5,040
245	235	**230**	4,752	5,040
250	240	**235**	4,896	5,040
255	245	**240**	5,040	5,040

The benefit is reduced to nil if the employee is required to, and does, make good all fuel provided for private use. There is no taxable benefit where the employer only provides fuel for business travel. The charge is proportionately reduced where the employee stops receiving free fuel part way through the tax year, but where free fuel is subsequently provided in the same tax year, the full year's charge is payable. The benefit is proportionately reduced where a car is not available or is incapable of being used for part of a year (being at least 30 days).

Mileage allowances

Advisory fuel rates for company cars

Engine size	Cost per mile		
	Petrol	Diesel	LPG
from 1 March 2013			
1,400cc or less	**15p**	**–**	**10p**
1,600cc or less	**–**	**13p**	**–**
1,401–2,000cc	**18p**	**–**	**12p**
1,601–2,000cc	**–**	**15p**	**–**
Over 2,000cc	**26p**	**18p**	**18p**
1 December 2012–28 February 2013			
1,400cc or less	15p	–	11p
1,600cc or less	–	12p	–
1,401–2,000cc	18p	–	13p
1,601–2,000cc	–	15p	–
Over 2,000cc	26p	18p	18p

Engine size	Cost per mile		
	Petrol	Diesel	LPG
1 September 2012–30 November 2012			
1,400cc or less	15p	–	10p
1,600cc or less	–	12p	–
1,401–2,000cc	18p	–	13p
1,601–2,000cc	–	15p	–
Over 2,000cc	26p	18p	17p
1 June 2012–31 August 2012			
1,400cc or less	15p	–	11p
1,600cc or less	–	12p	–
1,401–2,000cc	18p	–	13p
1,601–2,000cc	–	15p	–
Over 2,000cc	26p	18p	19p
1 March 2012–31 May 2012			
1,400cc or less	15p	–	10p
1,600cc or less	–	13p	–
1,401–2,000cc	18p	–	12p
1,601–2,000cc	–	15p	–
Over 2,000cc	26p	19p	18p
1 December 2011–29 February 2012			
1,400cc or less	15p	–	10p
1,600cc or less	–	12p	–
1,401–2,000cc	18p	–	12p
1,601–2,000cc	–	15p	–
Over 2,000cc	26p	18p	18p
1 September 2011–30 November 2011			
1,400cc or less	15p	–	11p
1,600cc or less	–	12p	–
1,401–2,000cc	18p	–	12p
1,601–2,000cc	–	15p	–
Over 2,000cc	26p	18p	18p
1 June 2011–31 August 2011			
1,400cc or less	15p	–	11p
1,600cc or less	–	12p	–
1,401–2,000cc	18p	–	13p
1,601–2,000cc	–	15p	–
Over 2,000cc	26p	18p	18p
1 March 2011–31 May 2011			
1,400cc or less	14p	13p	10p
1,401–2,000cc	16p	13p	12p
Over 2,000cc	23p	16p	17p
1 December 2010–28 February 2011			
1,400cc or less	13p	12p	9p
1,401–2,000cc	15p	12p	10p
Over 2,000cc	21p	15p	15p
1 June 2010–30 November 2010			
1,400cc or less	12p	11p	8p
1,401–2,000cc	15p	11p	10p
Over 2,000cc	21p	16p	14p

Engine size	Cost per mile		
	Petrol	Diesel	LPG
1 December 2009–31 May 2010			
1,400cc or less	11p	11p	7p
1,401–2,000cc	14p	11p	8p
Over 2,000cc	20p	14p	12p
1 July 2009–30 November 2009			
1,400cc or less	10p	10p	7p
1,401–2,000cc	12p	10p	8p
Over 2,000cc	18p	13p	12p
1 January 2009–30 June 2009			
1,400cc or less	10p	11p	7p
1,401–2,000cc	12p	11p	9p
Over 2,000cc	17p	14p	12p
1 July 2008–31 December 2008			
1,400cc or less	12p	13p	7p
1,401–2,000cc	15p	13p	9p
Over 2,000cc	21p	17p	13p
1 January 2008–30 June 2008			
1,400cc or less	11p	11p	7p
1,401–2,000cc	13p	11p	8p
Over 2,000cc	19p	14p	11p
1 August 2007–31 December 2007			
1,400cc or less	10p	10p	6p
1,401–2,000cc	13p	10p	8p
Over 2,000cc	18p	13p	10p
1 February 2007–31 July 2007			
1,400cc or less	9p	9p	6p
1,401–2,000cc	11p	9p	7p
Over 2,000cc	16p	12p	10p

[1]   Advisory fuel rates can be used to negotiate dispensations for mileage payments from 28.01.02 where:
   (a)   employers reimburse employees for business travel in their company cars; or
   (b)   employers require employees to repay the cost of fuel used for private travel.
   (In the case of (b) the figures may be used for reimbursements of private travel from 6 April 2001.)
[2]   Payments at or below these rates are tax and NIC free. The table figures will be accepted for VAT purposes.
[3]   Other rates may be used if the employer can demonstrate that they are justified.
[4]   Rates are currently reviewed by HMRC quarterly.
[5]   The 1 July 2008 rates can be used from 1 June 2008 if the employer wishes.

Authorised mileage rates

	Rate per business mile	
Cars	First 10,000 miles	Over 10,000 miles
2011–12 onwards[1]	**45p**	**25p**
2002–03 to 2010–11[1]	40p	25p

[1]   Where the employer pays less than the authorised rate the employee can claim tax relief for the difference (ITEPA 2003 ss 229–232, 235, 236).

	Rate per business mile
Car passengers Allowance for each fellow passenger carried	
2002–03 onwards	**5p**
Cycles	
2002–03 onwards[1]	**20p**
Motorcycles	
2002–03 onwards[1]	**24p**

[1]   Where the employer pays less than the authorised rate the employee can claim tax relief for the difference (ITEPA 2003 ss 229–232, 235, 236).

Charities and Community Amateur Sports Clubs (CASCs)

Gift Aid and Gift Aid Small Donations schemes

Under the **Gift Aid scheme** an individual donor can claim higher rate relief (and, if applicable, additional rate relief from 2010–11) on the grossed up amount of a monetary donation against income tax and capital gains tax. The charity or CASC claims basic rate relief on the grossed up amount of the donation. Donors must make a declaration that they are UK taxpayers to allow the charity to reclaim the repayment. One declaration can cover a series of donations to the same charity and the declaration can be made by writing, by electronic means or orally, although an oral declaration is not effective until a written confirmation is sent to the donor. New model written declaration forms were issued by HMRC on 24 February 2012, and only forms based on the new wording will be accepted from 1 January 2013. A declaration can be backdated for up to six years prior to the declaration for donations made after 5 April 2000. The basic rate tax deemed to have been deducted by the donor at source is clawed back if the donor's tax liability is insufficient to match it. Following the reduction of the basic rate to 20% for 2008–09 onwards, a transitional relief supplement of 2% of grossed up qualifying donations was payable to charities for 2008–09 to 2010–11. Donors may elect in their self-assessment tax returns for donations made after 5 April 2003 to be treated as made in the preceding tax year for higher rate (and if applicable, additional rate) relief purposes.

From April 2013 the **Gift Aid Small Donations scheme** allows charities and CASCs to claim a gift aid style payment on broadly £5,000 of small cash donations of up to £20 each in circumstances where it is often difficult to obtain a gift aid declaration, such as street collections. The donations must not have been the subject of a gift aid declaration and must not be deductible in calculating the individual's income.

From April 2004, taxpayers could nominate a charity to receive all or part of any tax repayment due to them. The nomination was made on the taxpayer's self-assessment tax return for 2003–04 and later years, with an indication of whether Gift Aid should apply to the donation. However, this scheme has been withdrawn for repayments due on tax returns for 2011–12 onwards, and for repayments made for earlier years on or after 6 April 2012.

Relief for payments falling due after 5 April 2000 under charitable covenants is given under the Gift Aid scheme. (ITA 2007 ss 413–430; FA 2012 s 50)

Gifts in kind

Relief is available for gifts by traders to charities, community amateur sports clubs or educational establishments of goods produced or sold or of plant or machinery used for the purposes of the trade (CAA 2001 s 63(2)–(4); ITTOIA 2005 ss 107–109; CTA 2009 ss 105–107; CTA 2010 ss 658–671).

Gifts of land, shares and securities etc

Relief is available where a person disposes of listed shares and securities, unit trust units, AIM shares, etc or of freehold or leasehold interests in land to a charity by way of a gift or sale at an undervalue. The amount deductible from total income is the market value of the shares etc on the date of disposal plus incidental disposal costs less any consideration or value of benefits received by the donor or a connected person. This is in addition to any capital gains tax relief (ITA 2007 ss 431–446).

Payroll giving

Under the payroll giving scheme, employees authorise their employer to deduct charitable donations from their pay and receive tax relief on their donation at their top rate of tax. From 6 April 2004 to 31 December 2006, the first £10 donated by each employee every month was matched for a period of six months. (FA 2000 s 38; ITEPA 2003 ss 713–715; SI 1986/2211 as amended.)

Inheritance tax relief see p 106. **Capital gains tax** see p 41. **Gifts of pre-eminent objects** see p 96.

Employment benefits

The following benefits on pp 85 to 89 cover some common benefits not detailed separately elsewhere. References to 'lower-paid' employees are those whose annual remuneration plus benefits is less than £8,500.

Accommodation, supplies, etc used in employment duties

(ITEPA 2003 s 316)

The provision of accommodation, supplies or services used by employees in performance of employment duties is not taxable provided:
- (a) if the benefit is provided on premises occupied by the employer, any private use by the employee (or the employee's family or household) is not significant; or
- (b) in any other case, the sole purpose of providing the benefit is to enable the employee to perform those duties, any private use is not significant and the benefit is not an excluded benefit (eg the provision of a motor vehicle, boat or aircraft).

Assets given to employees

(ITEPA 2003 ss 203, 204)

If new, tax is chargeable on the cost to the employer (market value in the case of a 'lower-paid' employee). If used, tax is chargeable on the greater of:
- (a) market value at the time of transfer; and

(b) where the asset is first applied for the provision of a benefit after 5 April 1980 and a person has been chargeable to tax on its use, market value when first so applied less amounts charged to tax for use up to and including the year of transfer.

Buses to shops

(SI 2002/205)

The provision of buses for journeys of ten miles or less from the workplace to shops etc on a working day is not taxable.

Cheap loans

(ITEPA 2003 ss 174–190)

A taxable benefit arises on employer-related loans to directors or employees earning £8,500 or more a year, on the difference between the interest paid and interest payable at the 'official rate' below. There is no tax charge where:
(a) all the employer-related loans (or all loans not qualifying for tax relief) do not exceed £5,000*;
(b) all the interest payable is or would be eligible for tax relief; and
(c) the loans are ordinary commercial loans.
* Proposed to be increased to £10,000 from 6 April 2014.

The provisions can apply to alternative finance arrangements entered into after 21 March 2006.

The 'official rate' is:

From 6 April 2010	**4.00%**
From 1 March 2009 to 5 April 2010	4.75%
From 6 April 2007 to 28 February 2009	6.25%
From 6 January 2002 to 5 April 2007	5.00%

The average rate for the tax year is:

2012–13	**4.00%**
2011–12	4.00%
2010–11	4.00%
2009–10	4.75%
2008–09	6.10%
2007–08	6.25%

From 2000–01 the official rate is set in advance for the whole of the following tax year, subject to review if the typical mortgage rates were to fall sharply during a tax year.

Childcare provision

(ITEPA 2003 ss 318–318D; SI 2006/882)

No liability arises:
(a) where the premises (which are not wholly or mainly used as a private dwelling) are made available by the employer or, where the scheme is provided under arrangements with other persons, by one or more of those persons; or
(b) where (a) does not apply, on the first £55 per week of registered or approved childcare, or where the employee joins the scheme after 5 April 2011, the first £55 (basic rate taxpayers), £28 per week (higher rate taxpayers), £25 per week (additional rate taxpayers, £22 per week before 6 April 2013) of registered or approved childcare.

Christmas parties and annual functions

(ITEPA 2003 s 264; SI 2003/1361)

Not taxable if cost does not exceed £150 per head per tax year and open to staff generally. Otherwise, fully taxable. Expenditure may be split between more than one function. (Not taxable on 'lower-paid' employees.)

Credit tokens

(ITEPA 2003 ss 90–96A, 363)

Where money goods or services are provided to employees through credit tokens, the cost to the employer, less any employee contribution, is taxable on the employee, except if they were used to buy certain non-taxable benefits.

Cyclists' breakfasts

(SI 2002/205; SI 2012/1808)

Before 6 April 2013 breakfast provided for employees arriving at the workplace by bicycle in recognition of having cycled to work is not taxable. No limit on number of such breakfasts per year. This exemption is removed from 2013–14 onwards.

Disabled employees

(ITEPA 2003 ss 246, 247; SI 2002/1596)

The provision of or payment for transport for disabled employees for ordinary commuting is tax free. From 9 July 2002, this also applies to the provision of equipment, services or facilities to disabled employees to help them carry out their duties of employment.

Emergency service vehicles

(ITEPA 2003 s 248A)

From 2004–05, there is no tax charge on any benefit arising from use of an emergency vehicle by an employee of an emergency service where private use is prohibited.

Employees' liability insurance

(ITEPA 2003 s 346)

This is non-taxable.

Eye tests and corrective appliances

(ITEPA 2003 s 320A; FA 2006 s 62)

From 2006–07, no liability arises where the provision of tests or special corrective appliances are required under health and safety legislation and are available as required to employees generally.

Homeworkers

(ITEPA 2003 s 316A)

From 2003–04, employer contributions to additional household costs not taxable where employee works at home. Supporting evidence required if contributions exceed £4 per week (£18 per month for monthly paid employees). Before 6 April 2012 the limit was £3 per week and before 6 April 2008 the limit was £2 per week.

Incidental overnight expenses

(ITEPA 2003 ss 240, 241)

Not taxable where employee stays away from home on business and payment from employer does not exceed:
- (a)   £5 per night in the UK; or
- (b)   £10 per night overseas.

Living accommodation

(ITEPA 2003 ss 97–113)

A taxable benefit (the '*basic charge*') arises on the annual rental value (or actual rent if greater) less any sums made good by the employee. There is an *additional charge* (if the basic charge is not calculated on the full open market rental value) where the cost of accommodation (including costs of any capital improvements less amounts made good by the employee) exceeds £75,000. The additional charge is the excess cost over £75,000 multiplied by the official rate for cheap loans (see above) in force at the start of the tax year less any rent paid by the employee in excess of the basic charge.

For leases of ten years or less entered into on or after 22 April 2009, a lease premium paid is to be treated as if it were rent and spread over the period of the lease accordingly.

The charges are apportioned in the case of multiple occupation or if the property is provided for only part of the year or part is used exclusively for business purposes.

Exemption: No taxable benefit arises where living accommodation is provided:
- (a)   for the proper performance of duties;
- (b)   by reason that it is customary to do so; or
- (c)   by reason of special threat to the employee's security.

The above exemptions apply to a full-time working director whose interest in the company does not exceed 5%, otherwise only exemption (c) applies to directors.

Living expenses

(ITEPA 2003 ss 313–315)

A taxable charge arises on the cost to the employer of the employee's living expenses. For the provision of assets such as furniture, see 'Use of employer's assets' below.

Where the exemption for living accommodation above applies, the tax charge relating to living expenses (including the provision of furniture and items normal for domestic occupation) is restricted to 10% of the employee's net earnings from the related employment less any sums made good by the employee.

Expenditure on alteration and structural repairs which are normally the landlord's responsibility do not give rise to a taxable benefit.

Long service awards

(ITEPA 2003 s 323; SI 2003/1361)

Not taxable provided the employee has at least 20 years' service and cost to the employer does not exceed £50 (£20 where made before 13 June 2003) for each year of service. No similar award may be made within ten years of such an award.

Meals

(ITEPA 2003 s 317)

Subsidised or free meals provided for staff generally at the workplace are not taxable. For 2011–12 onwards, however, this relief does not apply if the provision of meals is made under salary sacrifice or flexible remuneration arrangements.

Medical check-ups and insurance

(ITEPA 2003 ss 320B, 325; HMRC Employment Income Manual EIM21765)

Check-ups:

2009–10 onwards: One screening and one check-up each year not taxable.

2007–08 and 2008–09: By concession, HMRC continued the previous concessionary practice not to collect tax and NICs which might arise from the previous regulations.

2006–07 and earlier years: Routine health checks and medical screenings for employee (or members of the family or household) are not taxable.

Insurance: Premiums paid on behalf of employees (other than 'lower-paid' employees) are taxable unless for treatment outside the UK whilst the employee is performing duties abroad.

Personal expenses

(ITEPA 2003 ss 70–72, 336–341)

Unless covered by specific exemptions, payments to an employee by reason of his employment in respect of expenses or allowances are taxable. Deduction is allowed for expenses the employee is obliged to incur which are:

(a)   qualifying travelling expenses (broadly those necessarily incurred other than for ordinary commuting or private travel); or

(b)   other amounts incurred wholly, exclusively and necessarily in the performance of employment duties.

Relocation expenses

(ITEPA 2003 ss 271–289)

Qualifying removal expenses and benefits up to £8,000 per move in connection with job-related residential moves are not taxable. Included are expenses of disposal, acquisition, abortive acquisition, transport of belongings, travelling and subsistence, bridging loans and duplicate expenses (replacement domestic items).

Scholarships

(ITEPA 2003 ss 211–215)

An employee is taxable on the cost of any scholarship from a trust fund which does not satisfy a 25% distribution test or which is paid because of the employee's employment.

Subscriptions and fees

(ITEPA 2003 ss 343–345)

Not taxable where paid to professional bodies where employee has a contractual or professional requirement to be a member of the body.

Third party gifts

(ITEPA 2003 ss 270, 324; SI 2003/1361)

Gifts during the tax year of goods and non-cash vouchers up to £250 (£150 for 2002–03) not taxable where provided by a party unconnected with the employer and not for services provided in connection with employment.

Use of employer's assets

(ITEPA 2003 ss 203–206, 242, 244, 319, 320; FA 2005 s 17; FA 2006 ss 60, 61, HMRC Brief 02/2012)

Tax is chargeable on the annual rental value of land and, for other assets, at 20% of the market value when they are first lent or the rental charge to the employer if higher. No taxable benefit arises on:

(a)   the loan of a mobile phone for private use. From 6 April 2006 this is restricted to one mobile phone per employee and no longer extends to the employee's family or household but phones first loaned before 6 April 2006 are not affected by the change. HMRC's view from January 2012 is that exemption applies to smartphones with retrospective effect;

(b)   the use of works buses (see p 78);

(c)   cycles and cycle safety equipment (see p 78);

(d) to 5 April 2006, the loan of computer equipment for private use, provided use is not restricted to directors or senior staff and value of benefit does not exceed £2,500 (computers made available for private use before 6 April 2006 are not affected by the change).

From 6 April 2005, no benefit arises on the subsequent purchase by an employee at market value of computer or cycling equipment previously on loan.

Vouchers

(ITEPA 2003 ss 73–89, 95, 96, 268–270, 362; FA 2012 Sch 39)

Vouchers are taxable as follows.

(a)	Cash vouchers	On amount for which voucher can be exchanged.
(b)	Non-cash vouchers	On cost to employer less any contribution from employee (except where used to obtain certain non-taxable benefits).
(c)	Luncheon vouchers	Before 6 April 2013 on excess over 15p per working day[1].
(d)	Transport vouchers	On cost to employer less any contribution from employee.

[1] The 15p exemption on luncheon vouchers is repealed from 2013–14 onwards.

Employment income

PAYE and national insurance thresholds

	2008–09	2009–10	2010–11	2011–12	2012–13	2013–14
	£	£	£	£	£	£
Weekly NI	105	110	110	136/139	144/146	148/149
Weekly PAYE	116	125	125	144	156	182
Monthly NI	453	476	476	589/602	624/634	641/646
Monthly PAYE	503	540	540	623	675	787

The 2008–09 PAYE figures apply from 7 September 2008.

For full list of national insurance rates see p 109.

PAYE settlement agreements

(SI 2003/2682 Part 6)

These are voluntary agreements between the employer and HMRC under which the employer agrees to meet the tax payable on certain expenses and benefits in kind that are given to his employees. Once an agreement has been signed for a tax year, there is no need to:
- enter the items covered on form P9D or P11D;
- operate PAYE on them, or
- calculate a liability for included items which are liable for Class 1 or Class 1A NICs.

The employer pays Class 1B NICs on the items included in PAYE settlement agreements and on the total amount of tax payable. To be effective for a tax year, an agreement must be signed before 6 July following the end of the year and tax must be paid by 19 October following (or 22 October where paid electronically). They are most suited for payments and benefits provided on an irregular basis, or where benefits are for a group of employees and apportionment is difficult.

Personal service companies

(ITEPA 2003 ss 48–61)

These provisions affect 2000–01 and subsequent years. They are commonly known under the name 'IR35' and apply where personal services are provided to a client through an intermediary – normally the worker's personal service company. The effect of the legislation is to treat the worker as an employee of the client for working out the 'deemed employment payment'. The computation involves taking into account all payments and benefits, including those paid direct to the worker for a tax year other than by the intermediary for his services. Certain, restricted, allowable expenses, are deducted from 'earnings'. Finally, any payments or benefits received by the worker from the intermediary are deducted. Tax (under PAYE) and NIC is calculated and the amounts due are payable by the worker and his company. From 2013–14 the provisions are extended to office holders.

Managed service companies

(ITEPA 2003 ss 61A–61J)

Where an individual provides his services through a managed service company (as defined) all payments made to him by the company on or after 6 April 2007 are deemed to be employment income and PAYE and NIC have to be applied.

National minimum wage

Hourly rate

Age of worker	apprentice rate[3]	Under 18[1]	18–20[2]	21 or more
From 1.10.13	£2.68	£3.72	£5.03	£6.31
1.10.12–30.9.13	£2.65	£3.68	£4.98	£6.19
1.10.11–30.9.12	£2.60	£3.68	£4.98	£6.08
1.10.10–30.9.11	£2.50	£3.64	£4.92	£5.93
1.10.09–30.9.10	n/a	£3.57	£4.83	£5.80
1.10.08–30.9.09	n/a	£3.53	£4.77	£5.73
1.10.07–30.9.08	n/a	£3.40	£4.60	£5.52
1.10.06–30.9.07	n/a	£3.30	£4.45	£5.35
1.10.05–30.9.06	n/a	£3.00	£4.25	£5.05

[1] Applies to all workers under 18 who are no longer of compulsory school age.
[2] Applied to workers aged 18–21 before 1 October 2010. This rate also applied before that date to workers aged 22 or more, starting a new job with a new employer, doing accredited training.
[3] From 1 October 2010 the apprentice rate applies to apprentices aged under 19 and other apprentices in their first year of apprenticeship.

Basis of assessment

(ITEPA 2003 ss 14–41E)

	Services performed			
	Wholly in UK	Partly in UK	Partly abroad	Wholly abroad
Persons domiciled in UK				
Non-resident[2]	All	That part	None	None
Resident[2]	All	All[1]	All[1]	All[1]
Persons domiciled outside the UK				
UK employer				
Non-resident	All	That part	None	None
Meets requirement for 3-year period of non-residence[3]	All	That part	Remittances	Remittances
Resident	All	All[1]	All[1]	All[1]
Foreign employer				
Non-resident	All	That part	None	None
Meets requirement for 3-year period of non-residence	All	That part	Remittances	Remittances
Resident	All	That part	Remittances	Remittances

[1] Exemption for seafarers if at least half of qualifying period of over 364 days worked abroad (including 183 consecutive days). Deduction extended in April 2011 with retrospective effect to seafarers who are resident for tax purposes in a European Economic Area or European Union State, other than the United Kingdom. (ITEPA 2003 ss 378–385, HMRC Brief 10/2012).
[2] A statutory residence test is introduced from 6 April 2013 and ordinary residence is abolished from that date. Before 6 April 2013 resident but not ordinarily resident taxpayers were taxed broadly on all UK earnings and remittances for duties performed abroad.
[3] An employee meets the requirement for a 3-year period of non-residence for a tax year X if he has been non-resident for three consecutive tax years and year X is any of the three years immediately following that spell of non-residence.

Termination payments

(ITEPA 2003 ss 401–416)

The following lump sum payments are exempt from tax:
(a) Payments in connection with the cessation of employment on the death, injury or disability of the employee.
(b) Payments under tax-exempt pension schemes by way of compensation for loss of employment (or of earnings due to ill-health) or which can properly be regarded as a benefit earned by past service.
(c) Certain payments of terminal grants to members of the armed forces.
(d) Certain benefits under superannuation schemes for civil servants in Commonwealth overseas territories.
(e) Payments in respect of foreign service where the period of foreign service comprises:
  (i) 75% of the whole period of service; or
  (ii) the whole of the last 10 years of service; or
  (iii) where the period of service exceeded 20 years, one-half of that period, including any 10 of the last 20 years.
  Otherwise, a proportion of the payment is exempt, as follows:

$$\frac{\text{length of foreign service}}{\text{length of total service}} \times \text{amount otherwise chargeable}$$

(f)   The first £30,000 of genuine ex gratia payments (where there is no 'arrangement' by the employer to make the payment).

(g)   Statutory redundancy payments (included in computing £30,000 limit in (f) above).

Fixed rate expenses

For most classes of industry fixed rate allowances for the upkeep of tools and special clothing have been agreed between HMRC and the trade unions concerned. Alternatively, the individual employee may claim as a deduction his or her actual expenses (ITEPA 2003 s 367). (HMRC Employment Income Manual EIM32712.)

Industry	Occupation		Deduction from 2004–05 to 2007–08	Deduction from 2008–09
Agriculture	All workers[1]		70	100
Airlines	See note 5 below			
Aluminium	(a)	Continual casting operators, process operators, de-dimplers, driers, drill punchers, dross unloaders, firemen[2], furnace operators and their helpers, leaders, mouldmen, pourers, remelt department labourers, roll flatteners	130	140
	(b)	Cable hands, case makers, labourers, mates, truck drivers and measurers, storekeepers	60	80
	(c)	Apprentices	45	60
	(d)	All other workers[1]	100	120
Banks and building societies	Uniformed doormen and messengers (£40 before 2004–05)		45	60
Brass and copper	Braziers, coppersmiths, finishers, fitters, moulders, turners and all other workers		100	120
Building	(a)	Joiners and carpenters	105	140
	(b)	Cement works, roofing felt and asphalt labourers	55	80
	(c)	Labourers and navvies (£40 before 2004–05)	45	60
	(d)	All other workers	85	120
Building materials	(a)	Stone masons	85	120
	(b)	Tilemakers and labourers (£40 before 2004–05)	45	60
	(c)	All other workers	55	80
Clothing	(a)	Lacemakers, hosiery bleachers, dyers, scourers and knitters, knitwear bleachers and dyers	45	60
	(b)	All other workers	45	60
Constructional engineering[3]	(a)	Blacksmiths and their strikers, burners, caulkers, chippers, drillers, erectors, fitters, holders up, markers off, platers, riggers, riveters, rivet heaters, scaffolders, sheeters, template workers, turners, welders	115	140
	(b)	Banksmen, labourers, shop-helpers, slewers, straighteners	60	80
	(c)	Apprentices and storekeepers	45	60
	(d)	All other workers	75	100
Electrical and electricity supply	(a)	Those workers incurring laundry costs only	45	60
	(b)	All other workers	90	120
Engineering (trades ancillary to)	(a)	Pattern makers	120	140
	(b)	Labourers, supervisory and unskilled workers	60	80
	(c)	Apprentices and storekeepers	45	60
	(d)	Motor mechanics in garage repair shops	100	120
	(e)	All other workers	100	120
Fire service	Uniformed firefighters and fire officers		60	80
Food	All workers		45	60
Forestry	All workers		70	100
Glass	All workers		60	80
Healthcare staff in the NHS, private hospitals and nursing homes	(a)	Ambulance staff on active service	110	140
	(b)	Nurses and midwives, chiropodists, dental nurses, occupational, speech and other therapists, phlebotomists and radiographers	70	100
	(c)	Plaster room orderlies, hospital porters, ward clerks, sterile supply workers, hospital domestics, hospital catering staff	60	100
	(d)	Laboratory staff, pharmacists, pharmacy assistants	45	60
	(e)	Uniformed ancillary staff: maintenance workers, grounds staff, drivers, parking attendants and security guards, receptionists and other uniformed staff	45	60
Heating	(a)	Pipe fitters and plumbers	100	120
	(b)	Coverers, laggers, domestic glaziers, heating engineers and their mates	90	120
	(c)	All gas workers, all other workers	70	100
Iron mining	(a)	Fillers, miners and underground workers	100	120
	(b)	All other workers	75	100
Iron and steel	(a)	Day labourers, general labourers, stockmen, time keepers, warehouse staff and weighmen	60	80
	(b)	Apprentices	45	60
	(c)	All other workers	120	140

Industry	Occupation		Deduction from 2004–05 to 2007–08	Deduction from 2008–09
Leather	(a)	Curriers (wet workers), fellmongering workers, tanning operatives (wet)	55	80
	(b)	All other workers (£40 before 2004–05)	45	60
Particular engineering[4]	(a)	Pattern makers	120	140
	(b)	Chainmakers, cleaners, galvanisers, tinners and wire drawers in the wire drawing industry, tool-makers in the lock making industry	100	120
	(c)	Apprentices and storekeepers	45	60
	(d)	All other workers	60	80
Police force		Uniformed police officers (ranks up to and including Chief Inspector) (£110 for 2007–08 only) Community Support officers and other police service employees — see note 6 below	55	140
Precious metals		All workers	70	100
Printing	(a)	Letterpress section — electrical engineers (rotary presses), electro-typers, ink and roller makers, machine minders (rotary), maintenance engineers (rotary presses) and stereotypers	105	140
	(b)	Bench hands (periodical and bookbinding section), compositors (letterpress section), readers (letterpress section), telecommunications and electronic section wire room operators, warehousemen (paper box making section)	45	60
	(c)	All other workers	70	100
Prisons		Uniformed prison officers	55	80
Public service	(i)	Dock and inland waterways		
		(a) Dockers, dredger drivers, hopper steerers	55	80
		(b) All other workers (£40 before 2004–05)	45	60
	(ii)	Public transport		
		(a) Garage hands (including cleaners)	55	80
		(b) Conductors and drivers (£40 before 2004–05)	45	60
Quarrying		All workers	70	100
Railways		(See the appropriate category for craftsmen, eg engineers, vehicles etc.) All other workers	70	100
Seamen		Carpenters		
	(a)	Passenger liners	165	165
	(b)	Cargo vessels, tankers, coasters and ferries	130	140
Shipyards	(a)	Blacksmiths and their strikers, boilermakers, burners, carpenters, caulkers, drillers, furnacemen (platers), holders up, fitters, platers, plumbers, riveters, sheet iron workers, shipwrights, tubers, welders	115	140
	(b)	Labourers	60	80
	(c)	Apprentices and storekeepers	45	60
	(d)	All other workers	75	100
Textiles and textile printing	(a)	Carders, carding engineers, overlookers and technicians in spinning mills	85	120
	(b)	All other workers	60	80
Vehicles	(a)	Builders, railway vehicle repairers, and railway wagon lifters	105	140
	(b)	Railway vehicle painters and letterers, builders' and repairers' assistants	60	80
	(c)	All other workers	45	60
Wood & furniture	(a)	Carpenters, cabinet makers, joiners, wood carvers and woodcutting machinists	115	140
	(b)	Artificial limb makers (other than in wood), organ builders and packing case makers	90	120
	(c)	Coopers not providing own tools, labourers, polishers and upholsterers	45	60
	(d)	All other workers	75	100

[1] 'All workers' and 'all other workers' refer only to manual workers who have to bear the cost of upkeep of tools and special clothing. They do not extend to other employees such as office staff.

[2] 'Firemen' means persons engaged to light and maintain furnaces.

[3] 'Constructional engineering' means engineering undertaken on a construction site, including buildings, shipyards, bridges, roads and other similar operations.

[4] 'Particular engineering' means engineering undertaken on a commercial basis in a factory or workshop for the purposes of producing components such as wire, springs, nails and locks.

[5] With effect from 2006–07 a basic flat rate expenses allowance of £850 applies to all uniformed commercial pilots, co-pilots and other flight deck crew working in the UK (but not stewards/stewardesses). A further £100 allowance is allowed for the cost of travel to certain regular specified activities.

[6] From 2008–09 the allowance for police officers applies to community support officers. Other police service employees who must clean their own uniform can claim a deduction of £60 (£45 from 1998–99 to 2007–08).

Investment reliefs

Community investment tax relief

(ITA 2007 ss 333–382; CTA 2010 ss 218–269)

Investments made after 16 April 2002 by an individual or company in an accredited community development finance institution (CDFI) are eligible for tax relief up to 25%. The investment may be a loan or a subscription for shares or securities. Tax relief may be claimed for the tax year or accounting period in which the investment is made and each of the four subsequent years. Relief for each year is broadly the smaller of 5% of the invested amount, or the amount which reduces the investor's tax liability for the year to nil. From April 2013 any unused balance of the 5% annual relief can be carried forward, but not beyond the 5-year investment period, and only as long as some part of the investment remains within the CDFI. In addition, to comply with European State aid rules, from 1 April 2013 there is a limit on the amounts of relief a company can obtain in any 3-year period — the amount of CITR relief and any de minimis aid from other sources must not exceed €200,000.

Enterprise investment scheme

(ITA 2007 ss 156–257)

The EIS applies to investments in qualifying unquoted companies trading in the UK. Eligible shares must be held for at least three years from the issue date or commencement of trade if later (five years from the issue date for shares issued before 6 April 2000). The following reliefs apply subject to this and other conditions.

Relief on investment

Maximum investment:	From 2012–13	£1,000,000
	2008–09 to 2011–12	£500,000
	2006–07 to 2007–08	£400,000
Minimum investment:	From 2012–13	No minimum
	1993–94 to 2011–12	£500
Maximum carry-back to preceding year	From 2009–10	No restriction (subject to annual maximum)
(Up to $\frac{1}{2}$ amount invested between 6 April and 5 October)	2006–07 to 2008–09	£50,000
Rate of relief	From 2011–12	30%[1]
	1993–94 to 2010–11	20%[1]

[1] Given as a deduction against income tax liability.

Other reliefs (TCGA 1992 ss 150A–150C, Sch 5B)
- (a) A gain on a disposal of shares on which EIS relief has been given and not withdrawn is exempt from capital gains tax.
- (b) Deferral relief is available for gains on assets where the disposal proceeds are reinvested in eligible shares in a qualifying company within one year before and three years after the disposal.
- (c) A loss on a disposal of shares on which EIS relief has been given may be relieved against income tax or capital gains tax.

Seed enterprise investment scheme

(ITA 2007 ss 257A–257HG)

Between 6 April 2012 and 5 April 2017 SEIS applies to investments in companies with fewer than 25 employees and assets up to £200,000 carrying on or preparing to carry on new business. The following reliefs apply subject to this and other conditions.

Relief on investment

Maximum investment:	From 2012–13	£100,000
Maximum carry-back to preceding year	From 2013–14	No restriction (subject to annual maximum)[2]
Rate of relief	From 2012–13	50%[1]

[1] Given as a deduction against income tax liability.
[2] Carry back cannot therefore apply until 2013–14.

Other reliefs (TCGA 1992 ss 150E, 150G, Sch 5BB)
- (a) A gain on a disposal of shares on which SEIS relief has been given and not withdrawn is exempt from capital gains tax.
- (b) Reinvestment relief is available for certain gains on assets where the disposal proceeds are reinvested in SEIS (see p 41).

Venture capital trusts

(ITA 2007 ss 258–332)

An individual who subscribes for ordinary shares in a VCT obtains income tax reliefs at the rates in the table below subject to conditions. The shares must be held for at least five years (three years for shares issued before 6 April 2006 and five years for shares issued before 6 April 2000).

Relief on investment

Maximum annual investment:	**From 2004–05**	**£200,000**
	1995–96 to 2003–04	£100,000
Rate of relief:	**From 2006–07**	**30%**
	2004–05 to 2005–06	40%
	1995–96 to 2003–04	20%

Other reliefs

(a)   Dividends on shares within investment limit exempt from income tax (unless the investor's main purpose is tax avoidance – from 9 March 1999) (ITTOIA 2005 s 709).

(b)   Capital gains reliefs (see p 41).

Urban Regeneration Companies

Relief is available from 1 April 2003 for expenditure incurred by businesses in making contributions to designated Urban Regeneration Companies (ITTOIA 2005 ss 82, 86; CTA 2009 ss 82, 86).

Individual savings accounts ('ISAs')

(TA 1988 s 333; ITTOIA 2005 ss 694–701; SI 1998/1870; SI 2001/908)

Savers can subscribe to an ISA up to the following limits per tax year.

	1999–2000 to 2007–08	2008–09 to 2009–10*	2010–11	2011–12	2012–13	**2013–14**
Overall annual subscription limit	£7,000	£7,200	£10,200	£10,680	£11,280	**£11,520**
Cash limit	£3,000	£3,600	£5,100	£5,340	£5,640	**£5,760**

Before 2008–09 a limit of £4,000 (£3,000 before 2005–06) also applied to stocks and shares held in a mini-ISA. The subscription limit applies to each spouse or civil partner. Shares acquired under an approved share incentive plan, profit sharing scheme or SAYE option scheme may be transferred to a stocks and shares component of an ISA within 90 days without tax consequences. From 2008-09 PEPs are transferred into ISA accounts. For 2012–13 onwards the subscription limits are to be increased each year in line with the consumer prices index.

*For taxpayers aged 50 or over in 2009–10 the limits for 2010–11 apply for 2009–10 also, with effect from 6 October 2009.

Reliefs

(a)   Investments under the scheme are free from income tax and capital gains tax. When an investment is transferred to an investor he is deemed to have made a disposal and reacquisition at market value and any notional gain is exempt from capital gains tax.

(b)   Withdrawals may be made at any time without loss of tax relief.

Junior individual savings accounts (Junior ISAs)

(ITTOIA 2005 s 695A; SI 2011/1780)

A Junior ISA scheme was introduced from November 2011, available to all UK resident children under 18 who do not have a Child Trust Fund account. Children are able to have one cash and one stocks and shares Junior ISA at any time, with an overall annual contribution limit of £3,720 (£3,600 before 6 April 2013).

Personal equity plans ('PEPs')

(Subscriptions made **before 6 April 1999**: TA 1988 s 333; SI 1989/469; SI 1998/1869)

From 2008–09, all PEP accounts are transferred to ISA accounts.

Before 6 April 1999, subscriptions to PEPs could be made up to a maximum per year of £6,000 to a general plan and £3,000 to a single company plan. Dividend income is tax free and a 10% tax credit was payable until 5 April 2004 on dividends from UK equities. Interest on cash held is paid gross and is tax free if reinvested.

PEPs held at 5 April 1999 can continue to be held with the same tax advantages as an ISA (see above) and without affecting the amount that can be subscribed to an ISA.

National Savings Bank interest

(ITTOIA 2005 s 691; FA 2011 Sch 26)

Before 19 July 2011 the first £70 of any interest received from a National Savings Ordinary Account was tax free.

Miscellaneous reliefs

Employee shareholder status shares

The first £2,000 of the value of shares acquired through the adoption of the 'employee shareholder' employment status is not subject to income tax or national insurance. Applies from a date to be appointed, expected to be 1 September 2013. For the capital gains tax rules see p 41.

Foster carers and shared lives carers (Qualifying care)

(ITTOIA 2005 ss 803–828)

Generally, local authority payments to foster carers are not taxable to the extent they do no more than meet the actual costs of caring. In other cases, for 2003–04 onwards (and for shared lives carers from 6 April 2010):

- where gross receipts do not exceed the 'individual limit' and shared lives care is not being provided to more than three people, the carer is treated as having a nil profit and nil loss for the tax year concerned;
- where gross receipts exceed the 'individual limit' and shared lives care is not being provided to more than three people, the carer can choose to either be taxed on the excess or compute profit or loss using the normal business rules.

The 'individual limit' is made up of a fixed amount of £10,000 per residence for a full tax year plus an amount per adult or child for each week or part week that the individual provides qualifying care. The weekly amounts are £200 for a child under 11 years and £250 for a child of 11 or over and an adult.

For 2010–11 only, shared lives carers could choose to apply the simplified arrangements for adult placement carers.

Gift of pre-eminent objects

(FA 2012 Sch 14)

Individuals who gift pre-eminent objects to the nation will receive a reduction in their UK tax liability of 30% of the value of the object they are donating. The tax reduction can be against income or capital gains tax and can be spread forward across a period of up to five years starting with the tax year in which the object is offered. The legislation has effect in relation to liabilities for tax years and accounting periods beginning on or after 1 April 2012. The gift must be accepted as pre-eminent by the Arts Council under the Cultural Gifts Scheme.

Landlord's energy-saving allowance

(ITTOIA 2005 ss 312–314; CTA 2009 ss 251–253; SI 2007/831; SI 2007/3278; SI 2008/1520)

From 6 April 2004 to 5 April 2015 individual landlords who let residential property and pay income tax may claim a deduction from the property business profits for expenditure in the dwelling-houses let to install:

- loft insulation or cavity wall insulation; or
- (from 7 April 2005) solid wall insulation; or
- (from 6 April 2006) draught-proofing and insulation for hot water systems; or
- (from 6 April 2007) floor insulation.

Expenditure is restricted to £1,500 per building until 5 April 2007 and to £1,500 per dwelling-house from 6 April 2007.

The relief is extended to corporate landlords of residential property for expenditure on or after 8 July 2008.

Life assurance premium relief

(TA 1988 s 266, Sch 14 para 7; FA 2012 Sch 39)

For premiums due and payable **before 6 April 2015**, or payable before that date and actually paid before 6 July 2015, relief for premiums paid on qualifying life assurance policies for contracts made before 14 March 1984 is available by deduction of 12.5% from admissible premiums. Policies issued on or after 6 April 2013 will only be qualifying policies where the premiums payable for an individual into a policy or policies do not exceed £3,600 each year. Certain policies issued earlier may be affected.

Maintenance payments

(ITTOIA 2005 ss 727, 729; ITA 2007 ss 453–456)

Where either party to the marriage or civil partnership was born before 6 April 1935 tax relief may be claimed by the payer in respect of the lower of:

- the amount of the payments in the year concerned and
- the minimum amount of the married couple's allowance for the year concerned (see p 75).

The relief is restricted to 10% of the relevant amount. The payment must be made to the former/separated spouse or civil partner. It is made gross and is not taxable in the hands of the recipient.

Rent-a-room relief

(ITTOIA 2005 ss 784–802)

Gross annual receipts from letting furnished accommodation in the only or main home are exempt from tax up to a maximum of £4,250 (provided no other taxable income is derived from a trade, letting or arrangement from which the rent-a-room receipts are derived).

If the gross receipts exceed £4,250, the taxpayer can pay tax on the net receipts after deduction of expenses. Alternatively, the taxpayer can elect to pay tax on the amount by which the gross receipts exceed £4,250, without relief for the actual expenses.

An individual's maximum is halved to £2,125 if during the 'relevant period' for the year (normally the tax year) some other person received income from letting accommodation in that property.

An election can be made to disapply the relief for a particular tax year (for example, if the individual would otherwise make an allowable loss).

Capped income tax reliefs

From 2013–14 a limit on previously uncapped income tax reliefs is imposed. The limit is set at the greater of £50,000 or 25% of the individual's adjusted total income for the tax year. The specified reliefs which will be limited to the extent that they can be relieved by individuals against general income are:

> Trade loss relief against general income (ITA 2007 s 64)
> Early trade losses relief (ITA 2007 s 72)
> Post-cessation trade relief (ITA 2007 s 96)
> Property loss relief against general income (ITA 2007 s 120)
> Post-cessation property relief (ITA 2007 s 125)
> Employment loss relief against general income (ITA 2007 s 128)
> Former employees deduction for liabilities (ITEPA 2003 s 555)
> Share loss relief on non-Enterprise Investment Scheme / Seed Enterprise Investment Scheme shares (ITA 2007 Pt 4 Ch 6)
> Losses on deeply discounted securities (ITTOIA 2005 ss 446, 454)
> Qualifying loan interest (ITA 2007 Pt 8 Ch 1)

Pension provision from 6 April 2006

(FA 2004 ss 149–284, Schs 28–36)

From 6 April 2006, a new pension scheme tax regime fully replaced pre-existing rules for occupational pension schemes, personal (and stakeholder) pension schemes and retirement annuity schemes.

Tax relief on contributions

Individual contributions: Contributions to registered schemes are not limited by reference to a fraction of earnings and there is no earnings cap. There is no provision for the carry-back or carry-forward of contributions to tax years other than the year of payment.

An individual may make unlimited contributions and tax relief is available on contributions up to the higher of:

* the full amount of relevant earnings; or
* £3,600 provided the scheme operates tax relief at source.

Employer contributions: Employer contributions to registered schemes are deductible for tax purposes, with statutory provision for spreading abnormally large contributions over a period of up to four years. The contributions are not treated as taxable income of the employee, although from 6 April 2013 this relief does not extend to payments for the benefit of family members.

Special annual allowance charge: A special annual allowance charge applied for 2009–10 and 2010–11 for individuals with income of £130,000 or over. Tax relief above basic rate is recovered from pension savings above an individual's special annual allowance by the application of the special annual allowance charge. An individual's special annual allowance is the higher of their regular pension savings and £20,000 (or in certain circumstances, where contributions have been less regular than quarterly, £30,000).

Annual allowance

Each individual has an annual allowance as set out in the table below. If the annual increase in an individual's rights under all registered schemes exceeds the annual allowance, the excess is chargeable at the individual's marginal rate (40% for 2010–11 and earlier years). The individual is liable for the tax, unless, for 2011–12 onwards, he makes an election for the scheme to pay the charge if it exceeds £2,000. In such cases a consequential adjustment is made to the individual's entitlement to benefits.

Annual allowance	2008–09	2009–10	2010–11	2011–12	2012–13	**2013–14**
	£235,000	£245,000	£255,000	£50,000[1]	£50,000[1]	**£50,000[1]**

[1] From 2011–12 unused allowance can be carried forward three years. For these purposes the annual allowance for 2008–09 to 2010–11 is assumed to be £50,000.

[2] Allowance to be reduced to £40,000 from 2014–15.

Taxable benefits

'Tax-free' lump sum: The maximum 'tax-free' lump sum that can be paid to a member under a registered scheme is broadly the lower of:
- 25% of the value of the pension rights; and
- 25% of the member's lifetime allowance.

Lifetime allowance: Each individual has a lifetime allowance for contributions as set out in the table below. The excess over the lifetime allowance of the benefits crystallising (usually when a pension begins to be paid) is taxable at the following rates:
- 55% if taken as a lump sum;
- 25% in other cases.

Any tax due may be deducted from the individual's benefits.

Lifetime allow-ance	2008–09	2009–10	2010–11	2011–12	2012–13	**2013–14**
	£1,650,000	£1,750,000	£1,800,000	£1,800,000	£1,500,000	**£1,500,000**

[1] Allowance to be reduced to £1,250,000 from 2014–15.

Transitional. There are transitional provisions for the protection of lump sum and other pension rights accrued before 6 April 2006. A new form of protection is also available to protect pension rights from 6 April 2012 and from 6 April 2014 when the lifetime allowance is decreased.

Age restrictions

Minimum pension age: The minimum pension age is 55 (50 before 6 April 2010). A pension cannot be paid before the minimum age except on grounds of ill health. Those with existing contractual rights to draw a pension earlier will have those rights protected and there is special protection for members of pre-6 April 2006 approved schemes with early retirement ages. A reduced lifetime allowance will apply in the case of early retirement before minimum pension age except in the case of certain professions such as the police and the armed forces (to be prescribed by regulations).

Maximum benefit age: Before 2011–12 benefits must be taken by the age of 77 at the latest (age 75 before 22 June 2010). A member of a money purchase scheme may take a pension from the age of 77 (previously 75) by way of income withdrawal (known as an 'alternatively secured pension') instead of taking a scheme pension or purchasing a lifetime annuity. The maximum alternatively secured pension is 70% of a comparable annuity. These requirements are withdrawn for 2011–12 onwards.

Share schemes

Share incentive plans ('SIPs')

(TCGA 1992 ss 236A, 238A, Schs 7C, 7D Pt 1; ITEPA 2003 ss 488–515, Sch 2; FA 2003 s 139, Sch 21) Applications for approval of Share Incentive Plans could be made from 28 July 2000.

Free share plan

2000–01 onwards	annual maximum	£3,000

Partnership share plan

2000–01 to 2002–03	monthly maximum	£125 or 10% of monthly salary if lower
2003–04 onwards	annual maximum	£1,500 or 10% of annual salary if lower

Matching shares

2000–01 onwards	Maximum number of shares given by employer to employee for each partnership share bought	2

Shares are free of tax and NICs if held in the plan for five years. Dividends are tax free if reinvested in shares (restricted to a maximum of £1,500 per employee per tax year before 6 April 2013). Shares withdrawn from the plan at any time are exempt from capital gains tax and are treated as acquired by the employee at their market value at that time.

If shares are withdrawn within between three and five years (with exceptions such as on death, injury, disability, retirement, redundancy, or, from the date of Royal Assent to the Finance Bill 2013, certain cash takeovers), liability to income tax and NICs arises on the lower of their value on entering and on leaving the plan. If shares are withdrawn within three years (with similar exceptions), liability is on their value on leaving the plan.

Enterprise management incentives

(TCGA 1992 s 238A, Sch 7D Pt 4; ITEPA 2003 ss 527–541, Sch 5)

Certain independent trading companies with gross assets not exceeding £30 million may grant share options then worth up to £250,000 (£120,000 for options granted before 16 June 2012, £100,000 for options granted before 6 April 2008) to an eligible employee. The total value of shares in respect of which unexercised qualifying options exist must not exceed £3 million. An additional restriction, limiting the scheme to companies with fewer than 250 full-time equivalent employees, applies to options granted on or after 21 July 2008.

Where the conditions of the scheme are complied with:

(a) There is no charge to tax or NICs when the option is granted provided the option to acquire the shares is not at less than their market values at that date, and there is no charge on exercise providing the option is exercised within ten years.

(b) Capital gains tax will be payable when the shares are sold, though for disposals on or after 6 April 2013, shares acquired through exercising EMI options on or after 6 April 2012 are eligible for capital gains tax entrepreneurs' relief if certain conditions are met.

Approved save as you earn (SAYE) share option schemes

(TCGA 1992 s 238A, Sch 7D Pt 2; ITEPA 2003 ss 516–519, Sch 3; FA 2003 s 139, Sch 21)

The scheme is linked to an approved savings scheme, on which bonuses are exempt from tax, to provide funds for the acquisition of shares when the option is exercised at the end of a three or five-year contract. A five-year contract may offer the option of repayment on the seventh anniversary.

Monthly contributions to SAYE scheme

Minimum	£5–£10[1]
Maximum	£250

[1] The company may choose a minimum savings contribution between £5 and £10.

See the HMRC website (www.hmrc.gov.uk/shareschemes/saye-change-bonus.htm) for the bonus rates.

Where the conditions of the scheme are complied with, no income tax charge arises on the employee in respect of:

(a) the grant of an option to acquire shares at a discount of up to 20% of the share price at time of the grant;

(b) the exercise of the option (options must not be exercised before the bonus date subject to exceptions such as on injury, disability, redundancy, retirement, death or, from the date of Royal Assent to the Finance Bill 2013, certain cash takeovers); or

(c) any increase in the value of the shares.

Capital gains tax is chargeable on disposal of the shares: the CGT base cost is the consideration given by the employee for both the shares and the option.

Company share option plans ('CSOPs')

(TCGA 1992 s 238A, Sch 7D Pt 3; ITEPA 2003 ss 521–526, Sch 4; FA 2003 s 139, Sch 21)

Limit on value of shares under option held by employee at any one time

From 29 April 1996	£30,000

Scheme shares must be fully paid up, not redeemable and, for options granted before the date of Royal Assent to the Finance Bill 2013, not subject to special restrictions. Only full-time directors or qualifying employees may participate in the scheme.

Where the conditions of the scheme are complied with, no tax charge arises on the employee in respect of:

(a) the grant of an option to acquire shares[1];

(b) the exercise of the option[2]; or

(c) any increase in the value of the shares.

Capital gains tax is chargeable on disposal of the shares: the CGT base cost is the consideration given by the employee for both the shares and the option.

[1] At the time the option is granted the price at which shares can be acquired must not be less than the market value of shares of the same class at that time.

[2] The option must be exercised between three and ten years after the grant (or may be exercised less than three years after the grant where the individual ceases to be an employee due to injury, disability, redundancy or retirement, or, from the date of Royal Assent to the Finance Bill 2013, where there are certain cash takeovers of constituent companies). For options granted before 9 April 2003, the options must be exercised between three and ten years after the grant (without exception) and not less than three years after a previous exempt exercise of another option under the same or another approved company share option scheme.

Tax credits

From 6 April 2003, child tax credit and working tax credit replaced children's tax credit, working families' tax credit and disabled person's tax credit in addition to the child-related elements of certain social security benefits. Administered and paid by HMRC, they are non-taxable. Claims must be made after the commencement of the tax year and can be backdated for a maximum of one month (three months before 6 April 2012). Universal credit will replace tax credits. New claimants will start to claim universal credit from October 2013. Existing claimants will be gradually phased onto universal credit from April 2014, and this is expected to be completed by December 2017.

Child tax credit and working tax credit

	2012–13 Annual amount	2013–14 Annual amount
Child tax credit	£	£
Family element[1]	545	545
Child element (for each child or young person)	2,690	2,720
Addition for disabled child or young person	2,950	3,015
Enhancement for severe disabled child or young person	1,190	1,220
Working tax credit	£	£
Basic element	1,920	1,920
Lone parent and couple element	1,950	1,970
30-hour element	790	790
Disability element	2,790	2,855
Severe disability element	1,190	1,220
Childcare element – up to 70% (80% for 2006–07 to 2010–11) of eligible costs	**Weekly**	**Weekly**
– maximum eligible cost for one child	175	175
– maximum eligible cost for two or more children	300	300

[1] Only one family element per family. Before 2011–12, baby element payable in addition in the first year of the child's life.

Income thresholds and withdrawal rates	2012–13	2013–14
Income threshold for those entitled to CTC and WTC	£6,420	£6,420
Withdrawal rate	41%	41%
Income threshold for those entitled to CTC only	£15,860	£15,910
Income rise disregard	£10,000	£5,000
Income fall disregard	£2,500	£2,500

Calculation of award. Tax credits are awarded on an annual basis. They are initially based on the income of the claimant or joint claimants for the preceding tax year and then adjusted based on actual income in the tax year in which the credit is claimed. Income broadly includes all taxable income excluding the first £300 of income from pensions, savings, property or foreign assets. If current year's income is greater than the previous year's income by less than £5,000 (£10,000 for 2012–13 and 2011–12, £25,000 before 2011–12), the award is not adjusted. If current year's income is greater than the previous year's income by £5,000 or more (£10,000 for 2012–13 and 2011–12, £25,000 from 2006–07 to 2010–11), the award is adjusted to reflect current year's income less £5,000. An income fall disregard of £2,500 is introduced from 6 April 2012. This means that from 2012–13, where previous year's income exceeds the current year's income by not more than £2,500, the previous year's income will be used, but where the previous year's income exceeds the current year's income by more than £2,500, the current year's income plus £2,500 will be used. In any other case current year's income is used. Where circumstances change during a tax year and different rates apply, the award is recalculated on a proportional, daily basis. Such changes must be notified to HMRC within one month if tax credit entitlement will be reduced as a result. Before April 2007, this time limit was three months.

Eligibility. CTC is payable to UK resident single parents and couples responsible for a child or young person. WTC is payable to UK residents who are at least 16 years old and, in the case of single persons, who work at least 16 hours a week. In the case of a couple, from 6 April 2012, they must jointly work at least 24 hours a week and one must work at least 16 hours a week, or where only one of the couple works that person must work for at least 24 hours a week. Additionally, the claimant (or one of them if a couple) must either:
- be at least 25 years old and work at least 30 hours a week; or
- have a dependent child or children; or
- before 6 April 2012, be over 50 and qualify for the 50+ element; or
- have a mental or physical disability which puts them at a disadvantage in getting a job and have previously been in receipt of some form of disability benefit; or

- from 6 April 2011, be over 60 and work at least 16 hours a week, regardless of whether they have dependent children.

Renewal claim. Claims for tax credit must be renewed by 31 July.

Inheritance tax

Rates of tax

(IHTA 1984 s 7, Schs 1, 1A; HMRC Inheritance Tax Manual IHTM14544)

From 15 March 1988 onwards

Cumulative gross transfer rate:	Rate
for gross transfers on death over the cumulative chargeable transfer limit	40%
reduced rate for estates leaving 10% or more to charity for deaths on or after 6 April 2012	36%[1]
for gross lifetime transfers over the cumulative chargeable transfer limit	20%
Grossing-up net transfer rate for each £1 over the chargeable transfer limit:	
for net transfers on death not bearing own tax	2/3
for net lifetime transfers	1/4

[1] For deaths occurring on or after 6 April 2012 a reduced rate of 36% is introduced where at least 10% of the net estate is left to charity.

Cumulative chargeable transfer limits

Period	Limit	Period	Limit
	£		£
2013–14	325,000[1]	2000–01	234,000
2012–13	325,000	1999–2000	231,000
2011–12	325,000	1998–99	223,000
2010–11	325,000	1997–98	215,000
2009–10	325,000	1996–97	200,000
2008–09	312,000	1995–96	154,000
2007–08	300,000	10.3.92–5.4.95	150,000
2006–07	285,000	6.4.91–9.3.92	140,000
2005–06	275,000	1990–91	128,000
2004–05	263,000	1989–90	118,000
2003–04	255,000	15.3.88–5.4.89	110,000
2002–03	250,000	17.3.87–14.3.88	90,000
2001–02	242,000	18.3.86–16.3.87	71,000

[1] Any nil-rate band which is unused on a person's death can be transferred to their surviving spouse or civil partner for the purposes of the charge to tax on the death of the survivor on or after 9 October 2007.

[2] It is proposed to freeze the nil rate band at £325,000 until 2017–18.

Capital transfer tax nil rate bands

Period	Limit	Period	Limit
	£		£
6.4.85–17.3.86	67,000	26.3.80–8.3.82	50,000
13.3.84–5.4.85	64,000	27.10.77–25.3.80	25,000
15.3.83–12.3.84	60,000	13.3.75–26.10.77	15,000
9.3.82–14.3.83	55,000		

Estate duty nil rate bands (England, Scotland and Wales)

Period	Limit	Period	Limit
	£		£
22.3.72–12.3.75	15,000	9.4.62–3.4.63	4,000
31.3.71–21.3.72	12,500	30.7.54–8.4.62	3,000
16.4.69–30.3.71	10,000	10.4.46–29.7.54	2,000
4.4.63–15.4.69	5,000	16.8.14–9.4.46	100

Delivery of accounts: due dates

(IHTA 1984 s 216)

Type of transfer	Due date
Chargeable lifetime transfers	Later of: (a) 12 months after the end of the month in which the transfer took place; and (b) three months after the date on which the person delivering the account became liable
PETs which become chargeable	12 months after the end of the month in which the transferor died
Gifts with reservation chargeable on death	12 months after the end of the month in which the death occurred
Transfers on death	Later of: (a) 12 months after the end of the month in which the death occurred; and (b) three months after the date on which the personal representatives first act or the person liable first has reason to believe that he is liable to deliver an account
National heritage property	Six months after the end of the month in which the chargeable event occurred

Delivery of accounts: excepted transfers and estates

(SI 2004/2543; SI 2008/606)

Date of transfer or death	6 April 2000–5 April 2002	6 April 2002–5 April 2003	6 April 2003–31 Aug 2006	From 1 Sept 2006
Excepted transfers:	*Value below*	*Value below*	*Value below*	*Value below*
Total chargeable transfers since 6 April	£10,000	£10,000	£10,000	£10,000
Total chargeable transfers during last ten years	£40,000	£40,000	£40,000	£40,000
Excepted estates:				
Total gross value[1]	£210,000	£220,000	(see (a) below)	(see (a) below)
Total gross value of property outside UK	£50,000	£75,000	£75,000	£100,000
Aggregate value of 'specified transfers'[2]	£75,000	£100,000	£100,000	£150,000
Settled property passing on death	–	£100,000	£100,000	£150,000

For chargeable transfers after 5 April 2007, no account need be delivered where:

(i) the transfer is of cash or quoted shares or securities and the value of the transfer and other chargeable transfers made in the preceding seven years does not exceed the IHT threshold; or

(ii) the value of the transfer and other chargeable transfers made in the preceding seven years does not exceed 80% of the IHT threshold and the value of the transfer does not exceed the net amount of the threshold available to the transferor at the time of the transfer.

For footnotes see the list below.

Excepted estates

For deaths occurring after 5 April 2004, no account need be delivered where the deceased died domiciled in the UK provided either conditions (a) or (b) below are met, and both conditions (c) and (d) below are met.

<ol type="a">
<li>the aggregate of the gross value of the estate, and of any 'specified transfers'[2] or 'specified exempt transfers'[3] does not exceed the appropriate IHT threshold[4];</li>
<li>the aggregate of the gross value of the estate, and of any 'specified transfers'[2] or 'specified exempt transfers'[3] does not exceed £1,000,000; for deaths after 28 February 2011 at least part of the estate passes to the person's spouse, civil partner or to a charity; and after deducting from that aggregate figure any exempt spouse, civil partner and charity transfers and total estate liabilities, it does not exceed the appropriate IHT threshold[4];</li>
<li>the gross value of settled property or foreign assets do not exceed the limits in the above table; and</li>
<li>there were no chargeable lifetime transfers in the seven years before death other than specified transfers not exceeding the limits in the above table[5].</li>
</ol>

For deaths occurring after 31 August 2006 and before 6 April 2011, an estate will not be an excepted estate if the provisions for alternatively secured pension funds in IHTA 1984 ss 151A–151C (now repealed) apply by reason of the individual's death.

For deaths after 5 April 2002 and before 6 April 2004, no account need be delivered where the deceased died domiciled in the UK provided that:

<ol type="i">
<li>the aggregate of the gross value of the estate, and of any 'specified transfers' does not exceed the limits in the above table; and</li>
<li>the gross value of settled property or foreign assets do not exceed the limits in the above table; and</li>
<li>there were no chargeable lifetime transfers in the seven years before death other than specified transfers not exceeding the limits in the above table.</li>
</ol>

Where the deceased was never domiciled in the UK, no account need be delivered for deaths after 5 April 2002 provided that:

- the value of the estate in the UK is wholly attributable to cash and quoted shares and securities not exceeding £150,000 (£100,000 before 1 September 2006); and
- for deaths occurring after 31 August 2006 and before 6 April 2011, the provisions for alternatively secured pension funds in IHTA 1984 ss 151A–151C (now repealed) do not apply by reason of the individual's death.

[1] See table above — This limit applies to the aggregate gross value of the estate and of 'specified transfers' and 'specified exempt transfers'. For deaths after 28 February 2011 transfers treated as normal expenditure out of income made within 7 years before death and totalling more than £3,000 in any tax year will be treated as chargeable transfers for these purposes.

[2] 'Specified transfers' are chargeable transfers of cash, quoted shares and securities and, after 6 April 2002, interests in or over land and, after 5 April 2004, personal chattels or corporeal moveable property. For deaths after 28 February 2011 transfers treated as normal expenditure out of income made within 7 years before death and totalling more than £3,000 in any tax year will be treated as chargeable transfers for these purposes.

[3] 'Specified exempt transfers' are transfers in the seven years before death between spouses or civil partners, gifts to charity, political parties or housing associations, transfers to maintenance funds for historical buildings, etc or to employee trusts.

[4] For deaths after 5 April 2010 the IHT threshold for these purposes is increased by 100% where—
<ol type="a">
<li>the deceased is a surviving spouse or civil partner;</li>
<li>a claim has been made for the transfer of the unused nil-rate band of their deceased spouse or civil partner;</li>
<li>all of the first deceased spouse's or civil partner's nil-rate band was unused; and</li>
<li>the first deceased met certain other criteria similar to those listed above for excepted estates.</li>
</ol>

[5] For deaths after 28 February 2011 transfers treated as normal expenditure out of income made within 7 years before death and totalling more than £3,000 in any tax year will be treated as chargeable transfers for these purposes.

Excepted settlements

No account need be delivered of property comprised in an excepted settlement (i.e. one with no qualifying interest in possession) where a chargeable event occurs after 5 April 2007 and cash not exceeding £1,000 is the only property comprised in the settlement. Other conditions to be fulfilled are that, the settlor has not provided further property, the trustees are UK resident throughout the settlement's existence and there are no related settlements.

Reliefs

The following is a summary of the main reliefs and exemptions under the Inheritance Tax Act 1984 (Parts II and V). The legislation should be referred to for conditions and exceptions.

Agricultural property

Transfer with vacant possession (or right to obtain it within 12 months); transfer on or after 1 September 1995, of land let (or treated as let) on or after that date.	100% of agricultural value
Any other case.	50% of agricultural value

Note: The 100% relief is extended in limited circumstances by Concession F17.

Annual gifts £3,000

Business property

Unincorporated business.	100%		
Unquoted shares (including shares in AIM or USM companies) (held for 2 years or more).[1]	100%	Controlling holding in fully quoted companies.	50%
Unquoted securities which alone, or together with other such securities and unquoted shares, give the transferor control of the company (held for 2 years or more).[1]	100%	Land, buildings, machinery or plant used in business of company or partnership.	50%
Settled property used in life tenant's business.	100%		

[1] Tax charges arising and transfers occurring after 5 April 1996. 10 March 1992–5 April 1996 minority holding of shares or securities of up to 25% in unquoted or USM company qualified for 50% relief; larger holdings qualified for 100% relief.

Charities, gifts to Exempt

From 1 April 2002, Community Amateur Sports Clubs are treated as charities.

Marriage gifts

Made by:	parent	£5,000
	remoter ancestor	£2,500
	party to marriage	£2,500
	other person	£1,000

National purposes

Property given or bequeathed to bodies listed in IHTA 1984 Sch 3. Exempt

Political parties, gifts to Exempt

Potentially exempt transfers

Exempt if made 7 or more years before the date of death. Except for gifts with reservation etc, they include:
- (a) transfers by individuals to other individuals or certain trusts for the disabled;
- (b) transfers after 21 March 2006 by individuals to a bereaved minor's trust on the coming to an end of an immediate post-death interest;
- (c) transfers before 22 March 2006 by individuals to accumulation and maintenance trusts;
- (d) transfers by individuals into interest in possession trusts in which, for transfers after 21 March 2006, the beneficiary has a disabled person's interest; and
- (e) certain transfers on the termination or disposal of an individual's beneficial interest in possession in settled property (in restricted circumstances following FA 2006).

Quick succession relief

Estate increased by chargeable transfer followed by death within 5 years.

Death within 1st year.	100%
Each additional year: decreased by	20%
Small gifts to same person	£250

Spouses/civil partners with separate domicile (one not being in the UK)

Total exemption.	£325,000[1]

Tapering relief

The value of the estate on death is taxed as the top slice of cumulative transfers in the 7 years before death. Transfers on or within 7 years of death are taxed on their value at the date of the gift on the death rate scale, but using the scale in force at the date of death, subject to the following taper:

Years between gift and death	Percentage of full charge at death rates
0–3	100
3–4	80
4–5	60
5–6	40
6–7	20

For transfers of value before 6 April 2013 the total exemption was £55,000. From 6 April 2013 the limit is increased to the level of the prevailing IHT nil-rate band. For transfers of value made on or after 6 April 2013 individuals who are domiciled outside the UK and who have a UK-domiciled spouse or civil partner may elect to be treated as domiciled in the UK for the purposes of IHT.

Penalties see p 12.

National insurance contributions

From 6 April 2013

Class 1 contributions[1]				
Earnings limits and threshold		Weekly £	Monthly £	Yearly £
Lower earnings limit		109	473	5,668
Secondary threshold[3]		148	641	7,696
Primary threshold[3]		149	646	7,755
Upper earnings limit		797	3,454	41,450
Upper accruals point		770	3,337	40,040
		Not contracted out	**Contracted out** *Salary-related schemes[5]*	
Employees' contributions				
Weekly earnings:	Over £149.01–770	12%	10.6%	
	£770.01–£797	12%	12%	
	Over £797	2%	2%	
	– rebate £109–£149		1.4%[2, 5]	
Employers' contributions[4]				
Weekly earnings:	£148.01–£770	13.8%	10.4%	
	Over £770	13.8%	13.8%	
	– rebate £109–£148		3.4%[2, 5]	
Women at reduced rate				
Employees' contributions				
Weekly earnings:	£149.01–£797	5.85%		
	Over £797	2%		
Employers' contributions	Normal employers' contributions apply as above			
Class 1A and Class 1B contributions				13.8%

[1] Employees' rates are nil for children under 16 and those over state pensionable age but employers' contributions are still payable. Employees' NICs are not payable on earnings up to the primary threshold, employers' NICs are not payable on earnings up to the secondary threshold.

[2] The rebate is given on earnings between the lower earnings limit and the primary threshold for employees, and between the lower earnings limit and the secondary threshold for employers. The rebate for employees is given to employers to the extent that insufficient contributions have been paid by the employee for offset.

[3] From 6 April 2011 the primary threshold applies for employees' contributions and the secondary threshold applies for employers' contributions.

[4] An employer NIC 'holiday' applies to new businesses started in certain regions between 22 June 2010 and 5 September 2013. Between 6 September 2010 and 5 September 2013 the businesses may qualify for a deduction of up to £5,000 of their employer Class 1 contributions for each of the first ten employees hired in the first year of business.

[5] For 2012 to 2017 the rebates for defined benefit schemes (salary-related schemes) are 3.4% for employers and 1.4% for employees. Contracting out on a defined contribution basis (money purchase schemes) is abolished from 6 April 2012. Contracting out via a personal pension plan is also not possible from 6 April 2012.

From 6 April 2012–5 April 2013

Class 1 contributions[1]				
Earnings limits and threshold		Weekly £	Monthly £	Yearly £
Lower earnings limit		107	464	5,564
Secondary threshold[3]		144	624	7,488
Primary threshold[3]		146	634	7,605
Upper earnings limit		817	3,540	42,475
Upper accruals point		770	3,337	40,040
		Not contracted out	**Contracted out** *Salary-related schemes[5]*	
Employees' contributions				
Weekly earnings:	Over £146.01–770	12%	10.6%	
	£770.01–£817	12%	12%	
	Over £817	2%	2%	
	– rebate £107–£146		1.4%[2, 5]	
Employers' contributions[4]				
Weekly earnings:	£144.01–£770	13.8%	10.4%	
	Over £770	13.8%	13.8%	
	– rebate £107–£144		3.4%[2, 5]	
Women at reduced rate				
Employees' contributions				
Weekly earnings:	£146.01–£817	5.85%		
	Over £817	2%		
Employers' contributions	Normal employers' contributions apply as above			
Class 1A and Class 1B contributions			13.8%	

[1] Employees' rates are nil for children under 16 and those over state pensionable age but employers' contributions are still payable. Employees' NICs are not payable on earnings up to the primary threshold, employers' NICs are not payable on earnings up to the secondary threshold.

[2] The rebate is given on earnings between the lower earnings limit and the primary threshold for employees, and between the lower earnings limit and the secondary threshold for employers. The rebate for employees is given to employers to the extent that insufficient contributions have been paid by the employee for offset.

[3] From 6 April 2011 the primary threshold applies for employees' contributions and the secondary threshold applies for employers' contributions.

[4] An employer NIC 'holiday' applies to new businesses started in certain regions between 22 June 2010 and 5 September 2013. Between 6 September 2010 and 5 September 2013 the businesses may qualify for a deduction of up to £5,000 of their employer Class 1 contributions for each of the first ten employees hired in the first year of business.

[5] For 2012 to 2017 the rebates for defined benefit schemes (salary-related schemes) are reduced to 3.4% for employers and 1.4% for employees. Contracting out on a defined contribution basis (money purchase schemes) is abolished from 6 April 2012. Contracting out via a personal pension plan is also not possible from 6 April 2012.

From 6 April 2011–5 April 2012

Class 1 contributions[1]				
Earnings limits and threshold		Weekly £	Monthly £	Yearly £
Lower earnings limit		102	442	5,304
Secondary threshold[3]		136	589	7,072
Primary threshold[3]		139	602	7,225
Upper earnings limit		817	3,540	42,475
Upper accruals point		770	3,337	40,040
		Not contracted out	**Contracted out**	
Employees' contributions				
Weekly earnings:	Over £139.01–770	12%	10.4%	
	£770.01–£817	12%	12%	
	Over £817	2%	2%	
	– rebate £102–£139		1.6%[2]	
Employers' contributions[4]			*Salary-related schemes*	*Money purchase schemes*
Weekly earnings:	£136.01–£770	13.8%	10.1%	12.4%
	Over £770	13.8%	13.8%	13.8%
	– rebate £102–£136		3.7%[2]	1.4%[2]
Women at reduced rate				
Employees' contributions				
Weekly earnings:	£139.01–£817	5.85%		
	Over £817	2%		
Employers' contributions	Normal employers' contributions apply as above			
Class 1A and Class 1B contributions			13.8%	

[1] Employees' rates are nil for children under 16 and those over state pensionable age but employers' contributions are still payable. Employees' NICs are not payable on earnings up to the primary threshold, employers' NICs are not payable on earnings up to the secondary threshold.

[2] The rebate is given on earnings between the lower earnings limit and the primary threshold for employees, and between the lower earnings limit and the secondary threshold for employers. The rebate for employees is given to employers to the extent that insufficient contributions have been paid by the employee for offset.

[3] From 6 April 2011 the primary threshold applies for employees' contributions and the secondary threshold applies for employers' contributions.

[4] An employer NIC 'holiday' applies to new businesses started in certain regions between 22 June 2010 and 5 September 2013. Between 6 September 2010 and 5 September 2013 the businesses may qualify for a deduction of up to £5,000 of their employer Class 1 contributions for each of the first ten employees hired in the first year of business.

From 6 April 2010–5 April 2011

Class 1 contributions[1]				
Earnings limits and threshold		Weekly £	Monthly £	Yearly £
Lower earnings limit		97	421	5,044
Earnings threshold		110	476	5,715
Upper earnings limit		844	3,656	43,875
Upper accruals point		770	3,337	40,040
Not contracted out		**Employees' contributions**		**Employers' contributions**
Weekly earnings:	£110.01–£844	11%		12.8%
	Over £844	1%		12.8%
Contracted out			*Salary-related schemes*	*Money purchase schemes*
Weekly earnings:	£110.01–£770	9.4%	9.1%	11.4%
	£770–£844	11%	12.8%	12.8%
	Over £844	1%	12.8%	12.8%
	– rebate £97–£110	1.6%[2]	3.7%	1.4%
Women at reduced rate				
Weekly earnings:	£110.01–£844	4.85%	*as above*	
	Over £844	1%	*as above*	
Class 1A and Class 1B contributions				12.8%

[1] Employees' rates are nil for children under 16 and those over state pensionable age but employers' contributions are still payable. NICs are not payable on earnings up to the earnings threshold.

[2] The rebate is given on earnings between the lower earnings limit and the earnings threshold. The rebate for employees is given to employers to the extent that insufficient contributions have been paid by the employee for offset.

6 April 2009–5 April 2010

Class 1 contributions[1]				
Earnings limits and threshold		Weekly £	Monthly £	Yearly £
Lower earnings limit		95	412	4,940
Earnings threshold		110	476	5,715
Upper earnings limit		844	3,656	43,875
Upper accruals point		770	3,337	40,040
Not contracted out		**Employees' contributions**		**Employers' contributions**
Weekly earnings:	£110.01–£844	11%		12.8%
	Over £844	1%		12.8%
Contracted out			*Salary-related schemes*	*Money purchase schemes*
Weekly earnings:	£110.01–£770	9.4%	9.1%	11.4%
	£770–£844	11%	12.8%	12.8%
	Over £844	1%	12.8%	12.8%
	– rebate £95–£110	1.6%[2]	3.7%	1.4%
Women at reduced rate				
Weekly earnings:	£110.01–£844	4.85%	*as above*	
	Over £844	1%	*as above*	
Class 1A and Class 1B contributions				12.8%

[1] Employees' rates are nil for children under 16, men over 65 and women over 60 but employers' contributions are still payable. NICs are not payable on earnings up to the earnings threshold.

[2] The rebate is given on earnings between the lower earnings limit and the earnings threshold. The rebate for employees is given to employers to the extent that insufficient contributions have been paid by the employee for offset.

6 April 2008–5 April 2009

Class 1 contributions[1]				
Earnings limits and threshold		Weekly £	Monthly £	Yearly £
Lower earnings limit		90	390	4,680
Earnings threshold		105	453	5,435
Upper earnings limit		770	3,337	40,040
Not contracted out		**Employees' contributions**		**Employers' contributions**
Weekly earnings:	£105.01–£770	11%		12.8%
	Over £770	1%		12.8%
Contracted out			*Salary-related schemes*	*Money purchase schemes*
Weekly earnings:	£105.01–£770	9.4%	9.1%	11.4%
	Over £770	1%	12.8%	12.8%
	– rebate £90–£105	1.6%[2]	3.7%	1.4%
Women at reduced rate				
Weekly earnings:	£105.01–£770	4.85%	*as above*	
	Over £770	1%	*as above*	
Class 1A and Class 1B contributions				12.8%

[1] Employees' rates are nil for children under 16, men over 65 and women over 60 but employers' contributions are still payable. NICs are not payable on earnings up to the earnings threshold.

[2] The rebate is given on earnings between the lower earnings limit and the earnings threshold. The rebate for employees is given to employers to the extent that insufficient contributions have been paid by the employee for offset.

Class 2, 3 and 4 contributions

	2013–14	2012–13	2011–12
Class 2 (self-employed)			
Flat rate—per week	£2.70	£2.65	£2.50
Share fishermen—per week	£3.35	£3.30	£3.15
Volunteer development workers—per week	£5.45	£5.35	£5.10
Small earning exception—per year	£5,725	£5,595	£5,315
Class 3 (voluntary contributions)			
Flat rate—per week	£13.55	£13.25	£12.60
Class 4 (self-employed)[1]			
Lower annual profits limit	£7,755	£7,605	£7,225
Upper annual profits limit	£41,450	£42,475	£42,475
Rate between lower and upper limits	9%	9%	9%
Rate on profits above upper limit	2%	2%	2%
Maximum contributions			
Class 1 or Class 1/Class 2[2]	£4,121.28	£4,267.56	£4,312.08
– plus rate on earnings above upper limit	2%	2%	2%
Class 4 limiting amount[3]	£3,175.65	£3,278.75	£3,305.00
– plus rate on profits above upper limit	2%	2%	2%

[1] Not payable if pensionable age is reached by the beginning of the tax year.
[2] Where an earner has more than one employment (including self-employment), liability for Class 1 or Class 1 and Class 2 contributions cannot exceed a maximum amount equal to 53 employees' Class 1 contributions at the maximum standard rate, plus, from 2003–04 onwards, 2% (1% before 2011–12) on earnings over the individual's upper earnings limit (which varies depending on individual circumstances).
[3] Where Class 4 contributions are payable in addition to Class 1 and/or Class 2 contributions, liability for Class 4 contributions cannot exceed such an amount as, when added to the Class 1/Class 2 contributions payable (after applying the maximum if appropriate), equals the limiting amount. The limiting amount is the maximum Class 4 contributions payable (including, from 2003–04 onwards, 2% (1% before 2011–12) on earnings over the upper profit limit) plus 53 Class 2 contributions. If a contributor expects to exceed this amount he may apply for deferment of Class 4 contributions for the year in question. Deferment has no effect on the 2% (1% before 2011–12) payable on earnings over the upper profit limit, which is still payable.

	2010–11	2009–10	2008–09
Class 2 (self-employed)			
Flat rate—per week	£2.40	£2.40	£2.30
Share fishermen—per week	£3.05	£3.05	£2.95
Volunteer development workers—per week	£4.85	£4.75	£4.50
Small earning exception—per year	£5,075	£5,075	£4,825
Class 3 (voluntary contributions)			
Flat rate—per week	£12.05	£12.05	£8.10
Class 4 (self-employed)[1]			
Lower annual profits limit	£5,715	£5,715	£5,435
Upper annual profits limit	£43,875	£43,875	£40,040
Rate between lower and upper limits	8%	8%	8%
Rate on profits above upper limit	1%	1%	1%
Maximum contributions			
Class 1 or Class 1/Class 2[2]	£4,279.22	£4,279.22	£3,876.95
– plus rate on earnings above upper limit	1%	1%	1%
Class 4 limiting amount[3]	£3,180.00	£3,180.00	£2,890.30
– plus rate on profits above upper limit	1%	1%	1%

[1] Not payable if pensionable age is reached by the beginning of the tax year.
[2] Where an earner has more than one employment (including self-employment), liability for Class 1 or Class 1 and Class 2 contributions cannot exceed a maximum amount equal to 53 employees' Class 1 contributions at the maximum standard rate, plus, from 2003–04 onwards, 1% on earnings over the individual's upper earnings limit (which varies depending on individual circumstances).
[3] Where Class 4 contributions are payable in addition to Class 1 and/or Class 2 contributions, liability for Class 4 contributions cannot exceed such an amount as, when added to the Class 1/Class 2 contributions payable (after applying the maximum if appropriate), equals the limiting amount. The limiting amount is the maximum Class 4 contributions payable (including, from 2003–04 onwards, 1% on earnings over the upper profit limit) plus 53 Class 2 contributions. If a contributor expects to exceed this amount he may apply for deferment of Class 4 contributions for the year in question. Deferment has no effect on the 1% payable on earnings over the upper profit limit, which is still payable.

Employers' contributions: benefits in kind

Class 1A national insurance contributions are payable by employers on most taxable benefits in kind, excluding benefits:

(1) which are covered by a dispensation;
(2) included in a PAYE settlement agreement;
(3) provided to employees not earning more than £8,500 pa (including benefits in kind and expenses payments);
(4) otherwise not required to be included on a P11D;
(5) on which Class 1 national insurance contributions were due.

Class 1B contributions are payable by employers by reference to the value of any items included in a PAYE settlement agreement (PSA) which would otherwise be earnings for Class 1 or Class 1A, including the amount of tax paid. Income tax and Class 1B contributions on a PSA are payable by 19 October after the end of the tax year to which the PSA relates (or 22 October if paid electronically).

Common benefits subject to Class 1 and Class 1A NICs (CWG5 2012)

Benefit		NICs Class	PAYE or P11D
Assets transferred to employees but not readily convertible assets		1A	P11D
Assets placed at employee's disposal for mixed business and private use		1A	P11D
Car fuel supplied for private motoring in company car		1A	P11D
Car/van fuel supplied for private motoring in privately owned car	– supplied using company credit card, garage account, agency card or employer's own fuel pump	1A	P11D
	– any other circumstances	1	P11D
Cars available for private use		1A	P11D
Car parking facilities other than at or near place of work or as part of business travel		1A	P11D
Car parking fees paid for or reimbursed to employee other than at or near place of work or as part of business travel		1	P11D
Childcare where employer contracts with provider and either the value exceeds the permitted maximum or the qualifying conditions are not met		1A	P11D
Childcare where employee reimbursed or additional salary provided to meet cost		1	PAYE
Christmas boxes	– cash	1	PAYE
	– goods	1A	P11D
Clothing and uniforms			
cash payment to employee for clothing that can be worn at any time		1	PAYE or P11D[1]
– clothing provided by employer that can be worn at any time		1A	P11D
Council tax, unless employee provided with living accommodation which is not a benefit		1	P11D
Credit and charge cards – personal expenses on employer's card		1	P11D
Entertaining staff — expenses/ allowances	– employer contract with provider	1A	P11D
	– employee contract with provider	1	PAYE or P11D[1]
Expenses not covered by dispensation — any profit element in payment		1	P11D[4]
Food, groceries, farm produce	– employer contract with provider	1A	P11D
	– employee contract with provider	1	PAYE or P11D[1]
Goods transferred to employee	– employer contract with provider	1A	P11D
	– employee contract with provider	1	PAYE or P11D[1]
Holidays	– employer contract with provider	1A	P11D
	– employee contract with provider, or holiday vouchers	1	PAYE or P11D[1]
Income tax paid but not deducted from employee, or paid on notional payments not borne by employee within 90 days of receipt of each notional payment		1	P11D
Insurance premiums for pensions etc on employee's death or retirement, employee contract with provider		1	PAYE or P11D[1]
Living accommodation (beneficial)		1A	P11D
Loans	– non-qualifying	1A	P11D
	– written off	1	P11D

Benefit		NICs Class	PAYE or P11D
Meals vouchers (other than 15p a day of value before 6 April 2013)		1	P11D
Meals provided other than at canteen or at business premises open to all staff on a reasonable scale where all employees may obtain free or subsidised meal		1A	P11D
Medical, dental insurance or treatment provided in the UK by employer	– employer contract with provider	1A	P11D
	– employee contract with provider	1	PAYE or P11D[1]
Mobile phone[5] — cost of private calls, employee contract with provider		1	PAYE or P11D[1]
Personal bills		1	PAYE or P11D[1]
Readily convertible assets[2]		1	PAYE
Relocation payments	– qualifying over £8,000	1A	P11D
	– non-qualifying benefits or qualifying expenses paid after relevant day	1A	P11D
	– non-qualifying expenses	1	P11D
Round sum allowances (not identified as business expense)		1	P11D
Scholarships awarded to students because of parent's employment or payment of school fees	– employer contract with provider	1A	P11D
	– employee contract with provider	1	PAYE or P11D[1]
Social functions unless ITEPA 2003 s 264 satisfied		1A	P11D
Sporting or recreational facilities unless ITEPA 2003 s 261 satisfied		1A	P11D
Subscriptions, professional and fees not allowable as tax deduction	– employer contract with provider	1A	P11D
	– employee contract with provider	1	PAYE or P11D[1]
Telephones	– employer contract with provider, unless private use is insignificant or employee reimburses cost of all private calls	1A	P11D
	– employee contract with provider, unless used exclusively for business. If mixed use, not applicable to business calls if supported by evidence	1	PAYE or P11D[1]
Training payments	– employer contract with provider, unless work-related or encouraged by employer	1A	P11D
	– employee contract with provider, unless work-related or encouraged by employer	1	PAYE or P11D[1]
Vans available for commuting and other private use		1A[3]	P11D
Van fuel provided for use in van available for commuting and other private use		1A[3]	P11D
Vouchers (other than exceptions for childcare, meals, etc)		1	P11D

[1] Payments by employer to provider should be entered on P11D. Reimbursements to the employee are subject to PAYE.

[2] See detailed information in HMRC booklet CWG2(2012) para 34.

[3] No Class 1A due if van is available mainly for employee's business travel and commuting and other private use is insignificant.

[4] Specific and distinct business expenses within the payments should be recorded in appropriate section of P11D.

[5] No limit to number of mobile phones which employer can contract to provide NIC free solely for business with insignificant private use. Only one mobile per employee NIC free for private use where employer contracts.

Overseas

Average rates of exchange

Average for year ending	31.03.11	31.12.11	31.03.12	31.12.12	31.03.13
Abu Dhabi (Dirham)	5.7021	5.8887	5.8691	6.8312	7.0811
Afghanistan (Afghani)	68.543	69.079	69.855	76.7676	78.3810
Albania (Lek)	162.221	161.709	162.360	171.530	172.781
Algeria (Dinar)	114.760	117.054	117.306	123.093	124.787
Angola (Readj Kwanza)	143.686	150.194	150.405	150.805	151.532
Antigua (EC$)	4.1917	4.3288	4.3144	4.2716	4.2866
Argentina (Peso)	6.1478	6.6113	6.7074	7.1818	7.3432
Armenia (Dram)	569.704	595.023	602.532	635.239	643.669
Aruba (Florin)	2.7790	2.8699	2.8603	2.8319	2.8419
Australia (A$)	1.6526	1.5532	1.5274	1.5304	1.5443
Austria (Euro)	1.1779	1.1517	1.1582	1.2335	1.2438
Azerbaijan (New Manat)	1.2439	1.2666	1.2579	1.2416	1.2456
Bahamas ($ pegged to US$)	1.5535	1.6038	1.5958	1.5829	1.5898
Bahrain (Dinar)	0.5853	0.6243	0.6231	0.5965	0.5986
Bangladesh (Taka)	108.732	118.157	122.098	129.562	129.432
Barbados (BD$)	3.1049	3.2065	3.1958	3.1641	3.1752
Belarus (Rouble)	4,667.52	8,126.32	10,098.71	13,228.89	13,327.68
Belgium (Euro)	1.1779	1.1517	1.1582	1.2335	1.2438
Belize (Dollar)	3.0273	3.1651	3.1536	3.0510	3.0611
Benin (CFA Franc)	771.029	755.749	758.896	809.513	815.515
Bermuda ($ pegged to US$)	1.5535	1.6038	1.5958	1.5829	1.5898
Bhutan (Ngultrum)	70.8063	74.5576	76.2045	84.5328	86.5002
Bolivia (Boliviano)	10.8805	11.1260	11.0614	10.9317	10.9699
Bosnia-Herzegovina (Marka)	2.2990	2.2534	2.2628	2.4137	2.4316
Botswana (Pula)	10.5025	10.9159	11.1162	12.2967	12.5446
Brazil (Real)	2.6850	2.6776	2.7055	3.0916	3.2019
Brunei ($)	2.0707	2.0139	1.9994	1.9781	1.9773
Bulgaria (Lev)	2.2990	2.2534	2.2628	2.4137	2.4316
Burkina Faso (CFA Franc)	771.029	755.749	758.896	809.513	815.515
Burundi (Franc)	1,912.32	2,015.16	2,065.46	2,278.45	2,315.58
Cambodia (Riel)	6,411.57	6,475.58	6,475.17	6,389.11	6,412.63
Cameroon Republic (CFA Franc)	771.029	755.749	758.896	809.513	815.515
Canada (Can$)	1.5808	1.5844	1.5824	1.5836	1.5882
Cape Verde Islands (Escudo)	127.476	124.082	125.241	135.764	136.691
Cayman Islands (CI$)	1.2730	16.269	16.876	1.2973	1.3019
Central African (CFA Franc)	771.029	755.749	758.896	809.513	815.515
Chad (CFA Franc)	771.029	755.749	758.896	809.513	815.515
Chile (Peso)	778.013	771.550	771.868	770.078	771.858
China (Renminbi Yuan)	10.4195	10.3745	10.2339	9.9881	10.0173
Colombia (Peso)	2,919.66	2,959.41	2,918.79	60,320.53	73,260.13
Comoros (Franc)	578.272	566.813	569.174	607.135	611.636
Congo Brazzaville (CFA Franc)	771.029	755.749	758.896	809.513	815.515
Congo Dem Rep (Zaire) (Congolese Franc)	1,408.81	1,458.64	1,452.24	1,454.91	1,459.65
Costa Rica (Colon)	797.682	810.964	810.612	795.485	795.054
Cote d'Ivoire (CFA Franc)	771.029	755.749	758.896	809.513	815.515
Croatia (Kuna)	8.5942	8.5609	8.6416	9.2760	9.3297
Cuba (Peso)	1.5525	1.6033	1.5979	1.5821	1.5877

Average for year ending	31.03.11	31.12.11	31.03.12	31.12.12	31.03.13
Cyprus (Euro from 1.1.08)	1.1779	1.1517	1.1582	1.2335	1.2438
Czech Republic (Koruna)	29.3266	28.3142	28.6081	31.0509	31.2984
Denmark (Krone)	8.7744	8.5762	8.6238	9.1811	9.2621
Djibouti (Franc)	272.593	280.387	279.289	277.747	279.108
Dominica (EC$)	4.1917	4.3288	4.3144	4.2716	4.2866
Dominican Republic (Peso)	57.3989	60.8161	61.1402	61.9436	62.3545
Dubai (Dirham)	5.7021	5.8887	5.8691	6.8312	7.0811
Ecuador (US$)	1.5535	1.6038	1.5958	1.5829	1.5898
Egypt (£)	8.8874	9.5196	9.5564	9.5980	9.6543
El Salvador (Colon)	13.5802	14.0245	13.9777	13.8392	13.8877
Equatorial Guinea (CFA Franc)	771.029	755.749	758.896	809.513	815.515
Eritrea (Nakfa)	23.2870	24.0489	23.9685	23.7301	23.8132
Estonia (Euro from 1.1.11)		1.8004	1.1582	1.2335	1.2438
Ethiopia (Birr)	23.7448	27.1943	27.3735	28.1442	28.4456
European Union (Euro)	1.1779	1.1517	1.1582	1.2335	1.2438
Fiji Islands (F$)	2.9422	2.8741	2.8385	2.8347	2.8534
Finland (Euro)	1.1779	1.1517	1.1582	1.2335	1.2438
France (Euro)	1.1779	1.1517	1.1582	1.2335	1.2438
French Polynesia (CFP franc)	140.179	137.471	138.059	147.2666	148.3585
Gabon (CFA franc)	771.029	755.749	758.896	809.513	815.515
Gambia (Dalasi)	43.6735	45.4873	46.1451	49.3463	50.0122
Georgia (Lari)	46.9793	47.0579	47.1474	49.3209	49.8549
Germany (Euro)	1.1779	1.1517	1.1582	1.2335	1.2438
Ghana (Cedi)	2.2561	2.4716	2.5342	2.9353	3.0135
Greece (Euro)	1.1779	1.1517	1.1582	1.2335	1.2438
Grenada/Wind. Isles (EC$)	4.1917	4.3288	4.3144	4.2716	4.2866
Guatemala (Quetzal)	12.3875	12.4988	12.4276	12.4027	12.4776
Guinea Bissau (CFA Franc)	771.029	755.749	758.896	809.513	815.515
Guinea Republic (Franc)	9,528.78	11,127.68	11,045.72	11,031.34	10,987.18
Guyana (G$)	315.166	325.051	323.392	318.160	319.108
Haiti (Gourde)	61.8747	64.5992	64.5382	65.8809	66.6333
Honduras (Lempira)	29.3339	30.2872	30.2414	30.5512	30.8154
Hong Kong (HK$)	12.0853	12.4843	12.4121	12.2791	12.3307
Hungary (Forint)	324.947	321.141	328.864	356.921	357.238
Iceland (Krona)	185.726	185.767	187.988	181.908	179.505
India (Rupee)	70.8063	74.5576	76.2045	84.5328	86.5002
Indonesia (Rupiah)	13,976.90	14,037.29	14,013.84	14,803.46	15,015.79
Iran (Rial)	15,803.40	16,977.89	17,459.89	19,282.64	19,509.68
Iraq (Dinar)	1,812.31	1,872.54	1,863.11	1,838.80	1,844.89
Ireland (Euro)	1.1779	1.1517	1.1582	1.2335	1.2438
Israel (Shekel)	5.7496	5.7247	5.7699	6.1080	6.1623
Italy (Euro)	1.1779	1.1517	1.1582	1.2335	1.2438
Jamaica (J$)	133.470	137.120	137.063	139.788	141.452
Japan (Yen)	133.405	128.004	126.099	126.150	127.557
Jordan (Dinar)	1.0993	1.1359	1.1323	1.1206	1.1244
Kazakhstan (Tenge)	228.322	235.107	234.888	235.948	237.301
Kenya (Shilling)	124.987	142.141	142.959	133.744	134.456
Korea North (Won)	5.9760	6.1196	2.0773	2.0566	2.0638
Korea South (Won)	1,789.59	1,774.79	1,769.75	1,785.19	1,786.16
Kuwait (Dinar)	0.4425	0.4433	0.4410	0.6270	0.6708
Kyrgyz Republic (Som)	46.9793	47.0579	47.1474	49.3209	49.8549
Laos (New Kip)	12,629.81	12,823.65	12,758.14	12,601.88	12,647.16
Latvia (Lat)	0.8319	0.8140	0.8158	0.8605	0.8664
Lebanon (£)	2,330.14	2,413.90	2,407.45	2,380.24	2,388.62
Lesotho (Loti)	11.1799	11.5600	11.8049	13.0064	13.2799

Average for year ending	31.03.11	31.12.11	31.03.12	31.12.12	31.03.13
Liberia ($ pegged to US$)	1.5535	1.6038	1.5958	1.5829	1.5898
Libya (Dinar)	1.9555	1.9466	1.9392	1.9778	1.9914
Lithuania (Litas)	4.0586	3.9782	3.9947	4.2611	4.2927
Luxembourg (Euro)	1.1779	1.1517	1.1582	1.2335	1.2438
Macao (Pataca)	12.4303	12.8549	12.8021	12.6402	12.6831
Macedonia (Denar)	72.3545	70.8774	71.1307	76.0097	76.6256
Madagascar (Malagasy Ariary)	3,235.71	3,246.63	3,282.52	3,479.53	3,499.89
Malawi (Kwacha)	234.096	250.397	255.309	395.980	440.306
Malaysia (Ringgit)	4.8847	4.8993	4.8819	4.8899	4.9192
Maldive Islands (Rufiyaa)	19.8716	23.0937	24.0370	24.3159	24.3963
Mali Republic (CFA Franc)	771.029	755.749	758.896	809.513	815.515
Malta (Euro from 1.1.08)	1.1779	1.1517	1.1582	1.2335	1.2438
Mauritania (Ouguiya)	435.961	451.256	452.906	469.062	472.821
Mauritius (Rupee)	47.4584	46.0469	45.6847	47.7135	48.3212
Mexico (Peso)	19.3675	19.8679	20.1604	20.8757	20.9916
Moldova (Leu)	19.0176	18.8119	18.6449	19.1690	19.3536
Mongolia (Tugrik)	2,036.42	2,021.84	2,054.57	2,149.37	2,159.65
Montserrat (EC$)	4.1917	4.3288	4.3144	4.2716	4.2866
Morocco (Dirham)	13.1101	12.7406	12.7649	13.6812	13.7720
Mozambique (Metical)	53.4337	46.6306	44.6301	44.7312	45.4483
Myanmar (Burma) (Kyat)	9.9513	10.2769	10.2425	998.851	1,290.07
Nepal (Rupee)	113.132	119.028	121.368	135.203	138.256
Netherlands (Euro)	1.1779	1.1517	1.1582	1.2335	1.2438
New Caledonia (CFP Franc)	140.179	137.471	138.059	147.267	148.358
New Zealand (NZ$)	2.1253	2.0295	1.9819	1.9598	1.9707
Nicaragua (Gold Cordoba)	33.5288	35.9042	36.2063	37.2393	37.6033
Niger Republic (CFA Franc)	771.029	755.749	758.896	809.513	815.515
Nigeria (Naira)	235.513	249.169	250.633	251.436	251.944
Norway (Krone)	9.3501	8.9773	8.9649	9.2332	9.2568
Oman (Rial Omani)	0.5959	0.6173	0.6152	0.6091	0.6113
Pakistan (Rupee)	132.552	138.292	139.666	147.702	149.729
Panama (Balboa)	1.5525	1.6033	1.5979	1.5821	1.588
Papua New Guinea (Kina)	4.1689	3.7924	3.5751	3.2606	3.2646
Paraguay (Guarani)	7,336.74	6,744.83	6,668.88	7,021.56	7,014.83
Peru (New Sol)	4.3585	4.4165	4.3665	4.1775	4.1669
Philippines (Peso)	69.2370	69.4108	68.7961	66.9121	66.6941
Poland (Zloty)	4.6847	4.7312	4.8349	5.1694	5.1876
Portugal (Euro)	1.1779	1.1517	1.1582	1.2335	1.2438
Qatar (Riyal)	5.6514	5.8379	5.8186	5.7604	5.7806
Romania (Leu)	4.9798	4.8875	4.9379	5.5127	5.5900
Russia (Rouble-Market)	46.9793	47.0579	47.1474	49.3209	49.8549
Rwanda (R Franc)	914.593	961.775	961.237	971.316	979.920
Saotome & Principe (Dobra)	28,529.41	28,235.14	28,351.28	29,877.96	29,991.63
Saudi Arabia (Riyal)	5.8298	6.0147	5.9846	5.9361	5.9620
Senegal (CFA Franc)	771.029	755.479	758.896	809.513	815.515
Serbia (Dinar)	122.469	117.515	118.896	139.699	142.497
Seychelles (Rupee)	19.0717	19.8320	20.3733	21.7087	21.6401
Sierra Leone (Leone)	6,301.38	6,965.58	6,990.35	6,872.89	6,887.75
Singapore (S$)	2.0721	2.0153	2.0009	1.9808	1.9787
Slovakia Euro from 1.1.09	1.1779	1.1517	1.1582	1.2335	1.2438
Slovenia (Euro)	1.779	1.1517	1.1582	1.2335	1.2438
Solomon Islands (SI$)	12.1766	12.1145	11.8226	11.2242	11.2550
Somali Republic (Shilling)	2,385.47	2,510.12	2,511.69	2,491.09	2,497.64
South Africa (Rand)	11.1774	11.5787	11.8522	13.0070	13.2881

Average for year ending	31.03.11	31.12.11	31.03.12	31.12.12	31.03.13
Spain (Euro)	1.1779	1.1517	1.1582	1.2335	1.2438
Sri Lanka (Rupee)	174.212	177.075	178.794	202.164	207.292
St Christopher & Nevis (EC$)	4.1917	4.3288	4.3144	4.2716	4.2866
St Lucia (EC$)	4.1917	4.3288	4.3144	4.2716	4.2866
St Vincent (EC$)	4.1917	4.3288	4.3144	4.2716	4.2866
Sudan Republic (£)	3.6865	4.2308	4.2857	5.5950	6.0563
Surinam (Dollar)	4.3989	5.2053	5.2731	5.2209	5.2392
Swaziland (Lilangeni)	11.1799	11.5600	11.8049	13.0064	13.2799
Sweden (Krona)	10.9374	10.3955	10.4489	10.7413	10.7687
Switzerland (Franc)	1.5769	1.4214	1.4073	1.4870	1.4981
Syria (Pound)	72.2270	76.8639	80.3194	100.278	103.984
Taiwan (New T$)	47.9891	47.0816	47.0278	46.8585	46.9471
Tajikistan (Somoni)	46.9793	47.0578	47.1474	49.3209	49.8549
Tanzania (Shilling)	2,290.21	2,535.73	2,565.88	2,509.60	2,514.74
Thailand (Baht)	48.3929	48.8202	48.7955	49.2233	49.4121
Togo Republic (CFA Franc)	771.029	755.749	758.896	809.513	815.515
Tonga Islands (Pa'Anga)	1.6526	1.5532	1.5274	1.5304	1.5443
Trinidad and Tobago (TT$)	9.8754	10.2618	10.2329	10.1373	10.1744
Tunisia (Dinar)	2.2402	2.2536	2.2764	2.4768	2.5081
Turkey (Lira)	2.3646	2.6779	2.7522	2.8500	2.8622
Turkmenistan (New Manat)	30.3560	4.5608	4.5436	4.5008	4.5186
Uganda (New Shilling)	3,504.67	4,042.47	4,055.64	3,956.55	4,032.06
Ukraine (Hryvnia)	12.3143	12.7979	12.7843	12.7927	12.8607
United Arab Emirates (Dirham)	5.7021	5.8887	5.8691	6.8312	7.0811
Uruguay (Peso Uruguayo)	31.0534	30.8226	30.6354	32.1042	32.4913
USA (US$)	1.5535	1.6038	1.5958	1.5829	1.5898
Uzbekistan (Sum)	2,507.69	2,741.07	2,792.52	2,986.95	3,036.16
Vanuatu (Vatu)	153.126	149.979	148.545	149.246	150.209
Venezuela (Bolivar Fuerte)	6.6673	6.8855	6.8624	6.7942	6.8180
Vietnam (Dong)	30,237.45	33,063.93	33,256.91	33,021.29	33,125.30
Wallis & Futuna Islands (CFP Franc)	140.179	137.471	138.059	147.267	148.358
Western Samoa (Tala)	3.8095	3.7202	3.6667	3.6316	3.6520
Yemen (Republic of) (Rial)	340.988	345.071	345.455	341.023	341.167
Zambia (Kwacha)	7,497.68	7,779.14	7,907.84	8,132.81	8,138.51
Zimbabwe (Dollar)	587.473	606.220	604.136	598.385	600.614

Rates of exchange on year-end dates

	31.03.11	31.12.11	31.03.12	31.12.12	31.03.13
Australia (A$)	1.55	1.5159	1.5423	1.5657	1.4626
Canada (Can$)	1.5593	1.5825	1.5969	1.6185	1.5489
Denmark (Krone)	8.4221	8.8978	8.9259	9.1989	8.8392
European Union (Euro)	1.1296	1.1972	1.1998	1.233	1.1857
Hong Kong (HK$)	12.4681	12.0701	12.405	12.5991	11.826
Japan (Yen)	132.853	119.572	131.487	140.549	142.058
Norway (Krone)	8.8671	9.2748	9.1137	9.0463	8.8618
South Africa (Rand)	10.8351	12.5469	12.262	13.7914	13.9881
Sweden (Krona)	10.1121	10.6539	10.6016	10.5746	9.9125
Switzerland (Franc)	1.4665	1.4532	1.4442	1.4879	1.4439
USA (US$)	1.603	1.5541	1.5978	1.6255	1.5233

Note: The material on pp 117–120 is reproduced from information provided by HMRC and is Crown copyright.

Double taxation agreements (including protocols and regulations)

Agreements in force covering taxes on income and capital gains

Country	SI/SR & O	Country	SI/SR & O
Antigua & Barbuda	**1947/2865**		1996/3166
	1968/1096	France	**2009/226**
Argentina	**1997/1777**	Gambia	**1980/1963**
Armenia[1]	**2011/2722**	Georgia	**2004/3325**
Austria	**1970/1947**		2010/2972
	1979/117	Germany	1967/25
	1994/768		1971/874
	2010/2688		**2010/2975**[5]
Australia	**2003/3199**	Ghana	**1993/1800**
Azerbaijan	**1995/762**	Greece	**1954/142**
Bahrain	**2012/3075**	Grenada	**1949/361**
Bangladesh	**1980/708**		1968/1867
Barbados	**2012/3076**	Guernsey	**1952/1215**
Belarus[1]	**1986/224**		1994/3209
Belgium	**1987/2053**		2009/3011
	2010/2979	Guyana	**1992/3207**
Belize	**1947/2866**	Hong Kong	**2010/2974**
	1968/573	Hungary	**2011/2726**[6]
	1973/2097	Iceland	**1991/2879**
Bolivia	**1995/2707**	India	**1993/1801**
Bosnia Herzegovina[2]	**1981/1815**	Indonesia	**1994/769**
Botswana	**2006/1925**	Irish Republic	**1976/2151**
British Virgin Islands	**2009/3013**		1976/2152
Brunei	**1950/1977**		1995/764
	1968/306		1998/3151
	1973/2098	Isle of Man	**1955/1205**
Bulgaria	**1987/2054**		1991/2880
Canada	**1980/709**		1994/3208
	1980/1528		2009/228
	1980/1996	Israel	**1963/616**
	1985/1996		1971/391
	2003/2619	Italy	**1990/2590**
Cayman Islands	**2010/2973**	Ivory Coast	**1987/169**
Chile	**2003/3200**	Jamaica	**1973/1329**
China[4]	**1984/1826**	Japan	**2006/1924**
	1996/3164	Jersey	**1952/1216**
Croatia[2]	**1981/1815**		1994/3210
Cyprus	**1975/425**		2009/3012
	1980/1529	Jordan	**2001/3924**
Czech Republic[3]	**1991/2876**	Kazakhstan	**1994/3211**
Denmark	**1980/1960**		1998/2567
	1991/2877	Kenya	**1977/1299**
	1996/3165	Kiribati (and Tuvalu)	**1950/750**
Egypt	**1980/1091**		1968/309
Estonia	**1994/3207**		1974/1271
Ethiopia	**2011/2725**	Korea (South)	**1996/3168**
Falkland Islands	**1997/2985**	Kuwait	**1999/2036**
Faroes	**2007/3469**	Kyrgyzstan[1]	
Fiji	**1976/1342**	Latvia	**1996/3167**
Finland	**1970/153**	Lesotho	**1997/2986**
	1973/1327	Liechtenstein	**2012/3077**
	1980/710	Libya	**2010/243**
	1985/1997	Lithuania[1]	**2001/3925**
	1991/2878		2002/2847

Country	SI/SR & O	Country	SI/SR & O
Luxembourg	**1968/1100**	Romania	**1977/57**
	1980/567	Russian Federation	**1994/3213**
	1984/364	St Kitts and Nevis	**1947/2872**
	2010/237	Saudi Arabia	**2008/1770**
Macedonia[2]	**2007/2127**	Serbia[2]	**1981/1815**
Malawi	**1956/619**	Sierra Leone	**1947/2873**
	1964/1401		1968/1104
	1968/1101	Singapore	**1997/2988**
	1979/302		2010/2685
Malaysia	**1997/2987**		2012/3078
	2010/2971	Slovak Republic[3]	**1991/2876**
Malta	**1995/763**	Slovenia[2]	**2008/1796**
Mauritius	**1981/1121**	Solomon Islands	**1950/748**
	1987/467		1968/574
	2003/2620		1974/1270
	2011/2442	South Africa	**2002/3138**
Mexico	**1994/3212**		2011/2441
	2010/2686	Spain	**1976/1919**
Moldova[1]	**2008/1795**		1995/765
Mongolia	**1996/2598**	Sri Lanka	**1980/713**
Montenegro[2]	**1981/1815**	Sudan	**1977/1719**
Montserrat	**1947/2869**	Swaziland	**1969/380**
	1968/576	Sweden	**1984/366**
	2011/1083	Switzerland	**1978/1408**
Morocco	**1991/2881**		1982/714
Myanmar (Burma)	**1952/751**		1994/3215
Namibia	**1962/2352**		2007/3465
	1962/2788		2010/2689
	1967/1489	Taiwan	**2002/3137**
	1967/1490	Tajikistan[1]	**1986/224**
Netherlands	**2009/227**	Thailand	**1981/1546**
New Zealand	**1984/365**	Trinidad and Tobago	**1983/1903**
	2004/1274	Tunisia	**1984/133**
	2008/1793	Turkey	**1988/932**
Nigeria	**1987/2057**	Turkmenistan[1]	**1986/224**
Norway	**2000/3247**	Tuvalu (and Kiribati)	**1950/750**
Oman	**1998/2568**		1968/309
	2010/2687		1974/1271
Pakistan	**1987/2058**	Uganda	**1993/1802**
Papua New Guinea	**1991/2882**	Ukraine	**1993/1803**
Philippines	**1978/184**	USA	**2002/2848**
Poland	**2006/3323**	Uzbekistan	**1994/770**
Portugal	**1969/599**	Venezuela	**1996/2599**
Qatar	**2010/241**	Vietnam	**1994/3216**
	2011/1684	Zambia	**1972/1721**
			1981/1816
		Zimbabwe	**1982/1842**

[1] Following dissolution of the USSR, new agreements are in force with Azerbaijan, Estonia, Kazakhstan, Latvia, Lithuania, Moldova, the Russian Federation, Ukraine and Uzbekistan. *SI 1986 No 224* (former USSR agreement) treated as continuing to apply to Belarus, Tajikistan and Turkmenistan (for Belarus until coming into force of *SI 1995 No 2706*). It was similarly so treated by the UK until 31 March 2002 for Armenia, Georgia, Kyrgyzstan and Lithuania (none of which considered itself bound by that convention) but as ceasing so to apply after that date (but new treaties in force with Armenia, Lithuania and Georgia). (SP 4/01.)

[2] *SI 1981 No 1815* (former Yugoslavia agreement) treated as remaining in force between the UK and, respectively, Bosnia-Herzegovina, Croatia and Serbia and Montenegro. (SP 3/04.) Negotiations for new double taxation convention taking place with Croatia, Serbia and Montenegro (Revenue Press Release, 29 September 2004).

[3] *SI 1991 No 2876* (former Czechoslovakia agreement) treated as remaining in force between the UK and, respectively, Czech Republic and Slovak Republic. (SP 5/93.)

[4] *SI 1984 No 1826* does not apply to the Hong Kong Special Administrative Region, which now has its own agreement.

[5] Treaty replaces 1967/25 with effect from 1 January 2011 or 6 April 2011 depending on type of income. However, where a resident of Germany was, before 30 December 2010, in receipt of a UK pension (including State Pension) or annuity relievable under Article X of prior treaty 1967/25, the individual may elect for the terms of the prior treaty to continue to apply to the pension or annuity.

[6] New treaty effective in UK from 1 January 2012 for property income dividends, interest, royalties (and annuities not subject to PAYE), 6 April 2012 for pensions and annuities within PAYE. Prior treaty was 1978/1056.

Tax information exchange agreements in force

Country	SI	Country	SI
Anguilla	2010/2677	Guernsey	2009/3011
Antigua and Barbuda	2011/1075	Isle of Man	2009/228
Aruba	2011/2435	Jersey	2009/3012
Bahamas	2010/2684	Liberia	2011/2434
Belize	2011/1685	Liechtenstein	2010/2678
Bermuda	2008/1789	San Marino	2011/1688
British Virgin Islands	2009/3013	St Christopher and Nevis	2011/1077
Dominica	2011/1686	St Lucia	2011/1076
Gibraltar	2010/2680	St Vincent and Grenadines	2011/1078
Grenada	2011/1687	Turks and Caicos Islands	2010/2679

Tax information exchange agreements signed but not in force

Country

Curaçao, Sint Maarten and BES Islands (formerly the Netherlands Antilles)
Marshall Islands
Brazil

Tax information exchange agreements in force — EU savings directives

Country	SI	Country	SI
Aruba	2005/1458	Isle of Man	2005/1263
British Virgin Islands	2005/1457	Jersey	2005/1261
Gibraltar	2006/1453	Montserrat	2005/1459
Guernsey	2005/1262	former Netherlands Antilles (now known as Curaçao, Sint Maarten and BES Islands)	2005/1460

Agreements in force covering shipping and air transport profits

Country	SI/SR & O	Country	SI/SR & O
Algeria (air)	**1984/362**	Iran (air)	**1960/2419**
Armenia (USSR air)*	**1974/1269**	Kyrgyzstan (USSR air)*	**1974/1269**
Belarus (USSR air)*	**1974/1269**	Lebanon	**1964/278**
Brazil	**1968/572**	Moldova (USSR air)*	**1974/1269**
Cameroon (air)	**1982/1841**	Saudi Arabia (air)	**1994/767**
China (air)	**1981/1119**	Tajikistan (USSR air)*	**1974/1269**
Congo Democratic Republic	**1977/1298**	Turkmenistan (USSR air)*	**1974/1269**
Ethiopia (air)	**1977/1297**		
Georgia (USSR air)*	**1974/1269**		
Hong Kong (air)	**1998/2566**		
(shipping)	**2000/3248**		

* HMRC have confirmed that this Arrangement will be treated in the same way as the Convention covering income and capital gains (SI 1986/224). See note 1 p 122.

Agreements in force covering estates, inheritances and gifts

Country	SI/SR & O	Country	SI/SR & O
France*	**1963/1319**	Pakistan*	**1957/1522**
India*	**1956/998**	South Africa	**1979/576**
Ireland	**1978/1107**	Sweden	**1981/840**
Italy*	**1968/304**		1989/986
Netherlands	**1980/706**	Switzerland	**1994/3214**
	1996/730	USA	**1979/1454**

* Agreements pre-date UK inheritance tax/capital transfer tax.

Overseas income – basis of assessment

(ITTOIA 2005 Pt 8; ITEPA 2003 ss 573–576A)

	Professions, trades, etc	Pensions	Other income
Non-residents	Exempt	Exempt	Exempt
Residents			
(1) **Foreign domicile**[2]	Remittance	Remittance	Remittance
(2) **UK domicile**	Arising	90%[1] arising	Arising

[1] Pensions paid by the governments of the Federal Republic of Germany or of Austria to victims of Nazi persecution are exempt.

[2] Where from 6 April 2008, an individual not domiciled or not ordinarily resident in the UK who has overseas income (or, for non-domiciles only, gains) in excess of £2,000 claims the remittance basis, he will not qualify for personal allowances or the capital gains tax annual exemption. The claim for remittance basis must be made annually. If the individual is not UK domiciled (or before 6 April 2013, not ordinarily resident) in a year and has been resident in the UK for at least seven out of the last nine tax years and has overseas income or gains in excess of £2,000, there is an additional charge of £30,000. This charge is increased to £50,000 from 6 April 2012 for non-domiciles who have been UK resident for at least twelve tax years in the previous fourteen. (ITA 2007 ss 809A–809ZIO)

[3] A statutory residence test is introduced from 6 April 2013 and ordinary residence is abolished from that date. Before 6 April 2013 UK-domiciled taxpayers who were not ordinarily resident were taxed on the remittance basis.

Employment income liability of non-resident employees see p 89.

Tax-free (FOTRA) securities

Interest on all government stock is exempt from tax where the beneficial owner is not resident in the UK (FA 1996 s 154; FA 1998 s 161; ITTOIA 2005 ss 713, 714; CTA 2009 s 1279). Except in the case of 3$^{1}/_{2}$% War Loan 1952 or after, the exemption does not apply where the securities are held for the purposes of a trade or business carried on in the UK.

Social security benefits

Taxable state benefits

	Weekly 8.4.13	Total 2013–14 (52 weeks)	Weekly 9.4.12	Total 2012–13 (52 weeks)
	£	£	£	£
Bereavement benefits[1]				
Standard rate (widow's pension)	108.30	5,631	105.95	5,509
Widowed parent's allowance	108.30	5,631	105.95	5,509
Carer's allowance	59.75	3,107	58.45	3,039
– Adult dependency increase	35.15	1,827	34.40	1,788
Employment and support allowance[6]				
–under 25	56.80	–	56.25	–
–25 or over	71.70	–	71.00	–
Incapacity benefit[6]				
Long-term (after 52 weeks)	101.35	5,270	99.15	5,155
– Adult dependency increase	58.85	3,060	57.60	2,995
– Age increase: higher rate	10.70	556	11.70	608
lower rate	6.00	312	5.90	306
Short term				
– Under pension age: higher rate	90.50	–	88.55	–
– Adult dependency increase	45.85	–	44.85	–
– Over pension age: higher rate	101.35	–	99.15	–
– Adult dependency increase	56.65	–	55.45	–
Industrial death benefit[2]				
Widow's pension: higher rate	110.15	5,727	107.45	5,587
lower rate	33.05	1,718	32.24	1,676
Widower's pension	110.15	5,727	107.45	5,587
Invalidity allowance[3]				
Higher rate	20.70	1,076	20.25	1,053
Middle rate	13.30	691	13.00	676
Lower rate	6.65	345	6.50	338
Jobseeker's allowance[4]				
Single: under 25	56.80	–	56.25	–
25 or over	71.70	–	71.00	–
Couple: both under 10	56.00	–	56.25	–
both under 18 higher rate	85.80	–	84.95	–
one under 18, one under 25	56.80	–	56.25	–
one under 18, one 25 or over	71.70	–	71.00	–
both 18 or over	112.55	–	111.45	–
State pension				
Single person (Category A or B)	110.15	5,727	107.45	5,587
Single person (Category B lower) based on spouse's or civil partner's insurance	66.00	3,432	64.40	3,348
Adult dependency increase[7]	63.20	3,286	61.85	3,216
Non-contributory pension				
– single (Category C (higher) or Category D)	66.00	3,432	64.40	3,348
– single (Category C (lower))	39.45	2,051	38.50	2,002
Age addition (over 80) (each)	0.25	13	0.25	13
Statutory adoption pay				
Rate[5]	136.78	–	135.45	–
Earnings threshold	109.00	–	107.00	–
Statutory maternity pay				
Rate[5]	136.78	–	135.45	–

	Weekly 8.4.13	Total 2013–14 (52 weeks)	Weekly 9.4.12	Total 2012–13 (52 weeks)
	£	£	£	£
Earnings threshold	**109.00**	–	107.00	–
Statutory paternity pay				
Rate[5]	**136.78**	–	135.45	–
Earnings threshold	**109.00**	–	107.00	–
Statutory sick pay				
Rate	**86.70**	–	85.85	–
Earnings threshold	**109.00**	–	107.00	–

1. Paid to widows and widowers for up to 52 weeks.
2. For deaths before 11 April 1988 only.
3. When paid with retirement pensions. See note below on non-taxable benefits on p 129.
4. Where the allowance exceeds the amount shown above, the excess is not taxable.
5. The allowance is 90% of average weekly earnings if less than the above amount. In the first six weeks the rate of SMP is 90% of average weekly earnings even if higher than the standard rate.
6. Employment and support allowance replaces incapacity benefits for new claimants on or after 27 October 2008. Only contributory employment and support allowance is taxable. Income related allowance is not taxable.
7. Not available to new retirees from 6 April 2010. To be withdrawn completely on 5 April 2020.
8. **A cap will be placed on the total amount of benefit** that most people aged 16 to 64 can receive. Most local councils will be introducing this between 15 July and 30 September 2013. Bromley, Croydon, Enfield and Haringey Councils introduced it on 15 April 2013. The cap will apply to the total amount that the people in a household receive from certain benefits. The cap is £500 a week for couples (with or without children living with them), £500 a week for single parents whose children live with them, and £350 a week for single adults who don't have children, or whose children don't live with them. See www.gov.uk/benefit-cap.
9. **Universal credit** will be phased in gradually from 29 April 2013 and will replace some of the benefits above. Initially it will apply to new claimants in Greater Manchester and Cheshire but will be introduced to the rest of the UK from October 2013 and will be completed by 2017. See www.gov.uk/universal-credit.

Non-taxable state benefits

Weekly rates from	8.4.13	9.4.12
	£	£
Attendance allowance		
Higher rate (day and night)	79.15	77.45
Lower rate (day or night)	53.00	51.85
Child benefit[3]		
Eldest child	20.30	20.30
Each subsequent child	13.40	13.40
Child dependency addition		
Paid with state pension; widowed mothers/parents allowance; short-term incapacity benefit - higher rate or over state pension age; long-term incapacity benefit; carer's allowance; severe disablement allowance; industrial death benefit (higher rate);	11.35	11.35
Disability living allowance/personal independence payment[2]		
Care component — higher rate	79.15	77.45
middle rate	53.00	51.85
lower rate	21.00	20.55
Mobility component — higher rate	55.25	54.05
lower rate	21.00	20.55
Guardian's allowance	15.90	15.55
Incapacity benefit (short-term)[1]		
Under pension age – lower rate (first 28 weeks)	76.45	74.80
– Adult dependency increase	45.85	44.85
Over pension age – lower rate (first 28 weeks)	97.25	95.15
– Adult dependency increase	56.65	55.45
Maternity allowance (where SMP not available)		
Standard rate	136.78	135.45
MA threshold	30.00	30.00
Severe disablement allowance		
Basic rate	71.80	69.00
Age-related addition — higher rate	10.70	11.70
middle rate	6.00	5.90
lower rate	6.00	5.90
– Adult dependency increase	35.35	34.60

[1] Incapacity benefit replaced invalidity allowance from April 1995. The benefits are taxable except those paid in the first 28 weeks of incapacity and those paid to persons already receiving invalidity benefit on 13 April 1995 so long as they remain incapable of work.

[2] Disability living allowance is replaced by personal independence payments (PIP) in 2013–14.

[3] See note on p 73 regarding the income tax charge arising to certain child benefit claimants from 7 January 2013.

[4] **A cap will be placed on the total amount of benefit** that most people aged 16 to 64 can receive. Most local councils will be introducing this between 15 July and 30 September 2013. Bromley, Croydon, Enfield and Haringey Councils introduced it on 15 April 2013. The cap will apply to the total amount that the people in a household receive from certain benefits. The cap is £500 a week for couples (with or without children living with them), £500 a week for single parents whose children live with them, and £350 a week for single adults who don't have children, or whose children don't live with them. See www.gov.uk/benefit-cap.

Other non-taxable benefits include:

Bereavement payment (lump sum £2,000)

Child tax credit (see Tax Credits, p 100)

Christmas bonus (with retirement pension)

Cold weather payments

Council tax benefit (income related)

Earnings top-up

Housing benefit (income related)

Income support (income related)

Industrial death benefit

Industrial injuries disablement pension

Jobfinder's grant

Pension credit

Pneumoconiosis, byssinosis and miscellaneous disease benefits

Redundancy payment

Social fund payments

Television licence payment

Vaccine damage (lump sum)

War pensions

Winter fuel payment (£200, plus £100 for those aged over 80, for 2011–12)

Working tax credit (see Tax Credits, p 100)

Stamp taxes

Stamp duty land tax

Stamp duty land tax applies to contracts entered into (or varied) after 10.7.03 and completed after 30.11.03 and to leases granted after that date (FA 2003 ss 55, 56, Sch 5). With effect from 22.7.04, it also applies to the transfer of an interest in land into, or out of, a partnership and to the acquisition of an interest in a partnership where the partnership property includes an interest in land. With effect from 19.7.06, it applies to transfers of partnership interests only where the sole or main activity of the partnership is investing or dealing in interests in land.

Land transactions		Consideration[1]	
Effective date	Residential property[4]	Non-residential or mixed property	Rate
From 22.3.12	**Up to £125,000**	**Up to £150,000**	**Nil**
	£125,001–£250,000	**£150,001–£250,000**	**1%**
	£250,001–£500,000	**£250,001–£500,000**	**3%**
	£500,001–£1,000,000	**£500,001 or more**	**4%**
	£1,000,001–£2,000,000		**5%**
	£2,000,001 or more[5]		**7%[5]**
From 6.4.11–21.3.12	Up to £125,000	Up to £150,000	Nil
	£125,001–£250,000[2]	£150,001–£250,000	1%
	£250,001–£500,000	£250,001–£500,000	3%
	£500,001–£1,000,000	£500,001 or more	4%
	£1,000,001 or more		5%
From 1.1.10–5.4.11	Up to £125,000	Up to £150,000	Nil
	£125,001–£250,000[2]	£150,001–£250,000	1%
	£250,001–£500,000	£250,001–£500,000	3%
	£500,001 or more	£500,001 or more	4%
3.9.08–31.12.09	Up to £175,000	Up to £150,000	Nil
	£175,001–£250,000	£150,001–£250,000	1%
	£250,001–£500,000	£250,001–£500,000	3%
	£500,001 or more	£500,001 or more	4%
23.3.06–2.9.08	Up to £125,000	Up to £150,000	Nil
	£125,001–£250,000	£150,001–£250,000	1%
	£250,001–£500,000	£250,001–£500,000	3%
	£500,001 or more	£500,001 or more	4%
17.3.05–22.3.06	Up to £120,000	Up to £150,000	Nil
	£120,001–£250,000	£150,001–£250,000	1%
	£250,001–£500,000	£250,001–£500,000	3%
	£500,001 or more	£500,001 or more	4%

Lease rentals	On net present value of rent over term of lease (applying a discount rate of 3.5%)[3]		
Effective date	Residential property	Non-residential or mixed property	Rate
From 1.1.10	**Up to £125,000**	**Up to £150,000**	**Nil**
	£125,001 or more	**£150,001 or more**	**1%**
3.9.08–31.12.09	Up to £175,000	Up to £150,000	Nil
	£175,001 or more	£150,001 or more	1%
23.3.06–2.9.08	Up to £125,000	Up to £150,000	Nil
	£125,001 or more	£150,001 or more	1%
17.3.05–22.3.06	Up to £120,000	Up to £150,000	Nil
	£120,001 or more	£150,001 or more	1%
1.12.03–16.3.05	Up to £60,000	Up to £150,000	Nil
	£60,001 or more	£150,001 or more	1%

Premiums
The same tax is payable for a premium granted as for a land transaction. Special rules apply to a premium in respect of non-residential property where the rent exceeds £1,000 a year. For transactions before 12 March 2008, the rules applied to all property where the rent exceeded £600 a year.

[1]   Rates apply to the full consideration, not only to that in excess of the previous band.

[2]   For residential property, purchases by first-time buyers between 25 March 2010 and 24 March 2012 inclusive attracted a nil rate of SDLT for purchase consideration up to £250,000.

[3]   Rates apply to the amount of npv in the slice, not the whole value.

[4]   With effect from 19 July 2011, where a purchaser (or a connected person) of residential property acquires more than one dwelling from the same vendor (or a connected person) and makes a claim, the rate of SDLT will be calculated based on the mean consideration for each property, subject to a minimum rate of 1%.

[5]   **From 21 March 2012 a 15% rate applies to certain non-natural persons** acquiring a residential property where consideration exceeds £2,000,000. Relief is available for genuine property businesses so that the

charge is at 7% in certain cases. See p 65 for the annual tax on enveloped dwellings which also applies to such properties.

Exemptions and reliefs

No SDLT (or, where relevant, stamp duty) is chargeable on:

(1)   transfers to charities for use for charitable purposes.
(2)   transfers to bodies established for national purposes.
(3)   gifts inter vivos.
(4)   certain transfers on divorce or dissolution of a civil partnership.
(5)   transfers of property to beneficiaries under a will or an intestacy.
(6)   land transfers within groups of companies.
(7)   land transferred in exchange for shares on company reconstruction and acquisitions.
(8)   certain transfers to or leases granted by registered providers of social housing. (Although the relief is repealed for the old stamp duty rules for instruments executed on or after 6 April 2013, it still applies to stamp duty land tax).
(9)   sale and leaseback and lease and leaseback arrangements involving commercial and residential property.
(10) certain acquisitions of residential property by house building companies or property traders from personal representatives, or when people move into a new dwelling or a chain of transactions break down, or by employers involving employee relocations.
(11) for instruments executed before 6 April 2013, transfers on sale of residential property for a consideration of up to £150,000 in disadvantaged parts of the UK. This also applies to leases broadly, on rent where the relevant rental value does not exceed £150,000 and to premiums not exceeding £150,000. No claims can be made after 5 May 2014.
(12) from 1.10.07 until 30.9.12 for new zero carbon homes (including flats) with a purchase price of up to £500,000, there was no SDLT charged. Where the purchase price was in excess of £500,000, the SDLT liability on the purchase price was reduced by £15,000.
(13) from 25.3.10 until 24.3.12 purchases of residential property by first-time buyers for consideration of more than £125,000 but not more than £250,000 (see p 131).
(14) demutualisation of building societies and insurance companies.
(15) incorporation of limited liability partnerships.
(16) transfers of land between public bodies under a statutory reorganisation.
(17) compulsory purchase of land facilitating redevelopment.
(18) land transactions in compliance with planning obligations enforceable against the vendor and made within five years of the obligation where the purchaser is one of certain public authorities.
(19) transfers by a local constituency association in consequence of a reorganisation of parliamentary constituencies.
(20) purchases or leases of certain diplomatic or consular premises or headquarters premises of certain international organisations.

Relief from SDLT may also apply on:

(a)   right to buy transactions, shared ownership leases and rent to loan transactions.
(b)   alternative property finance schemes.
(c)   exercise of collective rights by leaseholders.
(d)   crofting community right to buy.
(e)   certain arrangements relating to land transactions involving public or educational bodies.
(f)   acquisitions of interests in land by certain National Health Service bodies.

Stamp duty

For contracts entered into (or varied) after 10 July 2003 and completed after 30 November 2003 and for leases granted after that date, stamp duty is abolished for all transfers other than stocks and marketable securities, and interests in partnerships. From 22 July 2004 stamp duty is also abolished for certain partnership transactions involving an interest in land. From those dates, transfers of land are subject to stamp duty land tax (see p 131).

Shares, etc	
Shares put into depository receipts or put into duty free clearance systems	1.5%
Purchase of own shares by company	0.5%
Transfers of stock or marketable securities	0.5%
Takeovers, mergers, demergers, schemes of reconstruction and amalgamation (except where no real change of ownership)	0.5%

[1]   It is proposed to introduce legislation in Finance Bill 2014 to abolish stamp duty on shares quoted on growth markets such as the Alternative Investment Market and the ISDX Growth Market.
(a)   Stamp duty is rounded to the next multiple of £5.
(b)   For instruments executed after 11 March 2008 stamp duty is not chargeable where the amount or value of the consideration is less than £1,000.

Fixed duties

Instruments affecting land transactions	£5

From 13 March 2008 fixed duties are generally abolished other than as above. The £5 rate applies to instruments effected from 1 October 1999.

Stamp Duty Reserve Tax (SDRT)

Agreements to transfer chargeable securities for money or money's worth (eg renounce-able letters of allotment)[1]	0.5%
Chargeable securities put into a clearance service[2] or converted into depositary receipts where the transfer is not an integral part of an issue of share capital[4]	1.5%
Dealings of units in unit trusts and shares in open-ended investment companies[3]	0.5%
Transfers of foreign currency bearer shares and agreements to transfer sterling or foreign currency convertible or equity-related loan stock issued by UK companies	0.5%

[1]   If the transaction is completed by a duly stamped instrument within six years from the date on which the charge is imposed, the SDRT will be cancelled or repaid.

[2]   Where the operator of a clearance service elects to collect and account for SDRT on the normal rate of 0.5% on dealing within the system the higher SDRT charge of 1.5% does not apply.

[3]   From 6 April 2001 transfers of units in a unit trust and surrenders of shares in open-ended investment trusts are exempt when held within individual pension accounts. It is proposed to introduce legislation in Finance Bill 2014 to abolish the stamp duty reserve tax charge on unit trusts and open-ended investment companies.

[4]   Following the cases of HSBC Holdings plc and the Bank of New York Mellon Corporation v HMRC and HSBC Holdings plc and Vidacos Nominees Limited v Commissioners for HMRC, SDRT of 1.5% is no longer applicable on issues of UK shares to depositary receipt issuers and clearance services. Claims for repayment of SDRT may be made.

Interest on unpaid tax

Stamp duty land tax. *From 26 September 2005:* Interest runs from the end of 30 days after the effective date of transaction (normally completion), or the date of a disqualifying event, until the tax is paid. In the case of a deferred payment, interest runs from the date the payment is due until the tax is paid. A penalty carries interest from the date determined until the date of payment.

Stamp duty. *For instruments executed from 1 October 1999:* Interest runs from the end of 30 days after the date the instrument is executed until the tax is paid. Amounts less than £25 are not charged.

Stamp duty reserve tax. Interest is charged from 14 days after the transaction date for exchange transactions and otherwise from seven days after the end of the month of the transaction. Amounts less than £25 are not charged.

Rates: see p 4.

Repayment supplement

Stamp duty land tax. *From 26 September 2005:* Interest is added to repayments of overpaid stamp duty land tax and runs from the date tax was paid or an amount was lodged with HMRC, or the date a penalty was made, to the date the order for repayment is issued.

Stamp duty. *For instruments executed from 1 October 1999:* Interest is added to repayments of overpaid stamp duty and runs from 30 days after the date the instrument is executed or the date of payment if later. Amounts less than £25 are not paid.

Stamp duty reserve tax. Interest is paid from the date the tax was paid to the date the order for repayment is issued.

Rates: see p 6.

Penalties

Offence	Penalty
Stamp duty land tax and stamp duty reserve tax	
Inaccuracy in return or other document (FA 2007 Sch 24).	See **Penalties — modernised penalty regime** on p 12
Inaccuracy in return or other document as a result of third party providing incorrect (or withholding) information (FA 2007 Sch 24).	See **Penalties — modernised penalty regime** on p 12
Failure to notify HMRC of an error in an assessment (within 30 days) (FA 2007 Sch 24).	See **Penalties — modernised penalty regime** on p 12
Failure to comply with HMRC investigatory powers with effect from 1 April 2010 (FA 2008 Sch 36).	(*a*) Initial penalty of £300; (*b*) if failure/obstruction continues, a further penalty of up to £60 per day; (*c*) if failure/obstruction continues after penalty under (*a*) imposed, a tax-related amount determined by the Upper Tribunal.
Provision of inaccurate information or document when complying with an information notice with effect from 1 April 2010 (FA 2008 Sch 36).	Up to £3,000 per inaccuracy.
Stamp duty – for instruments executed from 1 October 1999	
Failure to present instrument for stamping within 30 days after execution (or the day in which it is first received in the UK if executed outside the UK) (Stamp Act 1891 s 15B; SI 1999/2537). (Extended to instruments executed from 24 July 2002 for transfers of UK land and buildings, wherever executed (FA 2002 s 114).)	If presented within one year after the end of the 30-day period: the lower of £300 or the amount of the unpaid duty. If presented more than one year after the end of the 30-day period: the greater of £300 or the amount of unpaid duty.
Stamp duty land tax – contracts completed after 30 November 2003	
Failure to deliver a land transaction return by the filing date (FA 2003 Sch 10 paras 3, 4).	£100 if return delivered within three months of filing date, otherwise £200. If not delivered within 12 months, penalty up to amount of tax chargeable.
Failure to comply with notice to deliver return within specified period (FA 2003 Sch 10 para 5).	Up to £60 for each day on which the failure continues after notification.
Fraudulently or negligently delivering an incorrect return or failing to remedy an error without unreasonable delay (FA 2003 Sch 10 para 8).	*Up to the difference between the amount payable and the amount that would have been chargeable on the basis of the return delivered.* **Repealed and replaced by penalty under FA 2007 Sch 24 above after 31 March 2010.**
Fraudulently or negligently giving a self-certificate for a chargeable transaction or failing to remedy an error in respect of such certificate without unreasonable delay (FA 2003 Sch 11 para 3).	*Up to the amount of tax chargeable.* **Repealed for transactions after 11 March 2008.**
Failure to keep and preserve records under FA 2003 Sch 10 para 9 or Sch 11 para 4 (FA 2003 Sch 10 para 11, Sch 11 para 6).	Up to £3,000 unless the information is provided by other documentary evidence.
Failure to comply with notice to produce documents etc under FA 2003 Sch 10 para 14 (FA 2003 Sch 10 para 16).	(*a*) Initial penalty of £50; (*b*) further penalty for each day the failure continues up to £30 if penalty determined by HMRC, or £150 if determined by the court. **Repealed with effect from 1 April 2010. Penalties still apply after 31 March 2010 to notices issued before 1 April 2010.**
Failure (From 1 August 2005) to disclose certain SDLT proposals or arrangements (TMA 1970 s 98C; SI 2005/1868; SI 2005/1869; SI 2010/2743).	(*a*) Up to £600 per day during 'initial period' (but tribunal can determine a higher penalty up to £1 million); (*b*) further penalty up to £600 per day while failure continues. Both the initial penalty in (*a*) above and the secondary penalty in (*b*) above can be increased up to £5,000 per day that failure continues from 10 days after the order is made.
Failure (From 1 August 2005) to provide prescribed information relating to disclosure certain SDLT proposals or arrangements (TMA 1970 s 98C; SI 2005/1868; SI 2005/1869; SI 2010/2743).	(*a*) Initial penalty up to £5,000; (*b*) further penalty up to £600 per day while failure continues. This can be increased up to £5,000 per day after a tribunal has issued a disclosure order.

Offence	Penalty
Failure (From 1 August 2005) to provide scheme reference number relating to certain SDLT proposals or arrangements (TMA 1970 s 98C; SI 2005/1868; SI 2005/1869; SI 2010/2743);	(a) Penalty of £100 in respect of each scheme to which the failure relates;
for second failure, occurring within three years from the date on which the first failure began;	(b) penalty of £500 in respect of each scheme to which the failure relates;
for subsequent failures, occurring within three years from the date on which the previous failure began.	(c) penalty of £1,000 in respect of each scheme to which the failure relates.
Stamp duty reserve tax	
Failure to notify HMRC and pay tax (TMA 1970 s 93, SI 1986/1711 as applied in practice by HMRC; see under 'Penalties and appeals —stamp duty reserve tax' on HMRC website).	If notified within one year of the payment deadline: the lower of £100 or the amount of the unpaid duty. If notified more than one year after the payment deadline: £100 plus up to the amount of unpaid duty, subject to a reduction for mitigating factors.

Value added tax

Rates

(VATA 1994 s 2)

	From 4.1.11		1.1.10–3.1.11		1.12.08–31.12.09	
	Rate	VAT fraction	Rate	VAT Fraction	Rate	VAT Fraction
Standard rate	20%	1/6	17.5%	7/47	15.0%	3/23
Reduced rate (see p 142)	5.0%	1/21	5.0%	1/21	5.0%	1/21
Flat-rate scheme for farmers	4.0%*		4.0%[1]		4.0%*	

[1]   Flat rate addition to sale price

Registration limits

UK taxable supplies

(VATA 1994 Sch 1 para 1, Sch 1A para 1)

A person who is UK-established (from 1 December 2012[3], previously both UK and non-UK established persons) and makes taxable supplies is liable to be registered:
(a)   at the end of any month, or
(b)   at any time, if:

	(a) turnover in the past year[1] (b) turnover in the next 30 days[2] exceeds:	Unless, in the case of (a), turnover for next year not expected to exceed:
1.4.13 onwards	**£79,000**	**£77,000**
1.4.12–31.3.13	£77,000	£75,000
1.4.11–31.3.12	£73,000	£71,000
1.4.10–31.3.11	£70,000	£68,000
1.5.09–31.3.10	£68,000	£66,000
1.4.08–30.4.09	£67,000	£65,000
1.4.07–31.3.08	£64,000	£62,000

[1]   The value of taxable supplies in the year then ending.
[2]   If there are reasonable grounds for believing the value of taxable supplies will exceed limit.
[3]   For supplies made on or after 1 December 2012 non-UK established businesses are required to register for VAT regardless of the value of taxable supplies made in the UK.

Supplies from other EC countries ('distance selling')

(VATA 1994 Sch 2)

A business person in another EC country not registered or liable to be registered in the UK is liable to be registered on any day if, in the period beginning with 1 January in that year, the value of supplies by that person to non-taxable persons in the UK exceeds:

1.1.93 onwards	£70,000

Acquisitions from other EC countries

(VATA 1994 Sch 3)

A person not registered or liable to be registered under the above rules is liable to be registered:

    (a)   at the end of any month if, in the period beginning with 1 January in that year, the value of taxable goods acquired by that person for business purposes (or for non-business purposes if a public body, charity, club, etc) from suppliers in other EC countries exceeds the following limits; or

    (b)   at any time, if there are reasonable grounds for believing the value of such acquisitions in the next 30 days will exceed the following limits:

1.4.13 onwards	£79,000
1.4.12–31.3.13	£77,000
1.4.11–31.3.12	£73,000
1.4.10–31.3.11	£70,000
1.5.09–31.3.10	£68,000
1.4.08–30.4.09	£67,000
1.4.07–31.3.08	£64,000

Deregistration limits

UK taxable supplies

(VATA 1994 Sch 1 para 4)

A registered taxable person who is UK-established (from 1 December 2012[1], previously both UK and non-UK established persons) ceases to be liable to be registered if, at any time, HMRC are satisfied that the value of taxable supplies in the year then beginning will not exceed:

1.4.13 onwards	£77,000
1.4.12–31.3.13	£75,000
1.4.11–31.3.12	£71,000
1.4.10–31.3.11	£68,000
1.5.09–31.3.10	£66,000
1.4.08–30.4.09	£65,000
1.4.07–31.3.08	£62,000

Unless the reason for not exceeding the limit during that year is that the person will cease making taxable supplies or suspend making taxable supplies for 30 days or more.

[1] For supplies made on or after 1 December 2012 non-UK established businesses are required to register for VAT regardless of the value of taxable supplies made in the UK.

Supplies from other EC countries ('distance selling')

(VATA 1994 Sch 2)

A person registered under these provisions ceases to be liable to be registered if, at any time:
- (a) relevant supplies in year ended 31 December last before that time did not exceed following limit; and
- (b) HMRC are satisfied that value of relevant supplies in year immediately following that year will not exceed following limit:

1.1.93 onwards	£70,000

Acquisitions from other EC countries

(VATA 1994 Sch 3)

A person registered under these provisions ceases to be liable to be registered if, at any time:
- (a) relevant acquisitions in year ended 31 December last before that time did not exceed following limits; and
- (b) HMRC are satisfied that value of relevant acquisitions in year immediately following that year will not exceed following limits:

1.4.13 onwards	£79,000
1.4.12–31.3.13	£77,000
1.4.11–31.3.12	£73,000
1.4.10–31.3.11	£70,000
1.5.09–31.3.10	£68,000
1.4.08–30.4.08	£67,000
1.4.07–31.3.08	£64,000

Annual accounting scheme

(SI 1995/2518 regs 49–55)

A business may, subject to conditions, complete one VAT return a year. Before 1 April 2006, only businesses with taxable turnover up to £150,000 could join the scheme immediately; other businesses had to have been registered for 12 months.

	Can join if taxable supplies in next year not expected to exceed:	Must leave at end of accounting year if taxable supplies exceeded:
1.4.06 onwards	**£1,350,000**	**£1,600,000**
1.4.04–31.3.06	£660,000	£825,000
1.4.01–31.3.04	£600,000	£750,000

Cash accounting scheme

(SI 1995/2518 regs 56–65)

A business may, subject to conditions, account for and pay VAT on the basis of cash paid and received. It can join the scheme at any time as follows.

	Can join if taxable supplies in next year not expected to exceed:	Must leave at end of VAT period if taxable supplies in previous year exceed:	Unless turnover for next year not expected to exceed:
1.4.07 onwards	**£1,350,000**	**£1,600,000**	**£1,350,000**
1.4.04–31.3.07	£660,000	£825,000	£660,000
1.4.01–31.3.04	£600,000	£750,000	£600,000

Flat-rate scheme for small businesses

(SI 1995/2518 regs 55A–55V)

A business which expects its taxable supplies in the next year to be no more than £150,000 and (before 1 April 2009) its total business income to be no more than £187,500 (including VAT) can opt to join a flat-rate scheme. The appropriate percentage below is applied to total turnover generated, including exempt income, to calculate net VAT due.

Category of business	Appropriate %		
	From 4.1.11	1.1.10–3.1.11	1.12.08–31.12.09
Accountancy or book-keeping	14.5	13	11.5
Advertising	11	10	8.5
Agricultural services	11	10	7
Any other activity not listed elsewhere	12	10.5	9
Architect	14.5	13	11
Boarding or care of animals	12	10.5	9.5
Business services that are not listed elsewhere	12	10.5	9.5
Catering services, including restaurants and takeaways	12.5	11	10.5
Civil and structural engineer or surveyor	14.5	13	11
Computer and IT consultancy or data processing	14.5	13	11.5
Computer repair services	10.5	9.5	10
Dealing in waste or scrap	10.5	9.5	8.5
Entertainment or journalism	12.5	11	9.5
Estate agency and property management services	12	10.5	9.5
Farming or agriculture that is not listed elsewhere	6.5	6	5.5
Film, radio, television or video production	13	11.5	9.5
Financial services	13.5	12	10.5
Forestry or fishing	10.5	9.5	8
General building or construction services	9.5	8.5	7.5
Hairdressing or other beauty treatment services	13	11.5	10.5
Hiring or renting goods	9.5	8.5	7.5
Hotel or accommodation	10.5	9.5	8.5
Investigation or security	12	10.5	9
Labour-only building or construction services[1]	14.5	13	11.5
Laundry or dry-cleaning services	12	10.5	9.5

Category of business	Appropriate %		
	From 4.1.11	1.1.10–3.1.11	1.12.08–31.12.09
Lawyer or legal services	14.5	13	12
Library, archive, museum or other cultural activity	9.5	8.5	7.5
Management consultancy	14	12.5	11
Manufacturing fabricated metal products	10.5	9.5	8.5
Manufacturing food	9	8	7
Manufacturing that is not listed elsewhere	9.5	8.5	7.5
Manufacturing yarn, textiles or clothing	9	8	7.5
Membership organisation	8	7	5.5
Mining or quarrying	10	9	8
Packaging	9	8	7.5
Photography	11	10	8.5
Post Offices	5	4.5	2
Printing	8.5	7.5	6.5
Publishing	11	10	8.5
Pubs	6.5	6	5.5
Real estate activity not listed elsewhere	14	12.5	11
Repairing personal or household goods	10	9	7.5
Repairing vehicles	8.5	7.5	6.5
Retailing food, confectionery, tobacco, newspapers or children's clothing	4	3.5	2
Retailing pharmaceuticals, medical goods, cosmetics or toiletries	8	7	6
Retailing that is not listed elsewhere	7.5	6.5	5.5
Retailing vehicles or fuel	6.5	6	5.5
Secretarial services	13	11.5	9.5
Social work	11	10	8
Sport or recreation	8.5	7.5	6
Transport or storage, couriers, freight, removals and taxis	10	9	8
Travel agency	10.5	9.5	8
Veterinary medicine	11	10	8
Wholesaling agricultural products	8	7	5.5
Wholesaling food	7.5	6.5	5
Wholesaling that is not listed elsewhere	8.5	7.5	6

[1]   That is, services where value of materials supplied is less than 10% of turnover of such services; any other services are 'general building or construction services'.

[2]   Once in the scheme a business may continue to use it until its total business income exceeds £230,000, and if income does exceed this limit, the business can still remain in the scheme if the income in the following year is estimated not to exceed £191,500.

Partial exemption

(SI 1995/2518 regs 106–107)

A registered person who makes taxable and exempt supplies is partly exempt and may not be able to deduct (or reclaim) all his input tax. Where, however, input tax attributable to exempt supplies in a prescribed accounting period or tax year is within the de minimis limits below, all such input tax is attributable to taxable supplies and recoverable (subject to the normal rules).

De minimis limits	£625 per month on average and 50% of all input tax for the period concerned

Capital goods scheme

(SI 1995/2518 regs 112–116)

Input tax adjustment following change in taxable use of capital goods

Item	Value	Adjustment period
Computer equipment	£50,000 or more	Five years
Ships, boats or other vessels[1]	£50,000 or more	Five years
Aircraft[1]	£50,000 or more	Five years
Land and buildings	£250,000 or more[2]	Ten years (for adjustment periods commenced before 1 January 2011, five years where interest had less than ten years to run on acquisition)

[1]   Applies for goods acquired on or after 1 January 2011.

[2]   Figure reduced to £1 where owner ('O') of item or a person to whom O has granted an interest in that item:
    (a)   uses that item to make a grant falling within VATA 1994 Sch 9 Group1 Item 1(ka) (self-storage facilities excluded from exemption);
    (b)   decides, no later than 31 March 2013, to treat the item as a capital item; and
    (c)   makes a written record to that effect, specifying the date of the decision.

Adjustment formula where adjustment period begins before 1 January 2011

$$\frac{\text{Total input tax on item}}{\text{Length of adjustment period}} \times \text{adjustment percentage}$$

Adjustment formula where adjustment period begins on or after 1 January 2011

$$\frac{\text{Total VAT on item}}{\text{Length of adjustment period}} \times \text{adjustment percentage}$$

The adjustment percentage is the percentage change in the extent to which the item is used (or treated as used) in making taxable supplies between the first interval in the adjustment period & a subsequent interval. (The first interval generally ends on the last day of the tax year in which the input tax was incurred.) For goods acquired on or after 1.1.11 total VAT includes any non-business VAT & the extent to which a capital item is used for business purposes must be determined when ascertaining taxable use for each subsequent interval.

Zero-rated supplies

A zero-rated supply is a taxable supply, but the rate of tax is nil (VATA 1994 Sch 8).

Group 1 – Food

Group 2 – Sewerage services and water

Group 3 – Books etc

Group 4 – Talking books for the blind and handicapped and wireless sets for the blind

Group 5 – Construction of buildings etc

Group 6 – Protected buildings

Group 7 – International services

Group 8 – Transport

Group 9 – Caravans and houseboats

Group 10 – Gold

Group 11 – Bank notes

Group 12 – Drugs, medicines, aids for the handicapped etc

Group 13 – Imports, exports etc

Group 15 – Charities etc

Group 16 – Clothing and footwear

Group 18 – European Research Infrastructure Consortia (from 1 January 2013)

Reduced rate supplies

(VATA 1994 Sch 7A)

Group 1 – Domestic fuel and power

Group 2 – Installation of energy-saving materials

Group 3 – Grant-funded installation of heating equipment or security goods or connection of a gas supply

Group 4 – Women's sanitary products

Group 5 – Children's car seats and bases

Group 6 – Residential conversions

Group 7 – Residential renovations and alterations

Group 8 – Contraceptive products (from 1 July 2006)

Group 9 – Welfare advice or information (from 1 July 2006)

Group 10 – Installation of mobility aids for the elderly (from 1 July 2007)

Group 11 – Smoking cessation products (from 1 July 2007)

Group 12 – Caravans (from 6 April 2013)

Group 13 – Cable-suspended transport systems (from 1 April 2013)

Exempt supplies

(VATA 1994 Sch 9)

Group 1 – Land

Group 2 – Insurance

Group 3 – Postal services

Group 4 – Betting, gaming and lotteries

Group 5 – Finance

Group 6 – Education

Group 7 – Health and welfare

Group 8 – Burial and cremation

Group 9 – Subscriptions to trade unions, professional and other public interest bodies

Group 10 – Sport, sports competitions and physical education

Group 11 – Works of art etc

Group 12 – Fund-raising events by charities and other qualifying bodies

Group 13 – Cultural services etc

Group 14 – Supplies of goods where input tax cannot be recovered

Group 15 – Investment gold

Group 16 – Supplies of services by groups involving cost sharing (from 17 July 2012)

EC Sales Lists

(SI 1995/2518 regs 2, 21–23)

All VAT-registered businesses in the UK must provide HMRC with details of goods and services supplied to a VAT-registered customer in another EU country.

The requirement for returns is as follows:

Supplies of		Frequency
Goods	Supplies of goods are in excess of £35,000 (£70,000 before 1 January 2012) in any of the current or last four quarters	Monthly
Goods	Supplies of goods are below £35,000 (£70,000 before 1 January 2012) per quarter in the current and previous four quarters	Quarterly on 31 March, 30 June, 30 September and 31 December
Services supplied to a business where the place of supply is where the customer belongs		Quarterly as above
Goods and services where a business is required to submit monthly lists for goods		Monthly for all supplies, or monthly for goods and quarterly for services
Goods or services supplied by a business completing annual VAT returns	Total annual taxable turnover does not exceed £145,000; annual value of supplies to other EU countries not more than £11,000 (and do not include *New Means of Transport*)	On application — annual on agreed due date
Goods only supplied	Total annual taxable turnover does not exceed the VAT registration threshold plus £25,500; annual value of supplies to other EU countries not more than £11,000 (and do not include *New Means of Transport*	On application — annual in simple format on agreed due date

The due date for returns is 21 days after the end of the period if submitted online and 14 days after the end of the period if submitted on paper.

Country	Code
Austria[10]	AT
Belgium	BE
Bulgaria	BG
Cyprus[9]	CY
Czech Republic	CZ
Denmark[2]	DK
Estonia	EE
Finland[3]	FI
France[4]	FR
Germany[5]	DE
Greece[11]	EL
Hungary	HU
Ireland	IE
Italy[6]	IT
Latvia	LV
Lithuania	LT
Luxembourg	LU
Malta	MT
Netherlands[12]	NL
Poland	PL
Portugal[7]	PT
Romania	RO
Slovak Republic	SK
Slovenia	SI
Spain[8]	ES
Sweden	SE

[1] Countries not listed in the table above are not part of the EU VAT area and so sales to those countries should not be included on the EC sales list. The following are not part of the EU VAT area; Andorra, The

Channel Islands, Gibraltar, Mount Athos, San Marino, and Vatican City. The UK
of the EU VAT area, but sales to these should not be included on the list.
2   Does not include the Faroe Islands and Greenland.

3   Does not include Aland Islands.
4   Includes Monaco, but excludes Martinique, Guadeloupe, Reunion, St Pierre an⌐ᵤ
    Guiana.
5   Does not include Busingen and Isle of Heligoland.
6   Does not include communes of Livigno and Campione d'Italia and the Italian waters of Lake Lugano.
7   Includes the Azores and Madeira.
8   Includes the Balearic Islands but excludes Ceuta, Melilla, and the Canary Islands.
9   Includes British sovereign base areas of Akrotiri and Dhekelia, but excludes those areas in United Nations
    buffer zone and to the north of that where the Republic of Cyprus does not have effective control.
10 Includes Jungholz and Mittelberg.
11 Excludes Mount Athos.
12 Excludes Antilles (now Curaçao, Sint Maarten and BES Islands).

Intrastat

(SI 1992/2790)

All VAT-registered businesses in the UK must complete boxes 8 and 9 on the VAT return showing the total value
of goods supplied to and acquired from other EC member states respectively. Businesses with a total value of
such supplies or acquisitions exceeding a threshold must make supplementary declarations containing further
information each month. Thresholds are set for each calendar year and recent thresholds are shown below. If
a person's supplies or acquisitions in the previous calendar year exceeded the current year's threshold,
supplementary declarations must be made for the full current year. If the cumulative total of supplies or
acquisitions in a year exceeds that calendar year's threshold, supplementary declarations must be made for the
rest of the year, starting in the month in which the threshold is exceeded. From April 2012 declarations must be
submitted electronically and will be due 21 days after the end of the month in which there is EU trade to declare.

Year	Supplies threshold	Acquisitions threshold
2010 onwards	£250,000	£600,000
2009	£270,000	£270,000
2008	£260,000	£260,000
2007	£260,000	£260,000

Some of the EU country codes and the areas included for intrastat purposes differ from those used for EC sales
list purposes. The intrastat codes are as follows.

Country	Code
Austria	AT
Belgium	BE
Bulgaria	BG
Croatia[13]	HR
Cyprus[9]	CY
Czech Republic	CZ
Denmark[2]	DK
Estonia	EE
Finland[3]	FI
France[4]	FR
Germany[5]	DE
Greece[10]	GR
Hungary	HU
Ireland	IE
Italy[6]	IT
Latvia	LV
Lithuania	LT
Luxembourg	LU
Malta	MT
Netherlands[11]	NL
Poland	PL
Portugal[7]	PT
Romania	RO
Slovak Republic	SK
Slovenia	SI
Spain[8]	ES
Sweden	SE

United Kingdom[12]	GB

[1] Andorra and Liechtenstein are both outside the customs territory (and therefore the statistical territory) of the EU.

[2] Does not include the Faroe Islands.

[3] Includes Aland Islands.

[4] Includes Monaco, but excludes Martinique, Guadeloupe, Reunion, St Pierre and Miquelon, and French Guiana.

[5] Includes Isle of Heligoland but excludes Busingen.

[6] Does not include communes of Livigno and Campione d'Italia, the Italian waters of Lake Lugano and the Vatican.

[7] Includes the Azores and Madeira.

[8] Includes the Balearic Islands but excludes Ceuta, Melilla, and the Canary Islands.

[9] Includes UK sovereign base areas but excludes Northern Cyprus.

[10] Includes Mount Athos.

[11] Excludes all dependent and associated territories.

[12] Includes the Isle of Man and the Channel Islands but excludes Gibraltar.

[13] It is expected that Croatia will be joining the EU on 1 July 2013. Dispatches and arrivals to/from Croatia should be included from this date.

Car fuel

(VATA 1994 ss 56, 57, Schs 4, 6)

Where an employer pays mileage allowances, he may use the advisory fuel rates on p 82 to calculate the input VAT to reclaim on the fuel element. Receipts must still be retained.

VAT-inclusive scale figures can be used to assess VAT due on petrol provided at below cost price for private journeys by registered traders or their employees, where the petrol has been provided from business resources and accurate records of business/private mileage are not maintained. The figures represent the tax-inclusive value of the fuel supplied to each individual and relate to return periods beginning on the dates shown.

	12 months £	3 months £	1 month £
From 1 May 2013: CO_2 band			
120 or below	675	168	56
125	1,010	253	84
130	1,080	269	89
135	1,145	286	95
140	1,215	303	101
145	1,280	320	106
150	1,350	337	112
155	1,415	354	118
160	1,485	371	123
165	1,550	388	129
170	1,620	404	134
175	1,685	421	140
180	1,755	438	146
185	1,820	455	151
190	1,890	472	157
195	1,955	489	163
200	2,025	506	168
205	2,090	523	174
210	2,160	539	179
215	2,225	556	185
220	2,295	573	191
225 or above	2,360	590	196

	12 months £	3 months £	1 month £
1 May 2012–30 April 2013: CO_2 band			
120 or below	665	166	55
125	1,000	250	83
130	1,065	266	88
135	1,135	283	94
140	1,200	300	100
145	1,270	316	105
150	1,335	333	111
155	1,400	350	116
160	1,470	366	122
165	1,535	383	127
170	1,600	400	133
175	1,670	416	138
180	1,735	433	144
185	1,800	450	150
190	1,870	467	155
195	1,935	483	161
200	2,000	500	166
205	2,070	517	172
210	2,135	533	177
215	2,200	550	183
220	2,270	567	189
225 or above	2,335	583	194

	12 months £	3 months £	1 month £
1 May 2011–30 April 2012: CO_2 band			
120 or below	630	157	52
125	945	236	78
130	1,010	252	84
135	1,070	268	89
140	1,135	283	94
145	1,200	299	99
150	1,260	315	105
155	1,325	331	110
160	1,385	346	115
165	1,450	362	120
170	1,515	378	126
175	1,575	394	131
180	1,640	409	136
185	1,705	425	141
190	1,765	441	147
195	1,830	457	152
200	1,890	472	157
205	1,955	488	162
210	2,020	504	168
215	2,080	520	173
220	2,145	536	178
225 or above	2,205	551	183

	12 months £	3 months £	1 month £
1 May 2010–30 April 2011: CO_2 band			
120 or below	570	141	47
125	850	212	70
130	850	212	70
135	910	227	75
140	965	241	80
145	1,020	255	85
150	1,080	269	89
155	1,135	283	94
160	1,190	297	99
165	1,250	312	104
170	1,305	326	108
175	1,360	340	113
180	1,420	354	118
185	1,475	368	122
190	1,530	383	127
195	1,590	397	132
200	1,645	411	137
205	1,705	425	141
210	1,760	439	146
215	1,815	454	151
220	1,875	468	156
225	1,930	482	160
230 or above	1,985	496	165

	12 months £	3 months £	1 month £
1 May 2009–30 April 2010: CO_2 band			
120 or below	505	126	42
125	755	189	63
130	755	189	63
135	755	189	63
140	805	201	67
145	855	214	71
150	905	226	75
155	960	239	79
160	1,010	251	83
165	1,060	264	88
170	1,110	276	92
175	1,160	289	96
180	1,210	302	100
185	1,260	314	104
190	1,310	327	109
195	1,360	339	113
200	1,410	352	117
205	1,465	365	121
210	1,515	378	126
215	1,565	390	130
220	1,615	403	134
225	1,665	416	138
230	1,715	428	142
235 or above	1,765	441	147

149

	12 months £	3 months £	1 month £
1 May 2008–30 April 2009: CO_2 band			
120 or below	555	138	46
125	830	207	69
130	830	207	69
135	830	207	69
140	885	221	73
145	940	234	78
150	995	248	82
155	1,050	262	87
160	1,105	276	92
165	1,160	290	96
170	1,215	303	101
175	1,270	317	105
180	1,325	331	110
185	1,380	345	115
190	1,435	359	119
195	1,490	373	124
200	1,545	386	128
205	1,605	400	133
210	1,660	414	138
215	1,715	428	142
220	1,770	442	147
225	1,825	455	151
230	1,880	469	156
235 or above	1,935	483	161

Interest and penalties

Default interest

(VATA 1994 s 74)

Interest runs on the amount of any VAT assessed (or paid late by voluntary disclosure):
- from the reckonable date (normally the latest date on which a return is required for the period in question);
- until the date of payment (although in practice it runs to the date shown on the notice of assessment or notice of voluntary disclosure if paid within 30 days of that date).

The period of interest cannot commence more than three years before the date of assessment or payment.

The rates of interest are as follows:

Period	Rate
From 29 September 2009	3%
24 March 2009–28 September 2009	2.5%
27 January 2009–23 March 2009	3.5%
6 January 2009–26 January 2009	4.5%
6 December 2008–5 January 2009	5.5%
6 November 2008–5 December 2008	6.5%
6 January 2008–5 November 2008	7.5%
6 August 2007–5 January 2008	8.5%
6 September 2006–5 August 2007	7.5%
6 September 2005–5 September 2006	6.5%
6 September 2004–5 September 2005	7.5%
6 December 2003–5 September 2004	6.5%
6 August 2003–5 December 2003	5.5%*

Interest on VAT overpaid in cases of official error

(VATA 1994 s 78)

Where VAT has been overpaid or underclaimed due to an error by HMRC, then on a claim HMRC must pay interest:
- from the date they receive payment (or authorise a repayment) for the return period in question;
- until the date on which they authorise payment of the amount on which interest is due.

This provision does not require HMRC to pay interest on an amount on which repayment supplement is due.

The rates of interest are as follows:

Period	Rate
from 29 September 2009	0.5%
27 January 2009–28 September 2009	0%
6 January 2009–26 January 2009	1%
6 December 2008–5 January 2009	2%
6 November 2008–5 December 2008	3%
6 January 2008–5 November 2008	4%
6 August 2007–5 January 2008	5%
6 September 2006–5 August 2007	4%
6 September 2005–5 September 2006	3%
6 September 2004–5 September 2005	4%
6 December 2003–5 September 2004	3%
6 August 2003–5 December 2003	2%*
6 November 2001–5 August 2003	3%

* Due to an administrative error the rate of default and statutory interest was too high by one percentage point between 6 August 2003 and 5 September 2003. HMRC will not seek to recover amounts overpaid by HMRC and will seek to identify businesses overcharged (see Business Brief 17/05 as of 9 September 2005).

Repayment supplement – VAT

(VATA 1994 s 79)

Where a person is entitled to a repayment the payment due is increased by a supplement of the greater of:
- (i)   5% of that amount; or
- (ii) £50.

The supplement will only be paid if:

(a) the return or claim is received by HMRC not later than the last day on which it is required to be made;

(b) HMRC do not issue a written instruction making the refund within the relevant period; and

(c) the amount shown on the return or claim does not exceed the amount due by more than 5% of that amount or £250, whichever is the greater.

The 'relevant period' is 30 days beginning with the receipt of the return or claim or, if later, the day after the last day of the VAT period to which the return or claim relates.

Penalties and surcharges

Offence	Penalty
Inaccuracy in return or other document (FA 2007 Sch 24).	See **Penalties — modernised penalty regime** on p 12.
Failure to notify obligation to register for VAT, change in supplies made by person exempted from registration, acquisition affecting exemption, acquisition of goods from another member state and unauthorised issue of an invoice (FA 2008 Sch 41).	See **Penalties — modernised penalty regime** on p 12.
Inaccuracy in return or other document as a result of third party providing incorrect (or withholding) information (FA 2007 Sch 24).	See **Penalties — modernised penalty regime** on p 12.
Failure to inform HMRC of an error in an assessment within 30 days of the date of the assessment (FA 2007 Sch 24).	See **Penalties — modernised penalty regime** on p 12.
Failure to comply with HMRC investigatory powers with effect from 1 April 2009 (FA 2008 Sch 36).	(*a*) Initial penalty of £300; (*b*) if failure/obstruction continues, a further penalty of up to £60 per day; (*c*) if failure/obstruction continues after penalty under (*a*) imposed, a tax-related amount determined by the Upper Tribunal.
Provision of inaccurate information or document when complying with an information notice (FA 2008 Sch 36).	Up to £3,000 per inaccuracy.
Failure to submit a return electronically if required to do so by SI 1995/2518 reg 25 for prescribed accounting periods starting on or after 1 April 2012. Before 1 April 2012, failure of a *specified person* to make a *specified return* using an electronic return system for prescribed accounting periods ending on or after 31 March 2011 (SI 1995/2518 reg 25A). 'Specified person' was broadly a person registered for VAT on or after 1 April 2010, or one registered before that date who at 31 December 2009 or any later date has an annual VAT exclusive turnover of £100,000 or more. Penalty will only apply to prescribed accounting periods ending on or after 31 March 2013 where the person is required to make an electronic return only as a result of the removal of the turnover test from 1 April 2012.	Annual VAT exclusive turnover of: £22,800,001 or more — £400 £5,600,001 to £22,800,000 — £300 £100,001 to £5,600,000 — £200 £100,000 or under — £100
Failure to submit return or pay VAT due within time limit (where a return is late but the VAT is paid on time or no VAT is due, a default is recorded but no surcharge arises) (VATA 1994 s 59). Failure to pay tax due under the payment on account scheme on time (VATA 1994 s 59A).	The greater of £30 and a specified percentage of outstanding VAT for period, depending on number of defaults in surcharge period: first default in period 2%, second default 5%, third default 10%, fourth and further defaults 15%. (Surcharge assessments are not issued for sums of less than £200 unless the rate of the surcharge is 10% or more.) **Due to be replaced by penalties under FA 2009 Schs 55 and 56 from a date to be appointed.**
Evasion of VAT: conduct involving dishonesty (VATA 1994 ss 60, 61[1]).	*Amount of tax evaded or sought to be evaded (subject to mitigation).* *Repealed and replaced by penalty under FA 2007 Sch 24 for periods beginning on or after 1 April 2008 and ending on or after 1 April 2009 subject to the exceptions shown below[1].*
Issuing incorrect certificate stating that certain supplies fall to be zero-rated or taxed at the reduced rate (VATA 1994 s 62).	Difference between tax actually charged and tax which should have been charged.
Misdeclaration or neglect (VATA 1994 s 63).	*15% of VAT which would have been lost if inaccuracy had not been discovered.* *Repealed and replaced by penalty under FA 2007 Sch 24 for periods beginning on or after 1 April 2008 and ending on or after 1 April 2009.*

Offence	Penalty
Repeated misdeclarations (VATA 1994 s 64).	*15% of VAT which would have been lost if second and subsequent inaccuracies within penalty period had not been discovered.* **Repealed and replaced by penalty under FA 2007 Sch 24 for periods ending on or after 1 April 2008 and ending on or after 1 April 2009.**
Material inaccuracy in EC sales statement (VATA 1994 s 65).	£100 for each material inaccuracy in two-year penalty period (which commences following notice of second material inaccuracy).
Failure to submit an EC sales statement (VATA 1994 s 66).	Greater of £50 or a daily penalty (maximum 100 days) £5 for the first, £10 for the second, £15 for the third or subsequent failure in the default period.
Failure to notify liability for registration or a change in nature of supplies by person exempted from registration (VATA 1994 s 67).	*Greater of £50 and a specified percentage of the tax for which the person would have been liable, depending on the period of failure: nine months or less 5%; over nine and up to 18 months 10%; over 18 months 15%.* **Repealed after 31 March 2010 and replaced by penalty under FA 2008 Sch 41.**
Failure to notify acquisition of excise duty goods or new means of transport (VATA 1994 s 67).	*Greater of £50 and: 5% of the tax for which the person would have been liable if period of failure is three months or less, 10% if over three and up to six months and 15% if over six months.* **Repealed after 31 March 2010 and replaced by penalty under FA 2008 Sch 41.**
Unauthorised issue of invoices (VATA 1994 s 67).	*Greater of £50 and 15% of amount shown as or representing VAT.* **Repealed after 31 March 2010 and replaced by penalty under FA 2008 Sch 41.**
Breach of walking possession agreement (VATA 1994 s 68).	50% of VAT due or amount recoverable.
Failure to preserve records for prescribed period (VATA 1994 ss 69, 69B).	£500.
Failure to preserve records specified in HMRC direction (VATA 1994 ss 69, 69B).	£200 for each day of failure (maximum 30 days).
Breaches of regulatory provisions, including failure to notify cessation of liability or entitlement to be registered, failure to keep records and non-compliance with any regulations made under VATA 1994 (VATA 1994 s 69).	Greater of £50 and a daily penalty (maximum 100 days) of a specified amount depending on number of failures in preceding two years: £5* per day if no previous failures; £10* per day if one previous failure; £15* per day if two or more previous failures.
Where failure consists of not paying VAT or not making a return in the required time.	*1/6, 1/3 and 1/2 of 1% of the VAT due respectively, if greater.
Breaches of regulatory provisions involving failure to pay VAT or submit return by due date (VATA 1994 s 69).	Greater of £50 and a daily penalty (for no more than 100 days) of a specified amount depending on number of failures in preceding two years: greater of £5 and 1/6 % of VAT due if no previous failures; greater of £10 and 1/3% of VAT due if one previous failure, greater of £15 and 1/2% of VAT due if two or more previous failures.
Failure to comply with the requirements of the investment gold scheme (VATA 1994 s 69A).	17.5% of the value of transactions concerned.
Import VAT (FA 2003 ss 24–41):	From 27 November 2003:
– failures relating to non-compliance	maximum penalty of £2,500
– evasion.	maximum penalty equal to VAT sought to be evaded.
Failure to notify the use of a designated avoidance scheme (VATA 1994 Sch 11A paras 10, 11).	15% of the tax avoided (applies to businesses with supplies of £600,000 or more from 1 August 2004).
Failure to disclose certain schemes within 30 days of the due date or the first return affected (VATA 1994 Sch 11A paras 10, 11).	£5,000 (applies to businesses with supplies exceeding £10 million from 1 August 2004).

[1] Penalties under VATA 1994 ss 60, 61 will continue to be charged for acts or omissions not relating to an inaccuracy in a document or failure to notify HMRC of an under-assessment (SI 2008/568 and SI 2009/571).

Index